Social Media Playbook
for Business

Social Media Playbook for Business

Reaching Your Online Community with Twitter, Facebook, LinkedIn, and More

Tom Funk

 PRAEGER

AN IMPRINT OF ABC-CLIO, LLC
Santa Barbara, California • Denver, Colorado • Oxford, England

Library of Congress Cataloging-in-Publication Data

Funk, Tom, 1965-
    Social media playbook for business: reaching your online community with Twitter, Facebook, LinkedIn, and more / Tom Funk.
        p. cm.
    Includes bibliographical references and index.
    ISBN 978-0-313-38626-8 (hard copy : alk. paper)—ISBN 978-0-313-38627-5 (ebook) 1. Internet marketing. 2. Social media—Economic aspects. 3. Online social networks—Economic aspects. 4. Customer relations—Technological innovations. I. Title.
    HF5415.1265.F86   2011
    658.8′72—dc22   2010040755

ISBN: 978-0-313-38626-8
EISBN: 978-0-313-38627-5

15   14   13   12   11   1   2   3   4   5

This book is also available on the World Wide Web as an eBook.
Visit www.abc-clio.com for details.

Praeger
An Imprint of ABC-CLIO, LLC

ABC-CLIO, LLC
130 Cremona Drive, P.O. Box 1911
Santa Barbara, California 93116-1911

This book is printed on acid-free paper (∞)

Manufactured in the United States of America

To my daughters, Hannah, Molly, and Louisa, who are still waiting for something closer to Harry Potter.

Contents

Acknowledgments

Thanks to Jeff Olson for developing the idea for this book, and to my fine editor, Brian Romer, and publisher ABC-CLIO for bringing the project to fruition.

I'd also like to thank Nathan Focht and Blake Ellis, and the entire Timberline Interactive team, for affording me the conference-going and speaking schedule that played such a major role in collecting the case studies and anecdotal examples used in this book.

Speaking of conferences, I'm grateful to all the incredible people at Internet Retailer, both the magazine and the conference series, and to the DMA, Shop.org, and Mark Harvey and my other friends across the Pacific at Australia's Online Retailer conference. All have played a great role, not just in allowing me on their programs, but more importantly in supporting an industry and spreading best practices for e-commerce and social media to businesspeople like the ones I hope will be reading this book.

I'm grateful to Tim Parry at Multichannel Merchant for allowing me to contribute to his newsletters on an all-too-irregular schedule. And I owe a big thank you to all the people who generously shared their time and insights by granting me phone or e-mail interviews, including Phil Terry of Good Experience, Elisa Camahort Page of the BlogHer network, Max Kalehoff of Clickable, Max Harris of Gardener's Supply, Jeff Pape of WrestlingGear.com, Steve Elkins of WEBS Yarn.com, Mike Lyman of Signing Time, and many others.

Thanks to Seth Godin and Kurt Peters who were so helpful to my first book, *Web 2.0*, and without whom this title might never have been written.

Last but foremost, for patiently bearing with me during the long (and significantly underestimated!) hours of researching, interviewing, writing, and revising, I must thank my amazing wife Elizabeth and our fabulous daughters Hannah, Molly, and Louisa.

Chapter 1

Introduction

SOCIAL MEDIA: WHY DO IT?

Maybe you're trying to sort through all the hyperbole to judge objectively the costs and benefits of kicking your company's social-media program into high gear. Maybe you're already dabbling in social meda efforts for your business, but you're not sure how to proceed, or even whether it's worth the time. Or maybe you're already a firm believer in the promise of social media—but you need some ammunition to overcome the skeptics and naysayers at your firm.

Let's lay out the rationale for why your operation needs a strong social-media program and needs it now:

1. All the customers and prospects are participating in social-media Web sites.
2. Your competitors are already there, or will be soon.
3. The old marketing—interruption marketing—is in permanent decline. The new ways to reach customers are permission marketing, conversational marketing, and social marketing. Without participating in social media, your company simply cannot master the new skills of customer contact.
4. More important than selling in the social-media world is *listening* to your customer and communicating your brand directly and personally. The most exciting promise of social media for business is to let you connect more strongly to your best customers and spread the good word

about your company through a web that is more powerfully interlinked than ever before.

Social-networking sites have ridden an exponential growth curve, and today four out of five online Americans are creating, participating in, or reading some form of social media every month. Businesses have taken note: Dell Computer has tracked more than $3 million in sales from its Twitter posts, and products from Mentos to Blendtec blenders have soared thanks to viral videos on YouTube. The most active users of social media could likely be your best customers and best evangelists—but how do you reach them? And how do you adapt your approach to succeed in this free-wheeling space?

Though I call this book *Social Media Playbook for Business*, I don't mean to imply that companies can make a successful go of the social networks merely by remembering a bunch of scripted moves. For businesses and organizations to benefit from the new public square, the first play in the playbook is this: *listen*. Embrace social media as the world's best and newest listening post. It's the biggest, busiest, most interconnected hub of your customers and potential customers ever seen. It's a forum for immediate and informal one-to-one—but public—conversations with your customers.

Once you've spent enough time listening to understand the place and built your own reputation for generosity, politeness, sincerity, and authentic personality, and once you have a core community of friends, you can start using social media to speak your company's message. Social media can be a place to occasionally amplify and reinforce the messages you're making in your press releases and promotions—but that's far from the most effective way to talk on Twitter, Facebook, and the other networks. Social media is the *anti-marketing*. Social media is where you humanize your business. The best use of your voice in social media is to extend your brand in more personal, direct, and connective ways than is possible in advertising.

SERVING 80 PERCENT OF THE WEB—AND GROWING

We're all a little tired of giddy claims about the gigantic size and stratospheric growth of social media. But the numbers are true, and the phenomenon is just too big for any company to ignore.

Online networks like Facebook and LinkedIn and new media platforms like Twitter, Flickr, and YouTube today serve a stunning 80 percent of online Americans every month. That's 127 million people in the United States.

Collectively, social-media sites continue to grow at a furious pace—1,382 percent growth for Twitter and 513 percent for Facebook, for instance. Once the province of the young, social media is now growing fastest among older demographics.

Any ambitious business or organization should be trying to understand, participate in, and benefit from social media.

In March 2010, the traffic-monitoring firm Hitwise reported that Facebook had "reached an important milestone for the week ending March 13, 2010 and surpassed Google in the United States to become the most visited Web site for the week."[1]

Nielsen reports that social-media usage continues to grow—a full 73 percent of online adults participate at least once a week on blogs, social networks, and other social-media Web sites. That equates to a whopping 127 million U.S. adults.[2]

- Twitter has more than 100 million users.
- Facebook has more than 500 million users.
- There are 100 million videos on YouTube.
- There are 200 million active blogs.
- 54 percent of Web users post or tweet daily.
- Already, nearly 80 percent of Fortune 100 companies are active in at least one social-media channel.[3]

Social-media marketing spending in the United States is projected to grow at an annual compound rate of 34 percent through 2014, according to Forrester Research. By then, social-media marketing will amount to a $3.1 billion industry, surpassing e-mail marketing in terms of spending, Forrester said in a 2009 report.[4]

Most companies have already moved into social media. According to a 2010 survey by Econsultancy, 86 percent of respondents are marketing on Facebook, while 77 percent are tweeting and 58 percent are using LinkedIn.[5] If you are not already doing it, you're playing catch up.

STRENGTHENING CUSTOMER RELATIONSHIPS

So, if hundreds of millions of people are now frequenting social-media Web sites, what's the business opportunity here? Can we drive revenue through this new channel?

I'll get to that, but let me say that looking to social media for immediate sales generation is shortsighted. I spoke to several social-media pros and e-commerce executives in the course of writing this book, and a clear consensus emerged: For a business, the principal value of the social-media channel is in *strengthening the customer relationship.*

Yes, publicity, buzz, and sales could be the side effects of a social-media program run well. But your first aim should be to better understand your customer and connect with her more directly than you've ever been able.

Online social media developed for people, not businesses. But when businesses use these tools and Web sites with sensitivity and personality, they unlock powerful and unique benefits. For businesses and organizations, social media can be:

- An inexpensive and instant publishing channel
- Your real-time listening post to your market and your customers
- An informal, two-way communication channel between you and your customers

The first step of a corporate social-media program should be to listen. Increasingly, social-media Web sites are where your customers are, especially the most influential ones—and where tastes, opinions, and brand impressions are made and shared. Listen to customers and prospects. Listen to ongoing conversations about your market, your brand, and your competitors. Listen to absorb the culture and etiquette of the various platforms—Facebook, Twitter, MySpace, LinkedIn, the blogosphere, etc. Then you'll be able to start contributing as a true member of the community.

Interact and engage with others online, bring your company's brand values into the new social-media arena, and invest it with individual personality. In the process, you'll be tightening your connection to your customer, and only good things can come of that: Customer loyalty and positive word of mouth broadcast exponentially across the Web's new social networks.

LOW COST

Never has there been a communications medium offering business access to hundreds of millions of consumers that was so fast and so inexpensive.

Whether you launch your corporate blog or take your company's social-media program to Twitter, Facebook, and YouTube, you're harnessing publishing platforms that are so easy your grandmother could use them (and she may already be doing so!). They cost next to nothing and their informality challenges you to publish good stuff daily—as opposed to perfectly polished stuff once every blue moon. It gets you into the public mind and into the daily life of your best customers at a cost that is negligible.

Like many state government operations in the wake of the 2008 recession, Travel Michigan, the state tourism agency, saw its budgets slashed. So the agency went without a lot of its typical media buys and instead focused on more affordable social-media campaigns. Travel Michigan uses social media both as a means to reach a coveted younger demographic and to get the most for its media budget in these fiscally constrained times. "It is a low-cost way to engage to a younger audience," says the agency's managing director, Dave Lorenz.[6]

Merchants have seized on the importance of social media and have started investing time, manpower, and creative energy into the space. But they may not be entirely honest with themselves about the scope of their investments. Admittedly, since actual paid advertising on the social-media platforms is still in its infancy, nobody is spending much *money* on social media, at least not directly. But a recent study by Econsultancy indicates that merchants aren't really accounting for the true costs of their social-media efforts.

Two-thirds of respondents said they spent less than $5,000 a year on their social media. Some 32 percent of respondents actually claimed they spent nothing.[7]

The real cost is in staff time. "Most marketers said they spent between five and 10 hours per week on social media," says Rebecca Lieb, vice president for U.S. operations at Econsultancy, "and they plan to spend more time in social media in 2010."[8]

REVENUE OPPORTUNITY

Yes, there's ample evidence now that when a company does a good job engaging with people online in social networks, their sales benefit. It can work with companies big or small, and programs humble or ambitious:

- Dell Computer has rung up more than $3 million in sales through its @DellOutlet Twitter account.
- Wine of the Month Club rang up $1,000 of sales just from a single no-cost video of owner and winetaster Paul Kalemkiarian demolishing rejected wines with a bowling ball.

- Sony tracked $1.5 million to a Twitter promotion in which it offered 1,600 followers a 10 percent discount on custom Vaio laptops.
- Blendtec was an obscure blender-maker in Orem, Utah. "People didn't know a company called Blendtec, but we were making commercial blenders for years," said George Wright, director of marketing and co-brainchild of the company's ironic "Will it Blend?" YouTube videos. After the videos became a viral sensation, Blendtec sales grew fivefold.[9]
- The Georgia Aquarium sold 2,500 admission tickets through Facebook, Twitter, and MySpace in a 2009 campaign. The aquarium offered its followers and fans 25 percent to 40 percent off admission prices from February through May. The campaign used a specific URL for the promotion that allowed the aquarium to track sales directly, according to Dave Santucci, vice president of marketing and communication.

Countless other examples exist, and more are occurring daily. The companies that are best using social media are making positive brand impressions on their audience, and naturally some of that audience is responding by opening their wallets.

Research from the social-media platform Wetpaint and the Altimeter Group tracked an index of companies and measured their social-media activities and sales trends. They found that the firms with the highest levels of social-media activity—companies like Starbucks, Dell, eBay, and Nike—saw their overall sales climb 18 percent in 12 months, while those least active in social media saw sales drop 6 percent in the same period.[10]

Not surprisingly, connecting with a brand on social media is correlated with high likelihood to buy and recommend the brand's products. It may be a chicken-and-egg question (correlation does not prove causation), but it is nevertheless the sort of behavior any company should encourage, because the influence of our friends, in these interconnected online networks, is so powerful:

- 67 percent of Twitter users who become followers of a brand are more likely to buy the brand's products.[11]
- 60 percent of Facebook users who become fans of a brand are more likely to recommend the brand to a friend.[12]
- 74 percent of consumers are influenced in their buying decisions by the input of others on social networks.[13]

To me, these are heartening examples that people are embracing their favorite companies in their favorite social-networking sites, and sales are happening. But don't get too hung up on tracking and measuring revenue. Canadian social-media expert Danny Brown suggests we may be focusing on the wrong ROI: "Instead of return on investment," says Brown, "perhaps we should be more worried about the Risk of Ignoring."[14]

NETWORKING AND COLLABORATION

It's not just about the customer. Businesspeople have a lot to gain when they connect with each other online, too. Especially business-to-business execs can benefit from using the new online business networking tools, such as LinkedIn, Spoke, and others.

Reid Hoffman is the founder of the 65-million-member business network LinkedIn and an investor in scores of other social-media companies. He sees success on the Web 2.0 landscape as fundamentally a question of how much exposure you can achieve: "In real estate, the wisdom says 'location, location, location,'" says Hoffman. "In consumer Internet, think 'distribution, distribution, distribution.'"[15]

My focus in this book is on how businesses can harness the energy of online social networking to benefit their business—generating positive conversations among fans and prospective customers, and sparking buzz from nontraditional media (read: bloggers) and ultimately from mainstream media.

But another key business benefit of social media is that it helps organizations—especially far-flung multinationals and small "virtual" businesses—maintain an agile, multiperson conversation and push along complex projects.

A lot of cool online platforms now exist for working together on projects. Simplest of all is online document-sharing on Google Docs, where you can upload your latest press release or spreadsheet and invite specific people, or the public at large, to edit, revise, and shape it with you. For more ambitious projects calling on a larger team, wiki software—such as the platform that built Wikipedia, by far the world's largest and most up-to-date encyclopedia—can help you create and maintain truly massive software or publishing projects with a distributed and often volunteer workforce.

By embracing the nature and tools of social media, your business can communicate more fluidly throughout the organization; it can be more agile and more productive.

WHAT IS SOCIAL MEDIA AND HOW CAN MY ORGANIZATION GET INVOLVED?

The social Web is an enormous landscape today, and the opportunity to make interpersonal connections has been bolted onto everything from Web sites to mobile apps. You'll hear the terms "social networks" and "social media" used interchangeably, and the distinction between them is blurry indeed. Here are my definitions:

Social media: An umbrella term describing all Web-based and mobile services that give individuals the ability to establish a personal profile, connect with other users, and create, publish, and respond to content—whether to share with a network of friends or with the Internet as a whole.

Social-networking sites: Services that allow individuals to create a personal or business network. Social networks allow individuals to (1) establish a public or semipublic profile, (2) build a network of friends on the site, and (3) publish comments, messages, images, videos, and other content for their friends or the site at large. Examples of social-networking platforms include MySpace, Facebook, LinkedIn, and dating sites like Match.com.

Social-media sites: Services designed around a form of media—videos, photos, articles, and Web pages—that allow individuals to publish, rate, and comment upon the media. Examples of social media include YouTube video sharing, Flickr photo sharing, etc.

The blogosphere: The articles published by blogs and the microblog posts of Twitter are surely media, too, but I like to think of them as a distinct phenomenon.

Anyone who has spent any time on the Web at all will realize the shortcomings of hard-and-fast definitions like these, however. With its networking aspects of followers and direct messaging, Twitter may be as much a social network as it is a "micro-blogging" or social-media platform. Other hybrid beasts abound: With its wealth of customer ratings and reviews, public profiles, and friend networks, is Netflix a networking platform, or—since it's built around movies—is it a media platform? Of course, Netflix is really an e-commerce store, a pay video rental service that just happens to have built social-media tools into its DNA.

A BRIEF HISTORY LESSON

The Internet has always been social. Some of its very earliest applications, even before the invention of the World Wide Web, were social tools like discussion boards and forums.

When the Web made its commercial emergence in the mid-nineties, social applications like chat rooms were followed by private networking tools such as IM and ICQ, and finally by full-fledged social networks like SixDegrees in 1997 and Friendster in 2002.

Social-Media Timeline

1995:   Craigslist
1997:   SixDegrees
1999:   Live Journal, Black Planet, Blogger, Napster
2000:   MiGente
2001:   Ryze, Wikipedia, StumbleUpon
2002:   Friendster, Technorati
2003:   LinkedIn, Hi5, Wordpress, Skype, Furl, SecondLife
2004:   Facebook, Flickr, Digg, MySpace, Orkut, Yelp
2005:   YouTube, Bebo, Ning, MocoSpace
2006:   Twitter
2007:   iPhone, Friendfeed, Seesmic
2008:   AppStore, Tweetdeck, Groupon, SCVNGR
2009:   Foursquare, Google Wave, ChatRoulette

THERE'S NO SUCH THING AS SOCIAL-MEDIA MARKETING

"Social-media marketing" is a bit of an oxymoron. Purists say social media is for people, not businesses. Yet the social-network platforms themselves are so eager to monetize their sites (and the millions of eyeballs viewing them) that they have led the charge to give businesses more opportunities for publishing and advertising.

So it's not the mere presence of businesses on places like Facebook and Twitter that is a problem, it's just that the term "social-media marketing" is a misnomer. Companies establishing their pages on social-media sites should not be doing it for marketing, per se. For a business, social media is less about sales generation, more about customer service—customer outreach, R&D, focus grouping, shareholder services, and PR. Social media for business encompasses all these things, and of course a lot of intangibles as well.

Yes, there is a marketing component too: Spreading news of your latest products and discounts, hoping for some word-of-mouth marketing and endorsements from your fans. But to be successful, companies must first embrace the two crucial aspects of social media:

1. Honest, person-to-person communication, and
2. Content built around an idea that is "bigger than you."

As John Jantsh puts it, "We don't need social-media tools, social-media plans, social-media agencies, or social-media departments, we need marketing strategies and tactics that are informed by a terribly heightened customer expectation."[16]

WHAT'S THE BIG IDEA?

The number of companies with exemplary social-media programs just keeps growing. To me, one of the most exciting aspects is the focus that social media places on the *bigger idea* surrounding their business. Social media is a great place for niche companies to share in their customers' and fans' enthusiasm for a larger topic that goes beyond merely trying to sell the company's offerings.

Here are some great examples of companies whose social-media programs embrace a "big idea":

- **Gardener's Supply**: On Facebook, Twitter, and tens of thousands of customer ratings and reviews, it's not just about selling gardening stuff, but promoting gardening, educating, and celebrating gardeners.
- **Wine of the Month Club**: Uses Facebook, YouTube, Vimeo, and podcasts to satisfy its audience's enthusiasm for and curiosity about wine, food, and entertaining.
- **Hips & Curves plus-size lingerie**: Affirms the beauty and sexiness of the plus-size women to whom it caters, especially with its blog Curvy Confidential.
- **Sgt. Grit U.S. Marine specialties**: Its Web site, blog, YouTube channel, Facebook, Twitter, and MySpace serve a community of active-duty Marines, veterans, their families, and loved ones. Patriotism, tributes, reminiscences, and re-connections are all part of it—as are leatherneck jokes and tattoo sharing.
- **Yarn.com**: Through podcasts, a blog, Facebook, Twitter, and the niche network Ravelry, this family business shows knitters how to tackle new projects, shares tips, promotes classes, and energizes them about their hobby.

- **Patagonia**: YouTube video, a blog, Facebook, and Twitter are not about outdoor gear—it's about the outdoors, the beauty, thrill, and challenge of surfing, ice climbing, river kayaking, and the environmental conservation at the heart of the company.

The "bigger idea" can be a hobby, like woodworking or knitting, that stirs emotion, stimulates question-and-answer, and invites sharing of projects or collections among fellow hobbyists.

"Obsessional" product categories like gourmet or luxury items, cars, outdoor gear, indulgent treats, sexy lingerie, shoes, and clothes all generate emotional responses and strident opinions among their biggest fans.

And then there are products and services associated with a "bigger idea" or cause that stirs passion and connection. Businesses associated with causes and ideas like these are probably best suited of all for social media.

Since it's so novel a medium, it's easy to miss the fact that for businesses, the whole social-media trend is just a challenge to recommit to virtues that are not novel at all, but are rock-solid traditional: Customer focus. Authenticity. Responsiveness. Trustworthiness. And yes, the notion that business shouldn't be "all business," but should involve a higher calling—whether it's making the world a better place or just making it more fun.

WHO IS THE VOICE OF YOUR COMPANY?

Who is the voice of your company? A charismatic founder? The current CEO? A real or fictional ad pitchman, a celebrity endorser, a mascot? All of the above? Now if it's hard to answer that question, it'll be even harder to answer this one:

Who is the voice of your social-media efforts?

If you're lucky, and you're a small enough company blessed with a single powerhouse company voice (that colorful founder/inventor/evangelist) who also loves to explore new frontiers like social media—*and* this person has enough time, focus, and follow-through to execute on the program, congratulations! You've found the sweet spot, wherein the company's voice and its social-media voice are a single, real person.

Through the course of the book we'll look at many examples of programs whose success depended greatly on the personal qualities of their spokesperson.

These programs work best when the voice of the company is a colorful and committed founder or leader, like Wine of the Month Club's Paul

Kalemkiarian. Paul is a born showman, he's generous with his wine knowledge, and he has the authority that comes from tasting 4,000 wines a month to select the best for his members. His presence on the social networks is effective for him, but it's really just his tried-and-true message broadcast on a new medium.

And yes, your corporate social-media program can still be a success without a famous personality at the helm. The wonderful thing about social media is that the new online networks are places anyone can make new connections and build a reputation. As long as your social-media guru is authentic, generous, smart, interesting, helpful, and true to her word, she'll build a loyal following over time—both for herself and your brand.

Take Jim Deitzel. He's the face behind the logo at Rubbermaid's successful Twitter account. Deitzel isn't the founder, the CEO, or some ad spokesman. But he's a real person who has shown incredible instincts and sensitivities to connecting Rubbermaid with its audience on Twitter. And he makes no effort to hide his identity under a corporate veil: "There's always a person behind a Twitter account," he says. "I wanted people to know who they were talking with and I wanted them to get to know me personally. I wanted people to know they could count on me, not just a logo, to answer questions, talk about partnerships, and just feel connected."[17]

IT'S A MULTICHANNEL WORLD

The distinctions between on and offline, traditional marketing, and digital marketing are blurring and disappearing. Increasingly, any campaign you undertake will be multichannel—the same messaging will be consistent across all these media, supporting all other channels while taking advantage of the unique attributes of each. The walls between brick-and-mortar stores, Web sites, direct-mail catalogs, and the mobile experience are coming down. For a merchant, the world is not as neat and tidy as it once was: don't expect your print coupons, say, to be redeemed at retail stores and your e-mail codes to be used exclusively online. Customers expect to receive your marketing message in whatever form is handiest (e-mail, mobile text, catalog, and/or broadcast media), search for you in whatever means is handiest (Web search, local text search, local voice search, GPS, etc.), make their transaction wherever they prefer (Web site, mobile site, phone, in store, kiosk, pickup in store, etc.), and redeem your offer across channels (a physical gift card, gift certificate code, coupon code, and/or scanable bar code sent to their smart phone).

After the order is placed, they expect seamless customer service and fulfillment, so they can check order status by phone, online, or the mobile

Web and ask questions and make complaints wherever they wish—your Web site's online chat service, your Facebook fan page or Twitter stream, possibly even someone *else's* Web site, Facebook, or Twitter stream. Depending on the market, your CS people may need to be monitoring places from Yelp!, TripAdvisor, Epinions, the Better Business Bureau, the blogosphere, etc., to pick up signals far and wide of customer questions, complaints, or issues you need to address before you're the focus of the next egg-on-the-face Toyota recall.

This is an important point: Customer service has very much migrated to the Facebook page and Twitter stream. It's where your customers are and it's their first and easiest way to reach out to your company (finding your 1-800 number on the "contact us" page of your Web site is *so* 2005). If you're not prepared on your social-media platform to serve CS inquiries, soothe ruffled emotions, re-ship products, and grant discounts or credits, don't even start a corporate social-media program. Give your SM team the tools and authority they need to make customers happy.

For starters, it's just the right way to do customer service in the twenty-first century. And importantly, when customer service occurs publicly, as it now does on Facebook and Twitter and the other social-media platforms, your disgruntled customers do you public damage. On the other hand, your publicly resolved problems cast a public glow that is to your lasting benefit. The viral power of social media cuts both ways.

FAST, GOOD, CHEAP—PICK ANY TWO

Meet carpenter Ted Lylis, one of my Vermont neighbors. He combines the salt-of-the-earth qualities of a good New England builder with a quick smile, a hearty handshake, a mischievous look, and a bushy gray beard that would do Jerry Garcia proud. Top it off with a ball cap and a pair of suspenders. But what I like best about Ted is his folk wisdom. Haggling over the specs and budget for an addition a few years back, when my wife and I were expecting Louisa, our youngest daughter, Ted introduced us to an important concept in the construction biz:

"Fast, good, cheap," said Ted. "Pick any two."

Think about it. You can rush it and do it on the cheap, but it won't be any good. You can have it done well and on the fast track, but it will cost a premium. Or you can do a good job without spending a lot of money—but it will probably take back burner to other projects and, therefore, take forever.

So it is with social media.

Invest enough time in your social-media program to have a sensible, well-thought-out plan and a healthy understanding of the various networks. Invest enough money so that the effort doesn't stall and is professional enough that it doesn't tarnish your brand image. Above all, invest in quality: quality of message, quality of relationship.

In this book, I'll share tips for making the best use of the major social-media platforms, both for customer service and for marketing. I'll describe the efforts and successes (and some failures) of other companies.

Social media has many applications for community groups, nonprofits, political campaigns, and other organizations. My focus in this book is on for-profit businesses, large and small, but the book contains useful lessons for all sorts of groups.

For a business venturing into social media, the risks and potential rewards are high. People are passionate about this space; the most active social networkers are poised to be your brand's staunchest evangelists—or your most blistering critics. Some companies have made millions of dollars through smart and sensitive outreach in social media. Others have blundered into self-inflicted fiascos—PR nightmares that accelerate with the speed and force of a virus.

Here are some of the other topics we'll cover in this book:

- Embarrassing blunders of companies who got social media wrong
- Blogging 2.0—the new social-media features for your site
- Social shopping and the value of user-created ratings and reviews
- Adding social-media buzz to your PR campaigns, your online store, and your promotions
- Writing your social-media business plan

I've spent more than 15 years working in e-commerce, online marketing, and Web publishing. In this book, my goal is to help your business participate in this fastest-growing cultural trend of our time.

My aim is to separate the hype from the reality and offer some hands-on, practical advice for connecting with your customers and communicating your brand in the new social-media landscape. In the course of writing this book, I interviewed and researched businesses all over the country, from small mom-and-pops to big multinationals, so the book is populated with a lot of anecdotes, case studies, experiences, and results of actual online campaigns. I hope you'll find them as inspiring as I do, and that together they provide you a map to help you tap the promise of social media while sidestepping its landmines.

Chapter 2

Getting Started—The Strategy

LISTEN

Step one in your corporate social media program is to *listen*. Listen before you talk. Walk before you run.

Social-media platforms are for people, not companies. But times are changing, and the platforms are changing. The social networks are eager to make themselves more hospitable to businesses so they can finally start to make some money on their enormous audience.

And more heartening, *businesses* are changing. Business leaders like you are hearing the buzz about online social networking—and they're experiencing it firsthand in their personal lives, or in navigating LinkedIn or other business-networking sites in their professional lives. Social-media platforms are *not* for businesses that behave like faceless corporate behemoths eager to push a marketing message down the nearest convenient throat.

But social-media platforms *are* for businesses that behave like people.

That is, social media is a great place for businesses and organizations that genuinely care about what their customers and other people are thinking and saying about them. These are the kinds of businesses devoted to customer service and ready to perform great customer care through whatever new channels emerge.

Social media is also a welcoming place for firms that have a distinct, direct, personal culture and whose marketplace touches on a *higher purpose*—not just selling stuff, but also exhibiting social consciousness, displaying and sharing a unique corporate culture, or serving a market that is itself passionate and invested with a little something extra: companies with environmental consciousness, those serving a cultural or ethnic niche, lifestyle companies, and rabid hobbies can all fit the bill.

The social-media revolution has digitized our social lives and humanized our businesses!

So, as I said, step one is for you to listen. You definitely don't want to swoop in, guns blazing, with a business presence if you don't know these networks intimately already as a personal user. But nowadays, there is no reason to. You may still be a little unclear about what exactly the appeal is of Twitter, Facebook, or whatever. But if you turn to your left or right in the company cafeteria, no doubt your operation is staffed with a number of savvy technorati, people well versed in the mores and ways of social networking and ready for the new challenge of helping your company navigate it.

Participate on Twitter, Facebook, YouTube, and special-interest networks and blogs as a listener. Understand the culture. Make some friends.

Even Dell, the company that made headlines by generating $3 million in sales through its Twitter program, hastens to point out that social media isn't about selling. "The Dell philosophy is very much to listen," offers Dell's Marissa Tarleton, global head of online merchandising, small and medium business. She notes that Dell has more than *3 billion* customer interactions or conversations a year, and many of them are now occurring in social media. "We have a really robust process to filter those conversations and feedback and get it back into the organization to learn and improve."[1]

By listening, I mean two things:

1. Listening is the attitude you'll adopt when interacting with customers online. Your approach to social media is to value customer opinions and learn from them. In your corporate social-media program, you will put a higher priority on listening and learning than in getting your message out.
2. Monitoring will be a broad, systematic practice you'll adopt, with the help of the many social-media monitoring services, to collect, quantify, and make some sense out of what customers, *en masse*, are saying about you online. Your monitoring program is your ear to the ground, your first sign of emerging "sleeper" hits or of incipient PR disasters.

ESTABLISH YOUR SOCIAL-MEDIA BEACHHEADS

At this stage we're still committed to doing more listening than talking, more planning than executing. But there's one area I'll urge you to rush into: establishing the usernames and URLs for your company's social-media feeds and fan pages. Having intuitive, short, recognizable addresses for your social-media home pages is crucially important—and it will be an enduring frustration if some poacher reserves the best URLs before you do.

There are rules on Facebook and other platforms about how many fans you need before you can reserve your custom URL, but for the most part, the race is to the swift; you should waste no time in reserving accounts and usernames with addresses like these:

http://www.Twitter.com/yourcompany

http://www.Facebook.com/yourcompany

http://www.YouTube.com/yourcompany

http://www.MySpace.com/yourcompany

http://www.LinkedIn.com/in/yourname

WHO "OWNS" SOCIAL MEDIA?

Before your social-media program gets off the ground, you'll need to determine what departments and individuals will be responsible for its strategy and day-to-day management. Chances are, a lot of people at your organization are vying for some involvement in your new social-media program—and maybe some say over its direction. After all, Web 2.0 and social media are cool, cutting-edge fields. And they really do touch on virtually every corner of the enterprise: marketing, PR, shareholder relations, and customer service. And your IT and legal departments have some pretty good reasons to scrutinize the program as well.

Max Kalehoff, vice president of marketing for Clickable, a leading advertising tracking and analytics platform, puts it this way: "Social is something that transcends silos. It has to be coordinated across every business sector and function."[2]

Jim Tobin, author of *Social Media Is a Cocktail Party*, sees there being an immediate, short-term answer to the social-media staffing question and a different, longer-term solution. "Short-term companies are absolutely correct to bring on an expert or a small team assigned to social media . . . It takes a certain amount of expertise to understand it and utilize it without getting burned. In the long term, however, putting social media in a box like this, regardless of where you put it, won't work. That's because social media is a toolset, not a tactic, and a lot of people are going to benefit from using one or more tools in that toolset."[3]

Kalehoff notes, "Social is not necessarily a huge, scalable goldmine of opportunity. So social media isn't exclusively for marketers. It is also for PR people, brand managers, consumer insight, and CS and quality people."[4]

In my experience, it is generally marketers who are the first to latch onto social media as a potential channel for their business. So let me assume you're a marketer. Let's talk about some of the main parties in your company whom you'll need to invite to the social-media table.

GIVE CUSTOMER SERVICE A SEAT AT THE TABLE

The people most likely to champion the cause of corporate social media are either the top brass or the marketers. They have a natural appetite for the next big thing and an eagerness to reach out to find customers and prospects wherever they can be found.

But if the brain trust that starts your social-media program is composed exclusively of marketing types, you're in trouble. Social media is not a marketing channel or a branding channel. It's a communications platform. Good branding—and even good marketing and selling—can be *outcomes* of social media done well. But at its heart, social media is about communication, two-way, direct communication between a company and its customers and prospects.

These are the kind of conversations at which your CS team is expert. Engaging your head of CS in the challenges and opportunities of the social-media world is a great way to energize her and invest your program with all the service and communication skills that come naturally to a great CS person.

COOPERATE WITH INVESTOR RELATIONS, LEGAL, AND OTHER STAKEHOLDERS

When I was writing this book and posting about its progress, I was asked by investor relations professional Lynn Ricci: "I'm curious whether the book will include social media for public companies—specifically for the role of investor relations?" Ricci is investor relations director of Sound-Bite Communications, a Boston-area company that offers an integrated suite of voice, text, and e-mail for customer communications. With more than a dozen years of experience managing investor relations, Ricci has seen a lot of change in the IR landscape over the past decade, not least social media—it may be the most profound thing ever to hit corporate communications.

IR professionals have in the past several years faced Sarbanes Oxley and other securities regulations and disclosure challenges in a suddenly decentralized communications model where controlling the message and its channel is essentially impossible. The fondest hope of a marketing or PR person is that the decentralized word-of-mouth power of the Web will virally spread great news about the company. But the opposite is also true: Public relations execs and IR people also need to be on heightened response levels to react and try to contain and defuse virally growing bad news or scandal should it start to emerge.

"Investor relations has fallen behind in social media in general," points out Ricci. "Social media can be a new way to reach your investor base and keep them informed, but in many companies, it's seen as a marketing-only function. Companies are naturally more conservative around investor communications and become hesitant with the idea of Twitter or quick posts on blogs, since in the past everything had gone through legal."[5]

To keep up with industry developments, Ricci attends events like the annual conference of the National Investor Relations Institute (NIRI). At its 2009 and 2010 conferences, NIRI dedicated high-level panels to the role of social media in IR. In them, Laura Graves, director of global investor relations at Cisco, and Robert Williams, director of investor relations at Dell, addressed such questions as:

- How can I make use of social media and not get in trouble?
- How much time do I have to devote to social media to be effective?
- Does social media really have an impact on investment decisions and shareholder value?
- What is the future of social media in an IR context?

The biggest impact on IR is in handling a vastly decentralized flow of investor questions and comments, which now are as likely to pass through Twitter, Facebook, the Motley Fool, or Yahoo Finance as they might be to flow through the official corporate IR Web site. Social media now influences how individual and even institutional investors research companies. But caution is in order, too. Under some circumstances, information and statements posted to corporate Web sites and blogs is considered "fair disclosure" by the SEC.

The upshot: Investor relations absolutely should be comfortable with the tools of social media, incorporated into the back-and-forth communications involving shareholders, stakeholders, and the media. Using these tools skillfully and with sensitivity will help an IR professional tell her company's story, correct online misinformation, and become a valuable counterpart to investors and analysts.

And yes, legal needs a seat at the table, but in today's instant, decentralized, and humanized business environment, the last thing you should do is stifle the new customer relationship under a slow, overly cautious, and bureaucratic legal review of everything you propose to post. Social media doesn't work that way. It's a fast, personal, open, and authentic communications and publishing channel. Legal should no more scrutinize the social-media program than it would micromanage customer-service phone calls or internal e-mail messages.

What suffices, instead, is (1) for legal to have a strategic role in understanding the overall scope of the social-media program and advising on potential trouble spots, liabilities, and—most important—*helping craft the rules of engagement*; and (2) for legal to be well integrated with the social-media team, so that when potential legal issues arise or sensitive information is to be made public, they can give input and approval fast, in Internet time. Legal's role should be to help the team avoid pitfalls, but it should not fall into a pattern of wielding the veto pen or of slowing up an agile, customer-responsive communications and publishing channel.

Unfortunately, the young, Web-savvy staffers who will most likely lead business into the social-media age are not exactly the demographic to put your legal department at ease. Many studies, and tons of anecdotal evidence, show that the Millennial Generation has a casual attitude toward privacy, corporate IT and legal policies, and much else. In its research report *Millennials at the Gates*, Accenture said, "The results, in fact, show either a surprising lack of awareness or a blatant disregard for corporate policies regarding the use of information technology. More than half (60 percent) of Millennials say they are either unaware of their companies' IT policies or are not inclined to follow them."[6]

In its survey of Millennials' attitudes toward online posting of work or client information:

- Only 40 percent say their employers have published detailed policies related to posting work or client information on public Web sites.
- 31 percent don't know whether their company has such a policy.
- 17 percent say their employer hasn't published such a policy.
- 6 percent say the company policy is too complex to understand.
- 6 percent said they would ignore the company policy.[7]

Ed Moran, director of product innovation at Deloitte and an author of its "Tribalization of Business" survey, puts it this way:

> Going forward, [social channels] will be the primary way companies interact with their customers and future customers . . . Your whole enterprise should care, not just marketing. Your product-development people should be sitting right there saying, "What does this mean for the next revision of our product?" It'll help you get smart about support. "What are the bugs in our product, or what's not clear about the owners' manual?" You can correct that almost in real time through better integration with your support. Think about HR, even. People who are really engaged with your company's product and services and want to help; wouldn't those be great people to employ some day? So when you go across the enterprise and look at the different functions, every one of them should have a seat at the table.[8]

BEWARE OF SOCIAL-MEDIA DRIFT

So, we've just argued that basically every department deserves a seat at the table. But that can be a recipe for disaster—or at least inefficiency, contrary messages, and drift. In its *2010 Global Social-Media Check-Up*, the research and consulting firm Burson-Marsteller points out the dangers of competing, overlapping, and isolated social-media programs under the aegis of different departments and local offices:

> We found that each of these tools is being used extensively not only by corporate headquarters, but also by local market offices, various divisions of the company, and for one-time corporate events. To this extent, social media is providing great benefits and opportunities by helping different niches of a company reach their target audiences. But it is also introducing challenges by creating mixed messages and tones and by leaving abandoned Twitter accounts and Facebook fan pages that may be detrimental to the brand.[9]

HAVE A MISSION IN MIND

Every company has a mission statement nowadays, right? A short and to-the-point expression of a firm's goals and guiding principles. For Google, famously, it's:

- Organize all the world's information.
- Don't be evil.

Assuming your company already has a mission statement, display it prominently in the work area of your social-media guru or team. When you forge into SM, this statement will reinforce the purpose for reaching out to customers on these platforms, and the rules of engagement—the style and approach you'll take.

Maybe some of the core mission elements should also be in the e-mail signature of your social-media team members. Granted, it won't surface in interactions with your community on Twitter, Facebook, YouTube, or your blog, but the presence of a signature line is good for two reasons: (1) it reminds employees of the goal every day, and (2) social media done right often means interactions begun well on the SM platforms eventually evolve to other contact channels—your social-media team members and the pillars of their online community start to become friends, and get each other's direct e-mail, phone, and IM.

When you embrace a "bigger picture" mission statement, the reach, relevance, energy, and appeal of your social-media program will benefit. PETCO's mission statement, for instance, is "To promote the highest level of well-being for companion animals and to support the human-animal bond." So it's no wonder the roughly 35,000-fan Facebook community is enriched with uploaded pictures of members' pets, appeals for charities like Animal Rescue, and calendars of events ranging from Pet Cancer Awareness Day to the Miami Chihuahua Races.

In its social-media efforts and overall corporate communications, General Mills strives to be about more than just an array of food products. The company puts social action at the forefront of its message—focusing not just on their products, but on the more expansive topics of nutrition, health, and education.

Of course, don't craft your social-media mission statement without an ear to what your audience is most interested in, what they're responding to and expressing interest in.

"Your social-media program should be driven by fan feedback and what the followers ask for," says Best Buy's Mark Mosiniak.[10]

Start by restating your company's mission. Then ask yourself how that mission applies to a niche audience within the millions of people now active on social-media Web sites.

THE RULES OF ENGAGEMENT

That company mission statement is a great place to start, but it doesn't go far enough. Since social media is a new landscape with its own rules, you need social-media-specific rules for conduct. This will govern how you'll interact with customers. While being honest and authentic in these platforms is a must, you're still a company representative, and many things you might say without a second thought among friends might not be appropriate for your business SM program. So while everyone doing social-media posting and customer interaction should be at pains to let their own unique voice and personality come through, certain things are permanent no-nos. Nothing that gives any impression of sexism, racism, slander, or dishonesty can be tolerated.

Rudeness in a CS person isn't acceptable, but it happens. Your A-player customer service reps have probably already distinguished themselves, as have those C-minus players whose attitude and phone or e-mail manner are potentially damaging to the customer interaction and your brand. Even your top people can have bad days. CS staff are under more stress than just about anyone, and some days anybody will retaliate to a boorish or over-demanding customer. But today, if you do so in social media, your outburst is forever—if it is inflammatory enough, it will be enshrined forever like a bug in amber, and spread about and reposted throughout the Web.

One important rule for engagement is not the style of communication but its pace. How often will your people respond to online comments and questions? Like any CS operation, your social-media team must establish strong rules and monitoring for a 100 percent response rate in a set period of time.

Remember, your business is making its foray into social media for one reason: to get closer to your customers. So when your presence does what it's supposed to, and elicits feedback, you must participate. When your online community starts to talk to you, *always answer back*. It's the least you can do.

Many old hands have tried to instruct newcomers on how to comport themselves properly in this new social arena. Lizzie Post, the great-great-great granddaughter of Emily Post, offered tips on the etiquette of social networking on Facebook and MySpace. These things don't come naturally, and any mistakes made are made publicly and to some degree indelibly (yes, the swiftness of Internet time means that any faux pas quickly gets new content heaped in front of it). But they never go away, thanks to the forever-storage online, the tirelessness of search engines, and the fact that bad news now travels not just fast but *virally* fast.

If you think the social minefield is fraught for individuals, it's worse for businesses. There's a potential for reputational and indirect financial damage. The environment was not designed for business and has a hostile streak for business.

Many social-media etiquette guides for business play off the idea that proper behavior in social media isn't much different than proper comportment in life. There's the "social media is a cocktail party" analogy of Jim Tobin and Lisa Braziel. Or take Eric Fulwiler's "10 Things Your Grandmother Can Teach You About Social Media." Fulwiler, who blogs on business at OpinionatLarge.com and is a social-media strategist at Forbes.com, offers such grandmotherly chestnuts as "mind your manners," "send a thankyou card," and "think twice before you speak"—each seen through a socialmedia lens. Here's some additional Fulwiler advice, grandma-style:

- **Tuck in your shirt**. *How you present yourself is just as important in the virtual world as it is in the real world. Make sure you are always aware of how you appear to others.*
- **Whatever happened to a good old-fashioned** . . . ? *Sometimes all these new gadgets and thingamabobs aren't as important or effective as we make them out to be. Sometimes a good old-fashioned e-mail, phone call, or even in person "get-together" can accomplish things that social-media can't.*[11]

Make your list of rules of behavior in the social-media space. You could start with the Boy Scout Law (". . . trustworthy, loyal, courteous, kind, etc . . .")

Beyond outlining the general virtues you'll want to exemplify online, make a few specific rules of do's and don'ts. Make them clear enough that everyone interacting with customers, the media, other businesses, and the general public in the social-media space cannot misinterpret them in spirit or in letter:

No flaming/think twice: No matter how rudely someone addresses you in the social platforms, no matter how unfair or uncouth, you can't unload on him. When you post for a business, be yourself but behave professionally. Imagine anything you type potentially retweeted 5,000 times and then appearing as front-page news within 12 hours. Are you still comfortable with it, or do you want to take it down a notch or two before pressing post?

Reply to every question.

No posting about others without their permission. Retweeting is fine, linking to others' online content is fine, and digging is fine. But don't post about something said or done by a customer, coworker, rival company, etc.

Living within the confines of a 140-character Twitter post, and at the fast pace of an online chat, your social-media staff will no doubt rely on the acronyms of the social Web—the LOLs and TTYLs that have become universal abbreviations. These both make it functionally easier to post in social networks, and indicate that, yeah, you get the culture of the place. But you'll have to use good judgment; it's fine for your people to LOL, but depending on your brand image, it may not be okay to LMAO!

Megan Casey is editor-in-chief at Squidoo, the network of user-created (or as Squidoo likes to put it, user-curated) pages dedicated to every topic under the sun. Says Casey, "Remind yourself: people online are real people." She offers up a recipe for proper online etiquette. Among her prescriptions are these:

- Give people a break.
- The break you probably deserve yourself.
- People are out to do good 99 percent of the time.
- You probably are too.
- Say thanks out loud and a lot.
- Try making someone's day.
- Chances are they'll make yours in return.[12]

Derek Sivers, who founded the pioneering online music store CDBaby and is today a leader in the music and digital words, offers these thoughts:

> When we yell at our car or coffee machine, it's fine because they're just mechanical appliances. So when we yell at a Web site or company, using our computer or phone appliance, we forget it's not an appliance, but a person that's affected . . . at the end of every computer is a real person, a lot like you, whose birthday was last week, who has three best friends but nobody to spoon at night, and is personally affected by what you say.[13]

HUMANIZING THE ONLINE CS AGENT

E-mail and online chat—which are increasingly the province of your customer-service people—are devoid of the personal signals, emotional cues, and conflict-resolution aids we rely on in human conversation. Our million-plus years of evolution as a social, tribal animal have built in a welter of nonverbal social cues to establish connection and teamwork, the smiles and eye contact that indicate we're on the same team, working for a solution. Strip away those aids, and text-based communication can be a recipe for misunderstandings. A text message can inadvertently come off as rude, dismissive, cold, negative, or bureaucratic.

The emoticons of the early days of the Internet—those happy and sad faces constructed of colons, parentheses, and other marks of punctuation—arose to meet this need, to bridge the gap between online messages and their emotional tone. Emoticons have today evolved into a library of literally hundreds of custom expressions, from blushingly coy to furiously angry and everything in between. They can help grease the skids in online chat, and some light use of them in your company's social-media interactions can be fine, but overuse could make your team come off like a bunch of giddy preteens.

Vivid 3-D avatars for virtual worlds like Second Life make online person-to-person interactions not just more real, but surreal. And avatars are not the only way to present your CS people to your social-media audience. Online videoconferencing, VOIP phone, and video chat are all increasingly useful and well-adopted tools that combine the convenience of the Web with the personal touch of phone or face-to-face contact.

HAVE A PUBLISHING PLAN

Rules of engagement should also govern very clearly how often you will post. Nothing is sadder than a Facebook page, Twitter stream, or company blog begun in the blush of enthusiasm and good intentions, posted too frequently and with high-quality posts, only to see those posts become fewer, farther between, and less and less inspired. So the key to your social-media program is a simple plan.

Gardener's Supply's e-commerce director Max Harris says the company posts to its Facebook page seven times a week—and six out of seven posts are non-commercial in nature: how-to, helpful information, inspiring thoughts, and ruminations from gardeners. The one commercial message of the week is just that: a "Deal of the Week" that Facebook fans can be expected to pay greater attention to, thanks to its rarity. "Social-media programs are about community," he counsels his fellow marketers. "Keep promotion to a bare simmer."[14]

EXPLORE THE CORPORATE BLOGOSPHERE

Robert Scoble (aka Scobleizer) held the job title of technical evangelist at Microsoft from 2003–2006, when he blogged about the company and its products with such famous candor that:

1. He improved Microsoft's image—and humanized the company—in the eyes of many technology geeks, and
2. He largely defined corporate blogging, and set a new standard for it.

Later, Scoble and Shel Israel wrote an enormously helpful guide for corporate blogging, *Naked Conversations: How Blogs Are Changing the Way Businesses Talk with Customers.* "If you ignore the blogosphere," they pointed out, "you won't know what people are saying about you. You can't learn from them, and they won't come to see you as a sincere human who cares about your business and its reputation."[15]

In 2008, the Marriott hotel chain announced that its corporate blog, authored by CEO Bill Marriott, had been responsible for referring $5 million in bookings to the main site. But the value of most company blogs is not so much to drive revenue, but to engage with customers on a daily basis and in a more personal manner than typical corporate communications allow.

For your business, the advantages of blogging are manifold:

- Establish closer, more human contact with your customers and prospects.
- Quickly address emerging opportunities, timely events, and potential scandals or crises—you name it.
- By nature, blogs are richly interlinked with the fabric of the Web. Inbound links to your blog posts boost your search-engine rankings.
- Because of their timeliness, blog posts are picked up more quickly than static Web pages and rise more quickly to prominent rank in search results (they tend to recede quickly, too, like news items).

A 2009 study by HubSpot found that businesses that blog get 55 percent more traffic than non-blogging businesses, enjoy twice the number of inbound links, and have over five times the number of pages indexed by search engines.[16]

Launching a blog was never technologically difficult—from its very beginnings in 1997, when Jorn Barger coined the term "weblog" to describe an online diary, one of the most compelling attractions of blogging has always been its ease. No longer did daily or even hour-to-hour publishing present huge financial, technical, and operational hurdles. The barrier to entry is zero. With simple, free, and cheap blog platforms, individuals and companies alike have a communications platform that levels the playing field between huge operations—say multinational news operations staffed by hundreds or even thousands of journalists—and the stereotypical "guy in his pajamas."

So if blogging is so great and powerful, why am I merely suggesting that you "explore the blogosphere"? Why not jump in, as a corporate blogger, with both feet?

Because blogging is hard. Yes, pressing "publish" is easier than it's ever been. But the tasks of creating fresh material, researching, and writing it well have never been easy. And in blogging, persistence is everything. A stunning 95 percent of blogs are abandoned by their creators. For you to stick with it, and keep publishing at a regular frequency, will take extraordinary commitment—yet failing to do so will reflect badly on your brand.

The thing about establishing your company blog, hanging out your little shingle on the blogosphere, is that if it is lame or irregular—if weeks and months go by without a post—it will be an embarrassment to your company.

Even if you stick with it, doggedly, but you never generate the pleasure and passion for it that makes it fun and self-perpetuating, your corporate blog will be nothing but an albatross around your neck. You don't want that—so let's take it slow. Let's not plan to throw the big social-media party at our house yet. Let's recognize that the big party is currently at somebody else's house. Actually, countless other houses. Your job now is just to go out there and participate in those parties, take part in those conversations.

You'll learn a lot in doing that—following the leading blogs in your area of interest, getting to know their authors. Then, gradually, becoming known to their authors. Commenting, congratulating them for a post well written, and bringing up relevant points of your own.

Prior to launching your own blog, consider offering articles to trade publications or other blogs in your market. Post as a regular "guest blogger."

Frankly, as you build connections and participate in the conversation, you may decide that the blogosphere is rich enough without you needing to author your own blog.

And if, after all your legwork and networking in the blogosphere you feel ready and energized to add your company's blog to the mix, go for it. You will have a ready-built audience to read your work and spread it around, and more importantly you will have imbibed the generous, public-spirited, non-mercenary, and interconnected nature of the blogosphere. This will make you a better blogger and a more successful one.

SET UP GOALS AND A MEASUREMENT SYSTEM

When it comes to their social-media efforts, companies are chucking a lot of pasta at the wall, hoping some of it will stick. Big, full-fledged corporate social-media campaigns (especially for Fortune 400 companies) can be enormously complex and integrated affairs, requiring the work of expensive outside ad agencies, coordination with mobile devices, and the support of traditional media ad buys—plus ad spending on the social-network platforms themselves.

Sure, smaller companies are still doing social media on a shoestring. And many will say that this is the right way to do it—that ambitious, costly campaigns like T.G.I. Friday's hamburger giveaway or Pepsi's Refresh Project are too much noise.

But even smaller firms, making smaller investments, have recognized they need to track and measure social media's return on investment. If you're going to be investing time, effort, staff dollars, and other resources, how will you measure the success of your program?

What Web analytics tools exist to help companies measure social media?

- Facebook itself offers basic analytics for your fan page, and ad-tracking metrics.
- You can add Google Analytics tracking to your Facebook Page.
- Omniture has added a suite of features to support tracking and optimizing social media. WebTrends, Coremetrics, and others have done the same.
- You can use monitoring tools from Radian6, Jive, vocus, and a slew of others to track mentions of your brand across the blogosphere and social-media landscape
- Start-ups like Sometrics, Viralheat, and Sysomos specialize in comprehensive social-media tracking.

And of course, there are best practices for tagging the links from your social-media pages to your main site. Especially if you're doing e-commerce, your tagging is all-important to measure the impact of your social-media efforts.

What to Track in Social Media

There are three sets of metrics for businesses to track. You should establish target goals for each of these, and measure your progress toward them, probably monthly:

Measures of the popularity of all the social-media properties you manage:

- Twitter followers and Twitter lists
- Facebook fans

- Facebook engagement metrics (post quality and interactivity)
- YouTube subscribers and views
- Your corporate blog (visits, comments)

Impact of social-media traffic to your main Web site, and social behavior on your Web site. This is a tricky area, since correlation is not causation—social media did not necessarily create the traffic to your site; it could have been a round trip. But at the very least, these metrics capture a slice of your audience who are your engaged, online community—so they should be among your best customers, and growing them as a share of your total audience is good for your top and bottom lines. And it is also true that certain social-media campaigns, like contests or giveaways, are good at driving new visitors, e-mail signups, etc.

- Visits from social media
- Orders and sales
- E-mail newsletter sign-ups
- Catalog requests, leads, or inquiries
- Customer-submitted reviews (the raw number of reviews, and the average rating)

Measures of your brand visibility, and the impact on search-engine optimization

- External links
- Google Page Rank
- Brand mentions (the number of times your company is mentioned across the blogosphere and the rest of the Web—you can use Google Alerts, BackTweets, SocialMention, Radian6, or other tools to benchmark this data daily)

How to Track Social Media

For creating links from your social-media pages to your main Web site, there are five steps:

1. Find the right target on your Web site.

Table 2.1   Codes to track social media using Google Analytics

Argument	Explanation
utm_medium=social	All your social efforts, on whatever platform and whatever the campaign, are tagged "social"
utm_source=twitter	Separately track each platform you participate on—Twitter, Facebook, YouTube, your blog, etc.
utm_campaign= 20101228-newyears- resolutions	The campaign code describes your post and includes a date. The same campaign likely appears on several different networks.

2. Create tracking links your Web analytics package understands, to identify the source of traffic and the specific campaign or topic.

3. Put that big tracking link into a URL shortener like http://www.tinyurl .com.

4. When shortening links, you can also ask for a custom alias like http:// www.tinyurl.com/tennis-shoes so it looks nicer and takes up less of your limited space on Twitter.

5. Tag links from the social media to your site.

Here, for example (see Table 2.1), are the "medium," "source," and "campaign" codes I might use to track social media using Google Analytics.

WHAT'S THE ROI?

A 2009 study by Mzinga and Babson Executive Education found that while 86 percent of companies surveyed are using some form of social media in their business, almost none of them are tracking the return-on-investment. Only 16 percent were tracking the ROI of social media, while 84 percent were flying blind.[17]

Yet it's no wonder. At this point, you simply can't apply a clean, standardized equation to social-media ROI. As with superb customer service, you know social-media excellence is a virtue that is good for your business, but precisely *how good* is impossible to say.

The investment part is easy: Quantify the people-hours you're investing in social media, plus any dollars.

The return part is hard. I recommend totaling up the direct financial benefits of social media (direct sales referrals) and quantifying the likely worth or e-mail signups and catalog requests. Then try to attach a value to each new fan or follower. I would suggest that the annual value of a hard-core fan, compared to an average customer, can probably be teased out of your existing customer database. The revenue delta between a loyal customer and an average customer can then be prorated—maybe your social-media program deserves 20 percent of the credit for stimulating loyalty (the e-mail and catalog programs get the lion's share).

Positive brand mentions deserve some dollar value, too. So do external links—mainly because of their ability to boost your search-engine performance across the board.

All these numbers are going to be extremely arbitrary. But do come up with some model, then keep it consistent and track it. As long as you don't change your assumptions, your model will chart a useful trend line showing the business impact, month by month, of your social-media efforts.

IS MY COMPANY RIGHT FOR SOCIAL MEDIA?

When I interviewed him for my first book, Seth Godin told me social media was no place for business.

"Let's remember that social networks are about people, not about companies," Godin pointed out. "Nobody wants to 'friend' Ford Motor Company. As a result, companies, which are notoriously self-centered, have no place at all in a traditional social network. I'm not there to click on the ads, buddy."

"At the same time," Godin went on, "Google has made it easy for marketers to place anticipated, personal, and relevant ads in front of people who are looking for them. So, I guess the answer is:

• Make stuff that people will choose to talk about;
• Respect people's need for privacy and, yes, quiet;
• Make sure your ads show up in the right place at the right moment."[18]

The landscape has changed somewhat since then, but Godin is largely right: Social media is for people, connecting socially with people they know, or who share interests, for the purposes of communication, entertainment, or mission (think politics, social causes, etc.). Notably absent are businesses' typical goals of selling more stuff to more people.

But there *is* a place for business in social media, and there are seven sweet spots:

• Businesses or organizations run by a charismatic and well-connected leader, where the leader's social networking is a proxy for the prestige and principles of the business, or for natural showmen who make their business entertaining (such as Blendtec's, Tom Dickson, or Steve Spangler of Steve Spangler Science)

- Service businesses, B2B's, and consultancies where the person IS the business
- Social, political, and charitable causes—or businesses with a mission (Darius Goes West, LiveStrong) and brands that spring out of a cause or mission (SigningTime, The SCOOTER Store)
- Celebrities
- Entertainment businesses (video-based entertainment on YouTube, musicians on MySpace, writers on GoodReads)
- Lifestyle brands (Eesa snowboarding clothes, Nike, Performance Bike)
- Businesses that serve hobbyists, aficionados, or passionate special-interest communities (Yarn.com, Grunt.com, Bodybuilding, Wine of the Month Club)

Also, for *any* company, no matter how prosaic, there are a number of business tasks that are migrating to the Web, and to social media in particular, because that's where the people are:

- Customer-service questions
- Ratings and reviews
- Ads, product demonstrations, and how-to are migrating to YouTube

Finally, I'll rather grudgingly say there is a place for the big brand marketers, who have essentially bought themselves a seat at the table by being the first, most aggressive spenders on social-media advertising and creative campaign planning. These aren't niche players; they're big consumer-product companies whose products are marketed so broadly that their campaigns need to target broad "hot-button" interests in social media. Maybe it's lowest-common-denominator stuff, like sex appeal and entertainment, maybe it's a strong pocketbook appeal (free stuff!), or maybe it appeals to our better natures (charitable giving, environmental consciousness).

SOCIAL-MEDIA SCAMS AND PITFALLS

Rather than merely be a cheerleader for the benefits of social media, I should also point out that social media has its fair share of scams, frauds, and brand risks. One of the biggest reasons to participate in the major social-media networks is to be alert to fraudsters impersonating your company, or to respond to bona-fide customers posting unanswered complaints about you.

Sarah became a fan of "IKEA.com First 10,000 Fans to Register Get a $1,000 Gift Card!" on Facebook and suggested you become a fan, too.

It sounds good. Sarah is a friend, and she doesn't send you a lot of suggestions, so you pay it some attention in your crowded e-mail in-box. And $1,000 is serious money! You click through:

You Are Invited To Receive This Exclusive Offer For A Limited Time Only! Act Now To Get Your Free $1,000 IKEA Gift Card! This is only for a limited time, so be sure to enter right now! It's quick and easy; just follow these three simple steps:

Step 1: Become a fan.
Step 2: Invite all your friends. IMPORTANT*: If you do not invite ALL of your friends you may not be eligible. There's an easy way to quickly invite all your friends.* How to invite all friends.
Step 3: Register for your $1,000 gift card.
After a short registration process, your gift card will be mailed to you shortly. Thank you for your help!

Now, none of us want to spam our friends. But everybody has our price—and a $1,000 gift card, well that will quiet a lot of people's scruples. Plus, if it's an attractive offer to me, you reason, it'll be attractive to your friends and family too, right?

The problem is, this IKEA example turned out to be a complete scam. The page was created by a fraudster who had nothing to do with IKEA. The "short registration process" was actually an endless slew of schlocky side offers, from teeth whiteners to learn-at-home schemes, and two "trial offers" in which you had to enroll to qualify for the promised $1,000 gift card. But the pitches kept coming, the process was never complete—and of course, the promised gift card was a lie.

How fast does this kind of social-media scam offer catch on? Thanks to the viral power of social networks, it can grow exponentially. The sham IKEA page launched its offer on a Monday morning. I saw an e-mail like this at 9:45 Eastern time, and by noon when I visited it, the fake IKEA Facebook page had 2,600 fans.

The real IKEA quickly heard of it and began posting warnings about the scam. Chagrined users wall-posted cautionary messages like this one: "There is a page on FB that says it is advertising Ikea.com and is giving $1,000 gift cards to the first 10,000 fans. It is an absolute scam. . . . I totally fell for it . . ."

Within a few days of its appearance, the offer page was disabled by Facebook.

A similar scam targeted Whole Foods via fake fan pages with names like "Whole Foods FREE $500 Gift Card! Only Available for 36 hours!" and "Whole Foods Market Free $500 Gift Card Limited—first 12,000 fans only." As with the IKEA scam, these fan pages required users to invite all their friends, and then asked them to fill out forms with their personal information. The scam then used malware to crash users' computers and harvest their personal information.

The impact of scams like this is insidious: they damage the Facebook brand and lead customers to distrust its advertising as well as innocent suggestions made by friends.

In a survey of 500 companies by the security firm Sophos, 72 percent said they think social-networking sites like Facebook and Twitter pose serious risks to their data.

Sixty percent of respondents said Facebook was their most feared social-networking site when it came to scams and malware, followed by MySpace at 18 percent, Twitter at 17 percent, and LinkedIn at 4 percent.[19]

Scams like these also damage the brand of the scammed company. The real Whole Foods site posted prominent warnings against the scam, but many were suckered anyway. Perhaps most important, experiences like these leave customers with a lasting sense of shame for having spammed their connections with sleazy, misleading pitches. Once burned, twice shy; they will avoid passing any such offers to their network or responding themselves.

Fighting scams and frauds online is never easy, and the social-media sites will have to contend with it. Hopefully, with a combination of policing by the social-media networks, alertness and skepticism from users, and the "wisdom of the crowd," scams like these will be identified and shut down before they can gain any momentum.

These examples also highlight the importance of establishing your "listening" program early. When you're using social-media monitoring tools and watching them daily, you'll see signs of these scams early and can take steps to squelch them before they go viral.

HIRING YOUR SOCIAL-MEDIA GURU

While it's certainly not the *first thing* to attempt before kicking the tires on social media, before we wrap up our section on getting started, it's time to take a deep breath and open your checkbook. Thus far, you've been learning about social media, orienting yourself to the landscape, and absorbing the culture. You've established a few important beach heads on the niche and mass-market platforms.

But before you start creating content in earnest, you'll have to staff up.

Sure, up to now it has worked to fold social media into the responsibilities of your already overburdened marketing director or visionary founder—and if they love it and are good at it, they can hold onto some of the driving responsibility.

But as Mark Mosiniak of Best Buy Direct counsels, "Unless there's ownership, it doesn't happen. If it's 15 percent of someone's time, it will have zero results."[20]

You have to make a financial commitment, a salary budget. It can start in the form of a part-time focus, or well-managed intern—and in smaller companies, it may stay that way.

"Getting a dedicated person to make this 100 percent of their time is critical to success," says Mosiniak. Without a person at the helm of your social-media program and in the trenches, there is no way to roll out a coherent strategy, guarantee high-quality content, deliver consistent follow-up, and personally handle the praise, questions, and CS complaints that will come from customers and other online community members. And yes, it can be the same person at the helm and in the trenches, wearing different hats.

So who is the ideal person? And what's the job title?

This is an evolving field, and the job titles are all over the map, looking something akin to a MadLibs game using catchwords like "social," "community," "brand," and "evangelist." Here are just a few:

• Social-Media Manager
• Social-Media Specialist
• Chief Blogger
• Online Community Manager
• Online Media Manager
• Social-Media Community Manager
• Brand Evangelist
• Brand Community Manager
• Brand Advocate
• Digital Community Brand Advocate Web Manager
• Community Producer
• Community Executive
• Community Liaison Manager/Executive
• Community Host/Moderator

- Community Evangelist
- Community Developer
- Community Product Manager/Executive
- Community Support Manager/Executive
- Assistant Community Manager
- Community Content Manager
- Head of Interactions
- Chief Community Officer

Also, in larger or more specialized programs, you'll see more specific task-oriented jobs and internships ("Campus Rep," "Urban Street Photographer," "Mommy Blogger," "Social Video Expert," "Nightclub Event Social-Media Summer Intern," and the list goes on).

What's more consistent, as I see it, is the mosaic of qualities, qualifications, and responsibilities you'll need in this role.

What makes a great social-media guru, naturally, is social-media passion and know-how. A ton of energy and a voracious appetite for online socializing, posting, tweeting, commenting, and responding. They "get" the culture, they're part of it, they're natural people-persons, generous of spirit and optimistic by nature.

The ideal social-media professional also taps into a lot of the qualities and should exemplify the priorities found in job descriptions that far predate Web 2.0. A good social-media manager is one part PR director, one part loyalty/e-mail program manager, one part shareholder services expert, one part alumni relations director, and one part customer-service rep. Maybe they need a bit of "cruise director" thrown in. They have to simultaneously:

- Grasp and love the technologies and spirit of social media.
- Manage a high volume of daily communications—and in the process cultivate several high-quality, long-term relationships.
- Cherish the care and feeding of your most important stakeholders (PR outlets, best customers, investors).
- Take seriously even the most humble customer-service interactions.
- Recognize that in today's social-media landscape, behind even those humble interactions may be an influential VIP.

JVillage is a Web-development firm that helps synagogues, Jewish community groups, and not-for-profit organizations build and manage their

Web presences. When JVillage went looking for a social-media manager, the job description was a textbook example of the kind of person you need, in terms of responsibilities, talents, and passions:

"Do you tweet and use Facebook every day, all day? Is building social community so ingrained you just can't stop? Do you live and breathe the social-media world and have a solid understanding of all things social networking: blogs, networks, microblogging, wikis, podcasts—you name it. Do you have experience in Jewish culture? Come and participate in the membership engagement conversation at JVillage Network. Listen to our members, teach them, and facilitate the discussion. People and content are the main focus of this position."

When hiring a social-media person, here are some of the qualifications and responsibilities you might write into the job description:

- Create and manage pages on mainstream and niche social Web sites.
- Post high-quality and engaging content, regularly and on deadline.
- Conceive and execute creative events, contests, and promotions on the social sites.
- Manage fast and effective customer communications through social media, employing a centralized CRM system to measure performance.
- Incorporate social media into the corporate Web site, company events, conferences and exhibits, etc.
- Carry out growth strategy for social media, including paid advertising on social networks.
- Educate and advocate for social media within the organization.
- Set measurable goals for the program. Employ tracking tools and analytics platforms to measure progress toward those goals. Develop and distribute regular reports to key company execs.
- Discover new and cutting-edge social sites, tools, and tactics to better engage customers and further the company's goals.

THE SOCIAL-MEDIA INTERN

The notion of the social-media intern is already becoming passé, as firms have recognized that this social-media thing is big and is not going away and is deserving of the attentions of experienced staff. Time was, though, that interns were the gold standard of getting any sort of corporate social-media program going. After all, interns are cheap—so you didn't care if their ROI was unclear. And interns are young and hip; they "get" social media in a way that eludes their gray-haired bosses.

Interns can launch a fledgling social-media program where nobody on staff has much of a clue, but probably that's a recipe for disaster. One of the important aspects of social media when performed by business is that the outside world can communicate with and gain insight into a company insider. The higher up, the better. A here-today, gone-tomorrow intern, with no deep knowledge of what really makes a company tick, is a poor substitute.

But especially in cool, creative, cause-oriented companies, an intern can quickly fit in, can absorb the mission, and can really contribute to an existing social-media program. Eesa snowboarding apparel, the Rainforest Action Network, and Pizza Hut are just a few companies that have set interns loose on their social media. Blogger Aaron Uhrmacher's 10 Social-Media Tasks for Summer Interns could be a good list to start with:

1. **Overviews of social platforms**: Present opportunities to managers.
2. **Competitive analysis**: What are rival companies doing?
3. **Account creation and customization**: Get accounts set up on various platforms.
4. **Media research**: Which social-media platforms are your main media contacts using?
5. **Template creation**: If the intern knows Photoshop, try customized templates for Twitter or MySpace.
6. **RSS building**: Set up an RSS reader to monitor social-media activity around your brand, clients, or industry.
7. **Blog monitoring.**
8. **Blogging**: Showcase another side to your company, namely that you're empowering your interns.
9. **Web analysis**: A fresh set of eyes from your target demographic might be useful.
10. **Video**: Interns will likely be well versed in most types of online media, and most likely know how to edit video.[21]

THE SOCIAL-MEDIA CONSULTANT

What about hiring an outside consultant? Someone who knows the emerging landscape cold, who has built buzz for big multinational clients and knows how everything works, from Facebook advertising to social gaming widgets.

This is an emerging profession and it's attracting a ton of smart and motivated people with bona fide social-media stripes.

But the excitement and novelty surrounding the field mean that a number of shady little operations are out there, too, and what they have to sell is often very, very hard to distill into actual deliverables.

What I recommend is that you do your own research and dip your toe in the waters. You know your market best, and you probably already know some of the most prominent journalists, bloggers, and individual customers in it. Get started. Social media is a landscape for people to communicate with each other openly and informally and get to know each other. It's not a place you should fear venturing without the blessing of a highly paid consultant.

Where social-media specialists can really help you, I believe, is:

- Once you have dipped your toe, have begun your corporate social-media program, and have a modest track record, hire a consultant to assess your program and help you gauge your metrics and goals going forward.
- When you are ready to "take it to the next level," with integrated programs involving custom programming using Facebook and other developer tools, online stores hosted on social media, social widgets, and other complex projects.

INTERVIEW: PHIL TERRY

Creative Good was the world's first customer-experience consulting firm when Mark Hurst founded it in 1997. Since then, Creative Good has improved the customer experience—and measured improvements in key business metrics—for hundreds of companies, from Fortune 200 enterprises to dot-com start-ups. Creative Good CEO Phil Terry, who joined the firm in 1999, has been a longtime champion of good customer experience and has been exploring the opportunities of social movements online and offline since pretty much the dawn of the Web. He has written in *Harvard Business Review* on building communities, and recently moderated a customer-service panel at Twittercon.

Terry says, "I spend my workdays thinking about customer experience and about how executives can help each other, and I spend my evenings thinking about how adults can reignite their intellectual curiosity. At heart, I'm a community organizer building communities in the business world and elsewhere."

Phil and Mark are consummate networkers, generous and smart people full of energy.

Especially in technology fields, you encounter folks who aren't by nature extroverted—perhaps they are more comfortable at a computer screen for hours on end with a can of Mountain Dew at their side. But the experience of socializing, online or off, requires and reinforces a number of character traits: honesty, empathy, willingness to perform and return small favors, trustworthiness—and people need to be fun to be around: smart, funny, and sharing similar values or enjoying stimulating back-and-forth when they have different viewpoints.

What strikes me about Phil Terry and Mark Hurst is they are holistic, eclectic—they applaud and promote good experience wherever they find it, be it on a Web site, a person-to-person event, a road sign, or an instruction manual.

Over the years, Phil Terry's projects have included the private peer-to-peer helping and learning community he built for executives, dubbed the Councils; customer experience consulting at Creative Good; phone-based peer-facilitated reading groups at the Reading Odyssey, Inc.—and Slow Art Day, a global grassroots movement that organizes global museum meetups for the slow and thoughtful appraisal of works of art. He also contributes creative thinking at partner Mark Hurst's GEL conference.

Mark Hurst, founder of the GEL Conference (for Great Experience Live) has this to say about public speaking: "Here's the final measure of your success as a speaker: did you change something? Are attendees leaving with a new idea, some new inspiration, perhaps a renewed commitment to their work or the world?" It is this same ambition that they apply to all their work, including their social-media efforts.

Terry has always been a people-person, a champion of causes, and a builder of communities. At Occidental College in the 1980s, he was helping fight apartheid through protest and divestment, and spreading the word through bathroom fliers and other old-school messaging. But it wasn't long before he was tapping new forums, like CompuServe at the dawn of the commercial Internet, to get connected with like-minded people.

Creative Good is doing more social-media work. Can you tell me what the approach is?
Creative Good, the firm for which I'm CEO, has worked with more than 500 consulting clients in the last decade and we are working on some interesting new services for this challenging economy. One new area of work will be in social media. I started a Facebook group a year ago to celebrate Darwin's 200th birthday, which gathered 250,000 people and some of the world's leading scientists in 14 days. The lessons from this work combined with what we've learned building the Councils community and the Reading Odyssey are leading to a new practice area for clients.

The starting point is always on the consumer—observational research to discover behaviors and unmet needs.

The Councils are a business-networking group you formed and have helped nurture since 2002. What are they all about?
The Councils are a peer-learning and leadership network for executives, a cross-industry network of 450 members worldwide. My core message has always been about context and community. To build context and community, we have to set up an environment where it is safe to ask others for help. When you can do that, it is a transformative experience for everyone involved.

In the Councils, everyone understands trust is at the core.

Your slow art movement sounds a little like the slow foods movement. How does it work?
The basic idea is simple: Visit a museum. See a few pieces of art for 10 minutes or more. Have lunch and talk about it. Slow art is designed to help participants see art in a new way—to exercise their seeing, thinking, and listening muscle.

Slow Art Day involved 50 museums in cities all over the world. We promoted it largely on Facebook and other social media. One thing I like about slow art it's so inclusive and so disruptive at the same time. It supports museums, but it disrupts old ways of seeing.

Reading Odyssey is similar. We want to make it easy for adults to play with culture—read great books, discuss important ideas.

We run phone-based reading groups, lecture series, Facebook campaigns, and live events. They are a small seed, but down the road I hope they will affect thousands of adults.

Tell me about the strength of big networks. After all, it's one thing to maintain a tightly knit group of readers of great literature, or even some 450 council members, but what about the million-plus Facebook fans of T.G.I. Friday's restaurant, who friended the chain in exchange for a free cheeseburger?
A network that large is essentially a mailing list, not a community. In any community I've ever been a part of, there is a core community within the larger group.

The Darwin Group grew to 250,000 members in just 14 days. But within that group, the real community was 30 or 40 people behind the scenes who made it work. It was the community behind the community that kept the whole thing going, and they forged real connections.

The community behind the community is the engine for growth. Take Wikipedia, supposedly the work of millions of volunteer editors worldwide. There *aren't* millions of active editors, really. The vast majority of the work is done by a very small core of people.

It's the 80–20 rule—and in social media today it's really more like the 99–1 rule.

Create a community that is centralized, with a small group at its core.

This is not a new concept. Churches, civil rights workers, activists of any kind are always the small core of what becomes a larger group.

You have one foot in online media and one very firmly in person-to-person: organizing the councils, peer-to-peers, and Mark with GEL. Does the physical meetup make a difference? Or can you build a meaningful group that exists solely online?
My basic philosophy is that we live in the world we live in. The online/offline frame is artificial.

What is fundamentally new and powerful about online social media is the way you can now reach people and organize people and build communities so fast and in such scale.

Can social media communities be "scaled" for business—and should they?
In all this, the role of the marketer has fundamentally changed. In 1954, Peter Drucker was urging us to "create a customer"; that was a critical insight. Marketers' jobs used to be managing ad budgets and managing agencies. Now, marketers must become *community organizers*—that is a totally different set of skills. This person has to get out from behind his desk, go out there, and create customers and create communities. Obama used these skills to become president.

So, are social media just for customer service and communication, or can you use it to produce sales?
What you can do is listen well. That can inform and benefit many things—including sales.[22]

GUY KAWASAKI ON EVANGELISM

Whoever is in charge of your company's social media program, he or she should be at heart, an evangelist for your brand. One of the first people to wear the professional title of "Evangelist" (as an Apple Fellow at Apple Computer in the 1980s) was Guy Kawasaki.

Kawasaki is a serial entrepreneur, a round-the-clock tweeter, and the author of nine books on leadership, start-ups, and other business topics. Here are his tips for successful evangelism:

The future belongs to people who can spread ideas. Here are 10 things to remember:

1. Create a cause. A cause seizes the moral high ground and makes people's lives better.
2. Love the cause. "Evangelist" isn't a job title. It's a way of life. If you don't love a cause, you can't evangelize it.
3. Look for agnostics, ignore atheists. It's too hard to convert people who deny your cause. Look for those who are supportive or neutral instead.
4. Localize the pain. Never describe your cause by using terms like "revolutionary" and "paradigm shifting." Instead, explain how it helps a person.
5. Let people test drive the cause. Let people try your cause, take it home, download it, and then decide if it's right for them.

6. Learn to give a demo. A person simply cannot evangelize a product if she cannot demo it.

7. Provide a safe first step. Don't put up any big hurdles in the beginning of the process. The path to adopting a cause needs to be a slippery slope.

8. Ignore pedigrees. Don't focus on the people with big titles and big reputations. Help anyone who can help you.

9. Never tell a lie. Credibility is everything for an evangelist. Tell the truth—even if it hurts. Actually, especially if it hurts.

10. Remember your friends. Be nice to people on the way up because you might see them again on the way down.[23]

CRISIS MANAGEMENT IN THE SOCIAL MEDIA AGE

In his Twitter feed, the usability and customer-experience guru Mark Hurst commented "Interesting that @BP_America has 9,000 Twitter followers, while (parody) @BPGlobalPR has 104,000. Twitter amplifies parody over PR."

Hurst is right on—humor trumps most serious content on the Web. And serious or not, there's no excuse for being dry, boring, and devoid of personality. Sure, being responsible for the biggest oil spill in U.S. history means that British Petroleum isn't going to have the option of being irreverent, flip, or funny in its Twitter postings, or any public statements for that matter. But even in the teeth of an unprecedented catastrophe like BP's spill, it's possible to make an impression on your audience as an earnest and honest person—a real human being—trying to communicate openly.

And speaking of BP, let's turn our eye to the role social media is coming to play in corporate damage-control efforts. Since the Web is the main engine for news flow today, and the main engine for rapid, viral transmission of both positive buzz and negative scandal, it is only natural that the online social-media platforms will be an important stage for these issues to play out on.

During the gulf oil spill, BP gamely tried to put a human face on its company, from CEO Tony Hayward on down, doing the news and talk-show circuits, posting frequently on Twitter and Facebook, streaming live footage of the oil billowing out of the sea floor, and releasing YouTube videos depicting remote-controlled robot submarines hard at work trying to stop the leak.

Facebook, circa 2010, is not an ideal platform for dealing with serious corporate crises. The difference is telling, for instance, between Twitter, where people merely "follow" a stream of information, and Facebook, where users are obliged to "like" the source of information. During the worst days of the spill, when BP most needed to perform damage control both literally and figuratively, how many people—passionately interested in the news though they might be—were willing to "like" BP's page? About 7,000. That's 2,000 fewer than were following via Twitter, and in my experience it's typically the other way around. In its social-media survey of Fortune 100 companies, Burson-Marstetler found that the average corporate Twitter feed had 1,489 followers, while the average Facebook page has a whopping 40,884 fans.

When CEO Hayward was quoted saying "I want my life back," public outrage at BP as a company focused on Hayward as the public face of the company. His apology, posted to the BP Facebook page (among many other places), drew hundreds of comments, most of them negative and many of them abusively so. But scores of people "liked" the apology and stood up for Hayward, or praised rank-and-file BP employees and the company's efforts to fight the spill. That was a minority voice, to be sure, but the episode demonstrated that being part of the conversation allows even the most hated companies and execs to show their human side, make contrition, allow people to vent their anger, possibly spark a little exchange, and perhaps change a few perceptions.

BP also launched a full slate of resources on its Web site, and all in all, the spill offered some lessons of how to effectively reach out to people in the age of social media:

1. Provide plenty of information, in great detail, with frequent updates.
2. Be on every platform your customers and the general public are on.
3. Make top company execs participate in person.

REACHING THE MOMMY BLOGGERS

A major determinant of success for your social-media program will be how well you understand and target your audience. If you want an example of how social change has been ushered in by Web 2.0, look no further than the mommy blog phenomenon.

Of the 127 million U.S. social-media users, 68 million of them are women (77 percent of online women). An estimated 34 million of them are moms.

The Mom Blog Network, Mothers Click, and Mom Bloggers Club are just a few of the social networks that have sprung up to unite mom bloggers. The Mom Bloggers Club claims 9,500 bloggers as members.

BlogHer and SheBlogs are two major ad and PR networks bringing together women bloggers and the advertisers who covet their readers. Mommy blogs are the darlings of many a media buyer's blog ad spend, because women make 80 percent of household purchasing decisions.

BlogHer.com: 2,500 blogs reaching 20.5 million unique visitors per month

SheBlogs.org: 2,000 blogs reaching 20 million unique visitors per month

Women make up more than half the audience of the major social-media platforms, and they use the sites differently than their male counterparts. Experts say women employ social media to communicate, build connections, and share aspects of their personal lives. For men, the primary goals of online networking are to get information and to bolster their status.

"The whole world's gone social," says Facebook COO Sheryl Sandberg, "and women are more social than men." Women on Facebook have 8 percent more friends than men do, and they do 62 percent of the sharing. "The social world is led by women," says Sandberg. "If you reach women [online], they will tell their friends."[24]

I asked Elisa Camahort Page, one of three founders of the top blogging network BlogHer, to share her insights into this important demographic.

INTERVIEW: BLOGHER COFOUNDER ELISA CAMAHORT PAGE

What is it about women's blogs and their audience that makes them appealing to advertisers?
Part of it is old news: Women are responsible for over 80 percent of household spending. They control the purse strings, so consumer companies want to reach them.

Part of it is the more recent phenomenon of the Internet: All viewers, men and women, are spending more and more of their time online, less and less of it with other media channels.

And part of it is specifically about the profile of a woman who blogs. She is not only online and spending herself; she is sharing her advice, recommendations, and opinions with an *audience*. An audience of other women who trust what she has to say. And she is spreading her word across many online channels. A woman who blogs is statistically more likely to also tweet, and also post to Facebook, etc. It represents an amplified (and influential) word-of-mouth opportunity.

How has the women's blogging landscape changed in the years since you launched BlogHer—and what do you see coming down the pike?
When we launched BlogHer, part of our driving motivation was to once and for all answer a question we thought needed to die, namely: Where are the women who blog? And we honestly don't think people need to ask that question anymore. Does that mean people "get it?" Not always. It turns out that women are not as interested in putting themselves in neat little boxes as marketers, politicians, and the media! Women are not some monolithic bloc who act, think, vote, or blog the same.

You've sponsored a lot of research and you know this space better than just about anyone. Can you share some statistics about women bloggers and women in social media?
The BlogHer Network reached over 20 million unique visitors a month, and those women share these traits:

- They are cross-pollinating their voice and their work across multiple social-media tools. And that means they have an audience.
- After Internet search, they turn to blogs most frequently when making purchase decisions. And the information they find on blogs is highly influential . . . more influential than other media sources.
- They are motivated to blog for self-expression and community building. But we can't ignore the fact that the third top motivator is simply to have fun.
- Social networks definitely serve the purpose of keeping in touch with friends and family. Social networks are also a great source of fun. But blogs are considered a more suitable destination for a full range of other personal and pragmatic purposes . . . to keep up

with new trends and ideas, to seek and share opinion, advice and recommendations, and definitely to express one's self.

You can see the related percentages for the above points by reviewing our latest social-media study executive summary at http://www. blogher.com/files/Social_Media_Matters_2010.pdf.

What kind of brands or companies are successfully advertising on the BlogHer network? Can you tell a success story or two of campaigns that really took off?
We work with Fortune 500 brands across many different sectors. We offer the opportunity for broad reach across our entire network: deep engagement via sponsored video or text conversations on BlogHer. com *and* live interaction at our BlogHer conferences. I always like to share this particular case that capitalized on all of those: We worked with Ogilvy PR to help Tropicana launch a new product, Tropicana Trop50. We produced 24 weeks of a Web show, but also included media, contests, couponing, and sponsorship at our annual event. Here are some stats:

- Webisodes: 24 videos generated 5.6 million impressions
- Contest entries: 7,000+ on-topic contest entries
- BlogHer Conference Keynote: Provided 2,400 product samples, 1,200 women watched community-generated webisodes from tips filmed by 100 women at the Juice Studio at BlogHer '09
- Relevant awareness about Trop50's key message points increased 34 percent on BlogHer.com as a result of the Juice. Positive opinion increased 13 percent, and intent to purchase saw a 15 percent jump.

It seems offers and contests are especially popular. Are women particularly responsive to these kinds of ad campaigns?
Offers and contests can be popular if they are about or around a conversation that is relevant to women.
If you're interested in collecting e-mail addresses, that's one thing, but if you're interested in building an ongoing relationship with your customers, then tie your offer or your contest to a larger conversation. For example, right when the economy was imploding in late 2008, Prego sponsored a conversation on BlogHer.com. Not about

how you use Prego, but about sharing tips on how you save money at the grocery store. Yes, one person was going to win a grocery gift card, but members got very caught up in helping each other out with their tips and tricks. As it turned out, a percentage of the hundreds of comments the conversation generated actually mentioned the brand, but not because we asked them to.

Has the popularity of social media like Facebook and Twitter hurt traditional blogs by moving the conversation onto those networks? Or has it benefited blogs by stimulating more conversations and connecting more people?

We believe the popularity of any number of social-networking tools is extremely beneficial to bloggers, to brands, and to BlogHer itself. Now if someone likes what BlogHer does, they may blog about it, and if they do, they're likely to tweet that link. Then they may share that link on your Facebook fan page. They aren't just doing it necessarily to spread the word about us and the brands we work with. They're doing it to also spread the word about their own work. We are the lucky beneficiaries of this extended word-of-mouth network. Our study data shows that bloggers are the most likely social-media users to use *everything*. New social tools enable the amplification of what bloggers were already doing.

Can you offer any tips to businesses that want to appeal to women online?

Start by listening. The beauty of the blogosphere is that women are out there telling you exactly what they want and need and think. So, listen to them.

Then think really hard about how you can *join* the conversation, not interrupt it. Women have built communities online that are very significant in their lives. Trusted circles. Think about how you can add value to those communities, not about what value they bring you.[25]

BE REMARKABLE

I've saved this chapter's trickiest bit of advice for the last: Be remarkable.

Be funny. Be outrageous. Be generous of spirit and a true friend to those who follow you. Have an important social mission and pursue it unflinchingly.

"Remarkable almost never costs a lot," says Seth Godin, pointing to the success of Blendtec and its YouTube videos: "Blendtec has spent less than $1,000 to reach more than 20 million people with their videos. But there's no way they would work if the blender was lousy. Too many people jump ahead to the sexy part, without realizing that you don't get there without a product that's worth talking about."[26]

These are what make the social-media world go round, and they're no less applicable to businesses than they are to individuals. Maybe more so, since projecting the human side of your business doesn't come naturally. Your business, and the people behind it, can seem a step removed.

But that's not the way you want it to be. When your business steps out into social media, it must do it not as a faceless corporate entity, but as a real, living, breathing person.

Chapter 3

Getting Started—The Platforms

In this chapter, we'll go step by step through how best to participate in the major social networks and media-sharing platforms. This book is intended as a practical, across-the-board strategy guide for your business's social-media program—so we won't go into minute detail about each platform. If you need tactical how-to advice about a particular platform, we'll also recommend further reading dedicated to each, here and in appendix A.

According to Burson-Marsteller,[1] of the global Fortune 100 companies it surveyed:

- 65 percent use Twitter
- 54 percent use Facebook
- 50 percent use YouTube
- 33 percent maintain a company blog

"Understand the strengths of each different platform," recommends Mark Mosiniak, senior director of business development at Best Buy Direct. "We use Facebook mainly for marketing and customer relationship. We use Twitter predominantly, not so much for marketing but for customer service."[2]

FACEBOOK

Facebook is by far the most popular social network and one of the most visited Web sites in the world. According to Nielsen, 47 percent of Americans visit Facebook daily, nearly rivaling the 55 percent who watch TV. Facebook daily use easily beats out other traditional media like radio (37 percent) and newspapers (22 percent).[3]

- Facebook has more than 500 million active users.
- 50 percent of active users log on to Facebook in any given day.
- The average user has 130 friends and is connected to 60 pages, groups, and events.
- People spend more than 500 billion minutes per month on Facebook.
- The average user creates 70 pieces of content each month.
- About 70 percent of Facebook users are outside the United States.

15 FACEBOOK TIPS FOR BUSINESS

1. **Establish the company page—and the real people behind it**. The creator and administrators of a fan page are somewhat behind-the-scenes initially, but when they start responding to questions and replying to wall posts, their identities come to the fore. This can be a great opportunity for companies with well-known or visionary founders associated with their brands. And it's also a good thing to humanize the company by putting your social-media guru out there, front and center. But you may want to establish new Facebook accounts for the people managing your fan page, separate from their existing personal accounts.

2. **Post regularly**. Establish a publishing plan and stick to it—perhaps you'll post seven times a week, with one special promotion per week and the rest informative, newsy, or entertaining posts. You'll need to be flexible to post about relevant events at your company or in your market as they occur, but it's a good idea to sketch a rough plan. For instance, if you're an online pet supply store, picture a weekly schedule like this: pet-related news, new product, weekly special, how-to article, cute pet video, event promotion, and more pet-related news. You can let your company's promotional e-mail schedule drive some of your publishing plan. You can search Google News to come up with interesting pet-related items if you're at a loss for material.

3. **Invite your friends**. Individuals can suggest their company page to your friends. There are some cool JavaScript hacks out there that make it easier to invite all your friends in one fell swoop. But be careful. Nobody wants to be spammed, least of all by their friends, family, or peripheral colleagues. So do two things: First, make sure the site is an active, interesting place you're proud of, and second, invite only those friends you know well and feel comfortable suggesting the page for their benefit, not yours.

4. **Promote your Facebook page to existing customers**. You need to kick-start your fan base, and the best way is to tell your core customers about it. Add the Facebook logo to your Web site's navigation. Announce the fan page in an e-mail to your customers—maybe offer a discount to everyone who "likes" you.

5. **Set up a custom URL**. When you have at least 25 fans, you can reserve a good, recognizable URL, like http://www.Facebook.com/your company. You can establish the new URL by visiting http://www .Facebook.com/username/.

6. **Add a Facebook status widget to your home page and a Facebook logo link to your navigation**. These elements show your Web site visitors what's going on at your fan page and encourage them to join in—and it also makes it more fun for active participants when they see themselves on your site. I recommend making explicit calls to action: "Join Us on Facebook!" and "Follow Us on Twitter!"

7. **Add Facebook share and/or Facebook connect features to your site, and also display the "AddThis" widget on your pages**. A little bit of JavaScript added strategically to your Web site's page templates can add Facebook's "like," "share," and other features to your Web site, making it easy for Facebook users to promote your content or products to their friends. The "add this" widget does the same thing, but also for Digg, Twitter, MySpace, del.icio.us, StumbleUpon, and other social-media sites. When you launch a cool product or publish a noteworthy post, make it easy for your audience to share it with their friends. It's a fairly subtle way to show you're hip to social media and put the "network effect" to work. You'll attract more fans to your Web site and to your company Facebook page.

8. **Use Facebook's richness to your advantage**. Unlike Twitter, Facebook welcomes photos, videos, events, and limited HTML (or FBML, its unique Facebook Markup Language). Your Facebook page can be a rich and entertaining place. Make a point to upload a lot of the various

content types—such as photos from a recent company picnic. Create contest entry forms or e-mail signups so your fans don't have to leave the comfort of Facebook in order to connect with your company. See what people like and what they respond to.

9. **Staff for customer service**. Increasingly, fans of your brand will turn to Facebook—not your 1-800 number or your customer-support e-mail address—when they have questions they need answered. On the Facebook page of Bogner USA apparel, customers may ask about the availability of a new cosmetic bag or how to get a zipper repaired on a beloved ski parka. Bogner staffs its Facebook team so that such questions are picked up immediately and quickly and competently answered.

10. **Advertise for new fans using Facebook**. I was a skeptic about advertising on social media (and still am, when it comes to Twitter), but Facebook is getting it right. While I wouldn't recommend Facebook ads as revenue-generators, they've proven great for attracting new fans to your page, and also—in a $500 women's cycling wardrobe giveaway contest we ran for Terry Precision Bicycling—in generating e-mail signups. I estimate you can acquire new fans or contest signups for $0.50 to $1 apiece. Assuming you're cultivating a valuable relationship with them, and knowing that each fan has the potential to spread the word to their friends on Facebook, that's a very attractive number.

11. **Ask questions**. Some of your posts should pose a question to your audience. Asking your fans what they think, or asking for their own stories or experiences, is an easy and effective way to encourage more engagement.

12. **Have a contest or host an event or meetup**. It's so satisfying when your Facebook program helps you deepen the relationship with some members of your audience, from the passive (lurking and reading), to the casual (liking, commenting, and posting), to the active (participating in an event, entering a contest, or buying something from you). Whether you are driving some of your fans to a local retail event, or promoting something relevant to your market, like Green Up Day or Ride Your Bike to Work Day, brainstorm some in-person events you can throw your weight behind.

13. **Be active in the community**. This is where the identity of your administrator and the identity of your company intertwine. A company can't "friend" people on Facebook—only a person can. As your administrators get to know your fans, it is natural—and very good for the continued growth and popularity of your fan page—for them to be actively

friending your fans, joining relevant groups, and endorsing relevant causes. When they do these things, status updates percolate through their entire network, raising their visibility and that of your company.

14. **Monitor your quality scores**. Facebook displays a "post quality" and an "interaction" score for your fan page based on how many fans "liked" your posts or commented on them. It's a dead-simple approach to quality measurement, and it's really important. Challenge yourself to write good, compelling posts that your fans respond to!

15. **Try out FBML, the Facebook markup language**. You may have to bribe your resident codemonkey with a two-liter bottle of Mountain Dew to help you, but FBML is a useful and fairly well documented toolset to add new features to your Facebook page. You can use FBML to add inquiry forms, surveys, JavaScripts, and other elements to your page. You can also add existing Facebook widgets, or even dig into the very robust world of Facebook application development or online stores. More than any other social-media platform out there today, the sky is the limit.

T.G.I. Friday's leveraged the viral power of the Facebook group, saying "free burgers for everyone if we collect 500,000 fans." The nice thing about this is it incentivizes existing fans to spread the word before they can collect the free burger (and the incentive of a free burger is juicy enough that you don't feel too lame passing it to your friends and family).

The promotion was so successful that T.G.I. Friday's upped the ante, promising free burgers for up to a million fans. And sure enough, the company added a stunning 970,000 of them. Well done (pun intended).

TWITTER: IS IT A BLOG, OR IS IT E-MAIL MADE PUBLIC?

Spend any time at all in Twitterville (to borrow the homey term from Shel Israel) and you'll see three fairly distinct ways to compose a post:

- Microblog posts—observations conveyed in their entirety in 140 or fewer characters.
- Links to external pages, be they videos, longer-form blog posts or news items, or what have you.
- Direct messages—Containing the format @username, these posts are person-to-person messages visible not just by the recipient but by all the followers of the sender's Twitterstream.

I find this a fascinating aspect of the Twitter platform. With just three tools in the toolbox, inevitably most Twitter users will employ all three types of post. Yet the variation among users is enormous. Whole Foods is mostly messages to individuals, answering questions and conducting a friendly back-and-forth, only occasionally interspersed with a mention of grass-fed beef or favorite wines or cheeses.

Twitter is an odd bird (oops, another pun). The platform was born as an internal innovation at the Web start-up business Odeo. Co-founder Ev Williams had a problem: His developers, like developers the world over, were a decentralized and mercurial bunch, working weird hours and prone to go on all-night Mountain-Dew-fueled programming jags, then sleep through much of the workday. Williams needed something to facilitate better communication and coordination among the code-jocks and between them and the rest of the company. Odeo software architect Jack Dorsey came up with a simple messaging service that would work across the Web and as SMS texts to mobile devices. He dubbed it TWTTR.

As Shel Israel tells it in his excellent book *Twitterville*, "At the end of day one, a product designed for the internal use of a 12-member team had 20 users. The Odeo folks just couldn't resist sharing it with friends. Three years and two months after its public launch, there would be an estimated 32 million users."[4]

Twitter Strategies for Business

With more than 100 million members, and a structure designed perfectly for the rapid spread of information, Twitter is playing a leading role—perhaps the leading role—in the global transmission of news stories and cultural trends. Twitter has notched year after year of furious growth: 752 percent in 2008, 1,385 percent in 2009, 1,105 percent in early 2010.

Quite simply, Twitter is the fastest-growing communications medium in the history of the world. Your business should be part of the conversation.

Define Your Twitter Niche

Every Twitter account needs an "elevator pitch." If you can't concisely describe what it is and who it's for, don't bother. And then stick to the program. "I'm eating a bagel" isn't worthwhile content for anything but a very lame personal account.

For the e-commerce companies we work with, Facebook friends and Twitter followers are a subset—maybe 10 percent—of their house e-mail list. Presumably those fans are the really diehard enthusiasts, the evangelists. It's worthwhile to invest staff time on Twitter and other social-media platforms to:

1. Remind the evangelists about your offers,

2. Give them a platform to rave publicly about your stuff, and

3. Communicate with them, in a Web 2.0-style "customer-service/PR/ shareholder relations" effort.

Twitter Makes an Excellent Listening Post

Call it "microblogging" if you will, but Twitter is a lot more than a blog platform. It is, first and foremost, a communications platform. It's basically a public, internetworked e-mail system and SMS network. If you are using Twitter simply as a podium to publish blurbs linking to your company blog posts and press releases, you're missing the point.

Yes, you can and should use Twitter to publish short insights and news. And it's fine to link outside of Twitter if the item you're mentioning is longer than 140 characters.

But what you're missing, if you focus exclusively on getting your own word out, is the other side of the conversation. Just as in the real world, the online social-media world stops listening to narcissistic, self-infatuated speakers, the sort of people who pause in their monologue only long enough to say, "Enough about me—what do you think about me?"

Engaging in back-and-forth dialogue and spreading the word about what others are saying are both critically important parts of the Twitter ethos. Plus, it shows you to be generous of spirit, open-minded to what others are talking about, and well connected.

Yet research in *The Global Social Media Check-Up*, 2010, by the consulting and research firm Burson-Marsteller, indicates that too many companies are doing much more talking than listening. It found:

- 82 percent of corporate Twitter accounts are tweeting company news.
- Only 38 percent are actually responding to people's tweets.
- Only 32 percent are retweeting the posts of others.

Here are my 12 steps for avoiding pitfalls and building a successful Twitter program for your business:

Top 12 Tips for Successful Corporate Twittering

1. **Reserve a good, relevant username**. With only 15 characters or fewer to play with, and with, oh, about 106 million users earlier to the party, your most urgent task is to come up with a short, memorable, recognizable, intuitive Twitter handle: as close to @YourBusiness as you can get.

2. **Display a human face for your business**. I generally think the handle of your business Twitter account should be the name of your company, although others prefer names like @Jill_atCompany to humanize the account and to allow several people to tweet for a single company, an ideal approach for large firms. I like the example of @Rubbermaid, "currently tweeted by Jim Deitzel"—this approach is an ideal way to have your cake and eat it, too. You get the recognizable handle. You get the face behind the logo—the personality of the specific human being doing the tweeting. And if the staff member should, at some point, move on to a different role or a different company, the account can be "currently tweeted" by some new person, without disruption to the brand.

3. **Establish your specialty**. When I said you need an elevator pitch, I meant you need an area of focus, a specialty and a perspective that's easily expressed in just a few words. Your focus should be on benefits, not products. Sizzle, not steak. Your Twitter feed—indeed, all your social-media efforts—should ride the coattails of a bigger, more passionate lifestyle and social mission represented by the market you serve. Imagine you're writing little items for a fascinating lifestyle magazine in your niche. @organic_valley, a Wisconsin cooperative of 1,300 organic family farms, is not just hawking the products made by its farmers—it's sounding off on a wide range of topics related to world hunger, nutrition, deforestation, the impact of pesticides, bioengineering, and more.

4. **Post frequently**. Twitter is voracious. It demands at least daily postings to amount to anything. Keep it brief, don't overthink it, but feed it. Get into the habit. If you establish a schedule of seven posts a week for Facebook, say, plan to come up with 15 or 20 posts a week for Twitter. If you've done a good job of establishing your specialty above, you can simply set up news alerts to be informed of new developments in your market. Summarize them in under 140 characters and point a link to the article. You should also echo on Twitter every promotional e-mail you send out and every company blog post you make.

5. **Use hot-button keywords in your industry**. Heavy Twitter users troll through Twitter search results or set up alerts to follow topics of interest to them and the Tweeps who post about them. Keywords could be the name of high-profile people or celebrities, news events, companies, just the name of your market or industry, etc. Whether it's surfing, fat-free, Google Analytics, knitting, Scottish—whatever your niche, people on Twitter are searching for it daily and will follow you if you're a regular poster on it.

6. **Use popular hash tags, and promote your own**. A hash tag is a single, concatenated string prefaced with the # sign used to make it easier to find all tweets on a given topic or event. On the day of the Indy 500 auto race, the Twitterers at Indianapolis Motor Speedway pushed to get #indy500 to the top of the trending topics. Whether your topic or event is global in scope, or a niche business conference, giving it an easy-to-remember hash tag is key to helping your audience to stay in the loop.

7. **Follow!** It's not enough just to post and hope for the best. You've got to actively build a network on Twitter, and the best way to have people notice what you're doing is to take notice of them. Search for members posting on your topics of interest and follow them. Look at their own followers and select relevant folks to follow. Keep a focused network that aligns with your "elevator pitch" or area of specialty. When you follow people on Twitter, they'll generally follow you back.

8. **Recognize your followers**. When people follow you, take a moment to check them out. Some will be blank-slate newbies or evident spam artists, whom you can ignore. But when real people with an interesting stream of tweets follow you, follow them back. Send them a friendly direct-message thanking them for the follow and looking forward to getting to know one another. Maybe nothing will come of it—Twitter is the least reciprocal of the social-media platforms—but it's good form, and you never know what will come of these connections. For instance, Paul Kalemkiarian, owner of the Wine of the Month Club, reached out to one of his Twitter followers who ran a comparison Web site and they established a business relationship—and she ended up sending him $100,000 of holiday season business.

9. **Promote**. Give the Twitter icon prominent real estate on your Web site. Display the current feed widget on your home page. Pitch the Twitter feed in your e-mail newsletter, and maybe even your catalog or other print media.

10. **Retweet**. Be listening for references to your brand, and when people say something nice about you, retweet it. And also send a DM to thank them. Retweeting the good word is an easy, effective, daily discipline you should get into—it's a great way to spread any good buzz enjoyed by your brand, and it's unique to Twitter.

11. **Ask for retweets**. This can be a little crass, but if handled tongue in cheek or for a good cause, it can really spread the word. Example: Riding a wave of popularity for its Shape-Up fitness shoes, the Skechers shoe brand asked its followers "Retweet if you love your Shape-Ups!" This simple effort resulted in scores of positive, authentic, brand-building tweets, just for the asking.

12. **Attend or host a Tweetup**. One of the coolest elements of the surge in online social networking is that it hasn't turned us all into lonely, isolated mouse potatoes. Twitter fans have popularized the Tweetup, an in-person get-together of related Twitter users. For the most outgoing and connected among us, online social media is just a tool and a facilitator for the kind of personal and business networking that even your grandmother would recognize. Today there are more opportunities than ever to identify like-minded people in your vicinity—or those attending the same event as you—who are interested not just in exchanging Tweets, but in getting together in person, for drinks, a meal, a meeting, a hike or bike ride, a street protest, performance art, you name it. When the social connection deepens through in-person meeting, you're really taking the fullest advantage of social media's rich potential.

Customer Service, One Tweet at a Time

It's that last piece that is the weirdest: huge companies embracing micro one-on-one direct messaging, in public, and I can't help but think it is the novelty of the medium. They have dived into Twitter messaging with a few dozen customers; meanwhile, their outsourced phone centers may still give horrendous customer service to the masses.

But obviously some companies (Zappos, for instance) embrace the Twitter platform as just one part of a thoroughly good customer-service approach, whatever the channel.

I laugh off a lot of corporate Twittering, but sometimes I reconsider: Take Rubbermaid at http://twitter.com/Rubbermaid. They have an active community on Twitter and Facebook built around "organization"—food storage, closet organizing, etc., talking to mostly moms but also dads, professional organizers, etc. To me it sounds deadly boring. But if you check it out, there are real enthusiasts out there, and Rubbermaid seems to be building a sincere and healthy connection with them—600-some on Facebook and 6,000-some on Twitter.

That "reach" is a tiny drop in the bucket compared to the TV and magazine media buys they do, but I'll bet Rubbermaid is doing a lot to boost the relevance of their brand and also learn first-hand about their best customers.

Interestingly, Rubbermaid also operates an award-winning blog, whose positioning statement is "Adventures in Organization." Okay, it's not the sort of material to set your pulse racing and palms sweating. But it's a charmingly tongue-in-cheek yet clear mission statement that drives:

1. The company's choice of material and messaging, and
2. The customer's understanding of what the brand stands for.

LINKEDIN AND OTHER BUSINESS NETWORKS

The freewheeling and highly personal nature of Facebook, MySpace, and other social networks is an alien landscape for businesses. Your organization can fit in and thrive there, but it will take a lot of reconnaissance and slow acclimatization.

LinkedIn, by contrast, is a natural for you. It is the easiest place for any business to begin exploring the social-media landscape because it's designed specifically as a business-networking tool. And when I say business, I mean it in its very broadest sense; anything you do for a living will have its counterpart communities, colleagues, and vendors present on LinkedIn.

There are currently 65 million LinkedIn members, hailing from more than 200,000 companies, and the rate of adoption is growing at a blistering speed. Some of the growth may be coming from the troubled economy and job market. Pointing to month-over-month upticks of more than 20 percent, TechCrunch's Erick Schonfeld notes, "When times are tough, networking is a survival skill."[5]

But whether in a good economic climate or bad, the business networking resources on LinkedIn are a powerful help for anyone's career and daily productivity. How?

You'll notice I didn't say anything about customers. By and large, LinkedIn is not a place to go in search of customers—unless, of course, you are a business-to-business company, a consultant, or professional service. In that case, LinkedIn can be an enormously fertile ground for you.

Reid Hoffman is the perpetual-motion machine who founded LinkedIn and who, as an early stage angel investor, has his hands in Facebook, Digg, Ning, Technorati, Six Apart, Funny or Die, and literally scores of other Web businesses. With a BS in symbolic studies from Stanford and a masters in philosophy from Oxford, Hoffman combines big-picture thinking with deep technical know-how.

Hoffman, who has invested across the entire spectrum of social media, believes that people are likely to maintain two or three relatively distinct social-networking personas—and it is the business persona that LinkedIn so squarely targets. The clarity and discipline of LinkedIn as a haven for business networking is what makes it such an effective place.

The two value-added services from which LinkedIn draws its revenues are employment advertising placed by companies and recruiters and upgraded account fees. LinkedIn's other revenue source is from ads it displays on the site.

"Reid has a belief that every person is his or her own brand," said Matt Cohler, a former LinkedIn exec now at Benchmark Capital. "He means that in a good way, not a cheesy way. He believes that we are all our own organizations in the world today, and that the things that power and drive goodness in the world are relationships and trust."[6]

"I actually think every individual is now an entrepreneur, whether they recognize it or not," Hoffman told Charlie Rose in 2009. "Average job length is two to four years. That makes you a small business . . . You are the entrepreneur of your own small business. How do you get to your next gig? How do you do your career progression? All these things now fall on the individual shoulders. And so, they're essentially an entrepreneur."[7]

Some 25 percent or so of LinkedIn users are hiring managers or recruiters, but LinkedIn is about much more than jobs. LinkedIn also supports person-to-person networking, a very useful Q&A functionality, and professional groups. Not to mention, many business-to-business advertisers are promoting free webinars and other sometimes interesting and relevant things.

So you're ready to start using LinkedIn. Here are some tips to make the experience successful for you and your business:

Nine Steps for Making the Most of LinkedIn

1. **Connect to key people in your real-life professional network**—your most important colleagues with whom you have a special connection. Key vendors or clients. Past colleagues who have moved on to other employers, the people you're always glad to run into at conferences.

2. **Stay focused**. We all have varied interests and a broad range of people in our lives. Think of your Facebook network: Aunt Millie, an ex-high school sweetheart, some pals from work, college buddies, your boss (gulp!). Soon there's nothing you can post on your wall that feels comfortable, authentic, and relevant for everybody in your network. Don't let that happen to your LinkedIn network. One beauty of LinkedIn is that as a professional networking tool, it's inherently focused, as well as more discreet in tone. However, it's easy to get off base in the connections you seek out or the unsolicited ones that you accept. I work hard to connect with people I know, and know pretty well, in my industry and who likely share my business interests, goals, conference-going schedule, etc. I ignore most connection requests from people I haven't met, or who seem only trying to sell me something, or who just seem to be obsessive "people collectors." At the end of the day, I like to have an elevator pitch about my network. I can say it is comprised not exclusively but mostly of B2C e-commerce and marketing executives. They are a great group for me to ask questions about search-engine optimization or who is going to attend the Internet Retailer Web Design show. It's probably not a good network from which to recruit investment bankers or to get legal advice, but it suits my purposes. And the composition of your network isn't just for your benefit, but also to those select few you share it with. "Shared connections" is a great indicator of the overlap between people in the same industry or job, and it makes their connections richer and more useful because you're introducing your connections to others like them.

3. **Complete your profile**. This isn't number one on the list, because I want you to be a little familiar with the platform, and seeing whose profiles are most appealing, before you finish yours. What you choose to include in your LinkedIn profile, and what tone you adopt, is important. This is not a resume, per se. It is a professional biography, a business card, selling points, and a subtle window into who you are as a person.

4. **Post your status**. LinkedIn lets you check whether you want your status post to also go out as a tweet in your Twitter feed. That's a handy, laborsaving touch, and it's easily turned off if your LinkedIn post is going to be inappropriate for your Twitter feed or vice versa. Letting your connections know what you're working on, sharing a new development in your industry, or voicing your opinions on a topic of mutual interest is a great way to anchor each other in your professional worlds

and keep each other up-to-date. The status bar is also where I publish links to any blog post or article I've written. Without doing that, my blog would surely wither into obscurity, but by doing it, I give it a chance of getting some attention.

5. **Ask and answer questions**. LinkedIn questions are superpowerful. Answering questions well—and being selected as a "best answer" by the person who asked the question—is a nice little badge of courage on your profile.

6. **Provide and ask for recommendations—but sparingly**. A few well-chosen recommendations from past bosses, employees who reported to you, and clients or vendors who worked with you convey a more tangible sense of who you are and how good you are. It feels a bit narcissistic to ask for recommendations, but it's something you have to do—you'll never get any unless you ask.

7. **Join groups**. LinkedIn groups are a mixed bag, and the LinkedIn platform does not bestow a ton of useful functionality on groups. But nevertheless, if you can find relevant groups and start posting in discussions, you may find that you make connections that are useful and learn some useful things. Discussions you elect to "watch" are e-mailed to your in-box, which can be zero activity for many groups and can be terribly annoying in that rare overactive group that just takes off virally ("What is your favorite motivational quote?" was a discussion I was ready to slit my wrists over after a few dozen alerts).

8. **Use Amazon Reading List**. This is a handy feature that lets others see what books you are reading and what you think of them. If you do a lot of business reading—management, marketing, self-help, technical, how-to, etc.—share it. It's often a kickoff to some interesting interactions, and at the very least it signals something about what makes you tick intellectually and professionally.

9. **Use TripIt**. Another handy and easy to use application, TripIt lets you log your business travel schedule. If you travel much, it's of interest to your connections (it may cue them to connect with you at a shared conference or meeting). LinkedIn also reminds you of who among your connections lives in the city you're visiting. That's helpful, and it gets to one of the most powerful aspects of social networking: these connections are stronger and more satisfying when the digital connections are reinforced by occasional face-to-face meetings.

Avoiding LinkedIn Pitfalls

Of all the major social networks, it seems to me that LinkedIn has been the freest from privacy controversies, culture clashes, scammers, and parasites. There are a couple of reasons for this:

- LinkedIn is clearly and consciously a business platform, so your network is likely to be better defined, tighter, and more self-policing than on the general social sites, where business is just part (and a very small part) of the conversation.
- Requests for connections, though looser now than they once were, still expect requestors to know their invitees personally and to specify whether they know them as a colleague, business partner, fellow member of a LinkedIn group, or friend—and LinkedIn requires you to name the company or group specifically. Invitees are cautioned by LinkedIn not to connect to people they don't know.

Still, although LinkedIn is a less wild place than the mainstream social networks, there are potential pitfalls. Here are five lovely ways you can screw up on LinkedIn:

1. **Using LinkedIn to cold-call on business prospects**. This is a huge turn-off. When LinkedIn goes to the length it does to discourage connecting to strangers, a cold-call invite demonstrates that the person is selfish, socially clueless, and just plain doesn't follow directions. I never invite anyone to my network whom I have not either met in person, know through another friend, or have engaged in some back-and-forth communication by phone or e-mail.
2. **Oversharing of non-business info**. It's doubtful anyone on Twitter or Facebook really cares if you just ate a tuna sandwich. It's 100 percent guaranteed no one cares about it on LinkedIn.
3. **Oversharing of business or proprietary info**. Especially pronounced on LinkedIn is the risk of sharing proprietary information, tipping off competitors about your plans or whereabouts, being caught in a lie, leaking a sensitive press release, saying something disparaging about clients, vendors, conferences, job applicants, etc. Imagine tweeting that you flew into Pittsburgh to pitch yourself as a new vendor to a sporting goods company. It wouldn't take Dick's Sporting Goods current

vendors much to figure out that their account is in play—a fact that the client company has every right and reason to keep secret until a decision is made. On LinkedIn as on any social network, you need to be honest and straightforward. But you need also to recognize that LinkedIn posts become public in a flash. Think twice about that post. I can't tell you how many times I was on the verge of making a post when I took a moment and realized that it could have some negative repercussions or broadcast the wrong image or message. It is better to be safe than sorry.

4. **Being a connection whore**. LinkedIn has tried to slow individual network growth to keep connections strong and meaningful, discouraging users from asking for or accepting connections from users they don't personally know. But the unsanctioned group of mega-connectors known as LinkedIn LIONs pretty much go their own way. Unlike Facebook, Twitter, and other platforms, LinkedIn stops at "500+" when displaying your number of connections to the general public. Nonetheless, connection whores still make a point of bragging "over 10,500 connections" and so on, on their profiles. Big deal. Such pronouncements betray that you're after quantity, not quality. Especially on LinkedIn, I'm a huge believer that a smaller, well-focused network, where the members tend to share similar job descriptions or industry, is the best network to build. If you can't make a clear elevator pitch about the type of folks most commonly found in your network, your network is too big for its own good.

5. **Neglecting your profile**. LinkedIn is a pretty basic platform. The Q&A features, groups, status posts, and add-on applications like TripIt are nice touches, but they're window dressing to the main *raison d'etre* of the site: the professional profile. Your profile is your resume and business card, and it's not just for hiring managers and recruiters. It serves industry media, prospective customers, job applicants to your firm—everybody in your professional world. If your profile is a bare-bones recital of a few of your jobs, it hasn't been updated in three years, and you've got just a paltry few connections, it conveys the wrong message about you. Rather than describing the active, well-regarded, and well-connected professional you, it's a sad ghost town that makes you seem rather isolated, behind the times, and bad in the follow-through department. Better not to do LinkedIn at all than to do it lethargically.

OTHER BUSINESS NETWORKS

LinkedIn is the biggest business network by far, but there are a number of other worthwhile sites to look into, some of them with a niche focus on entrepreneurship:

- **Biznik**: Online community of entrepreneurs and small businesses.
- **cmypitch.com**: A UK-focused business Web site for entrepreneurs to exchange RFPs, quotes, and advice.
- **Cofoundr**: A global network of entrepreneurs, programmers, designers, investors, and others involved with start-ups.
- **eFactor**: At just under a million members, bills itself as the world's largest network of entrepreneurs and investors.
- **Ecademy**: A business and knowledge-sharing network with the motto "Community, Conversations, Commerce."
- **Entrepreneur Connect**: The online community sponsored by Entrepreneur.com.
- **Fast Pitch**: Business network oriented somewhat toward smaller businesses with an emphasis on sales, marketing, and lead generation.
- **Focus**: Oriented toward Q and A, to help marketing, IT, and other professionals make business decisions.
- **PartnerUp**: Small-business network with an emphasis on online forums.
- **Plaxo**: An in-the-cloud business address book tool that can sync with your Outlook contacts.
- **Ryze**: Business networking community and classified ad network with 500,000 members from 200 countries.
- **Spoke**: Uses spiders to build its database of 60 million businesspeople— one of whom could be you.
- **StartupNation**: Social network focused on start-up businesses, funding, and marketing.
- **Xing**: Global business networking and job search site with 9 million members.
- **Zoominfo**: Like Spoke, Zoominfo's profiles are initially built by spidering the Web for articles about people.

YOUTUBE

YouTube's own massive viewership is a compelling reason to be part of that online community—some 70 million people visit the site every month, viewing 2 billion videos every single day. In fact, every minute, 24 hours of video is uploaded to YouTube. But although the site is the 800-pound gorilla of social media (i.e., online media that users share, rate, and comment upon), YouTube is not an especially robust *social network*. That is, YouTube offers relatively few opportunities for interaction between users other than subscribing to channels and commenting upon, rating, and favoriting videos. YouTube is about as useful for nonmembers as it is for registered users in helping them spend countless hours watching two-minute clips of dancing babies, sports highlights, breaking news, and amateur stunts.[8]

There are three main angles that make YouTube particularly appealing to businesses and organizations:

1. Virality: Video is by far the most talked about and passed-around element of our modern digital life. When one catches on, whether it is as commonplace as a music video or as pivotal as an Iranian protester dying in the street, it can be seen by millions of people.

2. Search visibility: "Universal search" is the now well-established trend at Google, Yahoo, and Bing to intersperse traditional Web pages with many other content types within search results. These new content types are blog posts and news items, images, local results (with maps), products aka "shopping results," and videos. Search for just about anything, and you will see videos prominently displayed in the results set. If you're not uploading videos (and titling them with phrases commonly used by searchers), you're missing out on a source of traffic.

3. Inbound links: The best practice is to *upload* your video to YouTube, to take advantage of the thriving traffic and high page rank of the site—as well as its hosting and bandwidth—and then to *embed* a copy of it on your own Web site. Assuming it's any good, your video will serve as "link bait" among your target audience: Your customers and fans will link from their own blogs and other Web sites to your video page. Those external links will benefit your site's authority in the eyes of the major search engines, thus improving your search rankings.

What sorts of business should be posting videos on YouTube? Not necessarily only the big brands rehashing their Madison Avenue-produced TV ads. Sure, those ads that enjoy cult followings on TV get millions of views on YouTube, which is doubtlessly great for the brand. But for every big-budget ad, there are dozens of small-budget videos whose *only* distribution is online. That's where the democratic nature of the Web is helpful: A shaky hand-held video of a baby laughing his head off in his highchair has just as much chance for fame as a pricey broadcast ad. And probably *more* of a chance to make an impression.

Especially on YouTube, users seem genuinely in "discovery" mode, moving from one random but popular video to another. Unlike so much of the rest of the Web, which has become a Web of the familiar, YouTube seems unique in serving up fresh new content—the old notion of "surfing" the Web seems dead from the perspective of jumping from link to link, but it seems alive and well as far as surfing from one YouTube video to another is concerned. Ironically, this is quite similar to that other realm where we co-opted the term surfing: channel surfing the TV.

What kind of companies should be actively uploading videos to YouTube? What content should you consider uploading?

1. **Musicians, entertainers, comedians, TV shows, plays, movies, animation studios, and sports teams and leagues**. Anyone whose product is essentially video should be uploading trailers, highlights, and live concert footage. The entertainment industry still struggles with questions of intellectual property and how to be compensated for it, but it seems clearer and clearer that YouTube's potential to popularize media and performers is worth the risk of hurting the market by giving away free material. After all, the average YouTube video is just two minutes long—and amazingly, the typical user doesn't even sit through the whole thing, flitting from video to video every 3 minutes on average. If such a short fix satisfies the user's need without stimulating her to go see the movie or buy the song from iTunes, how much have you really given up?[9]

2. **Television commercials**. You've paid scads of money producing them—at least you can give them eternal life on the Internet. Your ad agency will have moved on to their next great idea, but consumers will still be out there in the thousands nostalgically clicking on ads of yore, rapping with Filet-O-Fish, watching the GoDaddy Girl suffer a wardrobe malfunction, or seeing VW's German engineers "UnPimp your Auto."

3. **How-to videos**. These needn't have big budgets or fancy production values to be popular and effective. If you are in the outdoor gear market, cookware, tools, crafts, or any do-it-yourself market—as well as many

business, technology, and software markets—you can probably envision several how-to topics that your audience would clamor for. Associating your company and products or services with these how-to videos, even if they are not actively being used or demonstrated on air, is a very positive move. Produce and upload a video assembly manual, instruction manual, or troubleshooting guide; the benefit for having such a resource available 24/7 on the public Web and easily found via search engines is a godsend. You generate good will and authoritative reputation in the eyes of your customers. You may also help them better use your products, turning potential customer-service headaches into happy customers and online praise. Sure, these workmanlike videos won't have the glitz and glamour of multimillion-dollar YouTube sensations, but they will be found by the niche audience that matters most to you.

4. **Product demos**. If you typically pitch your product or service by performing a demo, you probably have a worthwhile video in the making. Think about how you present your wares at a trade show or if your items sell in home-party settings. Real estate agents were quick to seize on the value of video walk-throughs to try to capture some of the appeal of a property that can otherwise only be seen in an in-person showing. The classic infomercial demonstrations of knives cutting through tin cans or vacuum cleaners tackling filthy carpets are not Oscar material, but they're visually memorable, and there's no other way to get the same message across as with video. One morning when my local Subaru dealer was digging out from a record-breaking blizzard, they made a point to videotape one of their all-wheel-drive Outbacks bursting free of more than a foot of fresh snow. No wonder the Subaru is the top selling car in snowy Vermont! While the Blendtec videos play more as entertainment than product demo, their subconscious demonstration value is strong: *Man it's fun to watch a blender shred a hockey puck (and that blender sure must be tough).*

5. **Highly visual markets**. Patagonia will be the first to tell you they are not about clothes—they're about the active outdoor sports you pursue in their clothes. So their Web site and their social-media program have leaned heavily on the power of video: about 200 YouTube uploads of breathtakingly shot and professionally produced adventure videos featuring surfing, ice climbing, bouldering, paddling, and more, from Chile to Siberia, from the Indian Ocean to, well, Patagonia. Their YouTube channel has more than 3,000 subscribers and has enjoyed more than a million views. Before the Internet, their print catalogs invested

more real estate in picturing real people pursuing outdoor adventures and text dedicated to eco-sensitivity than to mere product promotion. So it is with Patagonia's social-media outreach today. Almost any company stands to gain by focusing on the sizzle, not the steak—the video of the activity, not the product you designed for it. Other examples include David's Bridal and Ice.com.

THE VALUE OF VIDEO

Videos are good for your online business—whether you post them on your Web site to boost your e-commerce performance, or upload them to YouTube or Hulu for search-engine benefit, or in the hopes they'll become a viral success story.

- Online jeweler Ice.com found that visitors who chose to view product videos were 400 percent more likely to buy than those who did not. Ice.com also credits video with decreasing returns by 25 percent.[10]
- With proper optimization, video increases the chance of a front-page Google result by 53 times.[11]
- Among the benefits of online video, says eMarketer senior analyst Jeffrey Grau, are "lower numbers of abandoned shopping carts, reduced return rates, and higher sales."[12]

But of all the potential benefits of online video, the brass ring is "going viral." When a video goes viral, it becomes exponentially more popular thanks to the amplified word-of-mouth power of online social networks.

The favorite example is those Blendtec blenders. The "Will it Blend?" YouTube spots generated a 650 percent increase in traffic to the Blendtec Web site, around 10 million page views and coverage on the *Today Show* and the *Tonight Show*. Not to mention a significant jump in sales.

"When George approached me about actually filming extreme blending challenges and putting video clips out on the Web, I thought it would be fun, but I never imagined that it would take off like it did. In fact, when George said we were going to post videos on YouTube, I didn't even know what YouTube was," admits Blendtec president Tom Dickson. "'Will it Blend?' was not designed as a sales campaign—it was designed to be a branding campaign. The first six videos we produced and posted cost us about $50, and now they have been viewed by millions. This campaign put Blendtec on the map in just a few weeks."[13]

While the Blendtec story is often repeated, many new viral sensations are unfolding every month. A snapshot of some of the popular viral videos of 2010 reveals that most of them are big brands' big-budget television ads—but there's always a smaller brand or sleeper hit emerging:

- Lego World Cup—a stop-motion depiction of the United States versus England soccer match, starring Lego figures
- Adidas Originals ad—remaking the old *Star Wars* cantina scene
- A leaked iPhone 4 ad
- Samsung business-card throwing
- Heineken "Men with Talent"
- Greenpeace public-service spot

Who knows what will be the next Blendtec-style phenomenon? But one thing is for sure: it can't be you if you're not uploading anything.

YOUR COMPANY BLOG

A great primer for anyone planning a company blog is the book *Naked Conversations: How Blogs Are Changing the Way Businesses Talk with Customers* by Robert Scoble and Shel Israel. If nothing else, your blog is an unparalleled means for expressing your company's perspective in your unique company voice.

"The most valuable and powerful tool a business has is its voice," says Ben Cohen, the iconic founder of Ben & Jerry's ice cream and a lifetime proponent of socially responsible business.[14]

Authoring a company blog may be the most time-consuming single piece of the social-media program outlined in this chapter. Yes, filming and editing YouTube videos can take a big investment of time, and in some cases outside resources. And yes, posting and direct-messaging to Twitter every few minutes, as the top twitterati do, can add up to a ton of hours. But writing frequent, high-quality blog posts that make a difference—and that have the potential to spread—is a big job.

Scoble and Israel point out that in comparison to traditional corporate communications platforms—public relations campaigns and advertising, for instance—blogs are positively cheap, easy, and quick.

Authors, when asked how long a book or a chapter should be, often answer "as long as a piece of string." And so it is with blog posts—there is no correct answer as to the ideal length.

The best traditional blogs still require relatively long-form posts—although readers reward the best, most thoughtful, and most original posts by Digging and spreading the word. Glenn Allsopp, a viral marketing blogger in South Africa, analyzed average post lengths of the most popular blogs (as measured by Technorati) across eight industries, and saw a great deal of variation, with posts on celebrity gossip blogs or sites dedicated to tech gadgets or political news opting for lots of shorter posts—from about 180 to 465 words a post, but with a frequency of several posts a day.[15]

In industries valuing depth over immediacy, expect to spend more time researching and writing, and plan to write longer, more significant posts. In Allsopp's analysis, blogs about investing, marketing, and self-improvement averaged about 1,200 to 1,500 words per post. But, Allsopp notes, these blogs typically see a posting rate of just one to seven posts a week.

That said, attention spans are getting ever shorter. The trends we're seeing on offline and online media alike, for shorter-form media, will likely continue, accelerated by the success of microblogging platforms like Twitter. However, there is no substitute for quality—whether blog posts get shorter or not.

Allsopp also performed an interesting analysis of the most popular blog posts across several industries (as measured by external links), and there he found a number of common themes. Admittedly, his analysis revealed less about what makes a great blog post than what attracts external links. Some of the impact here may be that blog headlines that match common search phrases (like "best places to live" or "hot growth stocks for 2010" or "how to write a cover letter") tend to perform well in search-engine results, so are therefore seen by more people, so are therefore linked to by more people.

Not every post you issue can be a "top 10" or a "beginner's guide." That said, here are some tips for blog topics and headlines:

- Tips
- How to
- Contests or giveaways
- Comparisons

NING: THIS IS YOUR COMPANY BLOG ON STEROIDS

Blogs as a phenomenon were certainly overhyped a few years back. Douglas Quenqua wrote in the *New York Times* that according to a 2008 survey, only 7.4 million out of the 133 million blogs the *Times* tracks had been updated in the past 120 days—with "95 percent of blogs being essentially abandoned."

The fact is, very few people or companies are doing things interesting enough to justify frequent posting—or have the writing skills, persistence, and work ethic to pull it off. While I strive to keep my own Timberline blog off the DOA list, it ain't easy!

That said, I still encourage anyone with a passion for their topic, with a story to tell, and an enthusiastic audience of customers, members, or other "community," to go for it. Blogs are still a terrific, low-cost, and high-speed way to publish online and to elicit comments and other feedback.

The Ning platform, which marries a traditional blog with all the ingredients of a niche social network, makes life easier because your online community does some of the writing for you.

Ning offers a constellation of built-in social-media features: members who can maintain their own profiles and establish friendships with one another; discussion forums; video and photo sharing; and an events calendar.

The Ning platform is the brainchild of Marc Andreesen, who, in the early days of the Web, created the Netscape browser.

All of Ning's social features combine to create more dynamic sites less likely to be DOA—because your community helps generate content. Of course, a healthy community requires care and feeding, cajoling and cheerleading. But the network effect is a powerful tailwind once you get it established.

One plus: Most niche companies already do a great job of stimulating a sense of community among their customers. And if the niche is tightly defined, even a small group—say a couple dozen members—can still feel very vibrant and energizing.

DASHBOARDS AND LINKED ACCOUNTS: SOCIAL-MEDIA PUBLISHING MADE EASIER

With the rapid increase in social-media Web sites, businesses and ordinary people alike can now easily become fatigued and spread too thin. They're on too many platforms to post to any of them with regularity. One step the major social platforms are now making is integration between one another: link your Facebook account to your Twitter account, and your Facebook posts will appear automatically, abbreviated to 140 characters if need be, on Twitter.

Link Twitter to LinkedIn and your tweets automatically appear as status updates on LinkedIn.

The advantage of account linking is clear: it's fast and convenient. Time spent managing your social-media program at its most elemental level—writing and publishing your posts—is cut to a fraction.

The problem is that managing your program at this most elemental level is important. Each of the social platforms is its own beast with its own culture. Your networks on each platform will overlap, no doubt, but they'll also contain a lot of different people who come to each platform with different expectations.

A typical Facebook wall post is a longer, more leisurely post than is possible on Twitter; often on Facebook your posts will be illustrated with an image. On Twitter, the 140-character limit imposes a disciplined "haiku" style post, getting across a main point *and* the author's emotional perspective in a bare minimum of words and abbreviations.

When your Facebook posts are fed automatically to Twitter, often all that appears will be fluff, with the most crucial content chopped off abruptly and a random "short URL" link stuck in its place.

You may forget your Twitter account is hooked to LinkedIn, and publish breezy, trivial, or unprofessional tweets that send an awkward message on your more business-minded LinkedIn account. Do you really want your clients, vendors, colleagues, and business prospects to know that you're listening to Bob Marley in your bare feet while finishing that big proposal?

More important, perhaps, is that being on these platforms is an important part of, well, *being* on the platforms—seeing the status posts of your fans and those you follow scroll by. Seeing what topics are trending on Twitter. Seeing which of your business contacts are traveling to an important conference or publishing new blog posts on a topic of interest to you.

Remember, we're on the social networks to be social—to perk up our ears to ongoing conversations, to read the posts of others and comment in an encouraging and constructive way, to build relationships, and to receive and answer customer inquiries, praise, or complaints as fast as possible. If you overuse the new tools for the sake of efficiency, but as a consequence fail to log into each account and become an authentic member of the online community there, you'll have been penny-wise but pound-foolish.

My advice to anyone starting a program is to leave accounts unlinked for at least the first six months or year of your social-media endeavors. That way you'll establish a real community consisting of genuine, personal connections. You'll understand the unique culture of each platform and how to be more effective in each one.

When you do link accounts, do it sparingly and only temporarily. You should only share posts that are "for everybody" and feel like they work equally well everywhere. When you're done sharing those posts, unlink your accounts so you don't forget about the linkage in the future and share an inappropriate comment across multiple networks.

One excellent solution is to use a social media dashboard like HootSuite to make your publishing easier—without sacrificing the quality of your posts to each network. HootSuite and other dashboards integrate with social networks like Twitter or Facebook to make publishing easier and add some powerful scheduling, monitoring, and tracking tools. On Hoot-Suite, you can:

- Manage several different Twitter accounts from one publishing platform.
- Publish to Twitter, Facebook, and LinkedIn from one platform.
- Queue and schedule social-media posts ahead of time—for the entire upcoming week, say.
- Manage workflow among the members of your social-media team.
- Monitor what's being said by others about your brand or products.
- Get statistical reports of how your program is performing.

CUSTOMER RATINGS AND REVIEWS

If you have a product to sell, the social networks can seem a very round-about way to pursue your main goal. You don't generate a lot of editorial content and maybe you don't have an overriding social mission. You just want to encourage people to buy! Well, user ratings and reviews are for you.

Pioneered almost from its very start by Amazon.com, user reviews and ratings are an incredibly powerful tool. Today, if you want them on your site—and syndicated to the Web at large—you don't have to pour into the effort the millions of bucks Amazon did. Many e-commerce platforms have now built the feature into their software. If yours has not, the quickest and easiest approach may be a third-party service, the two most notable being PowerReviews and Bazaarvoice.

Both work roughly the same: users review your product qualitatively and give it an overall one-to-five star rating that will be displayed on the product detail page. Your product page will invite visitors to review the product. Best practices are also to solicit product feedback via e-mail when you send customers their order confirmation and shipping confirmation e-mails.

USER-GENERATED CONTENT 101

Encouraging your Web site visitors to post their own comments, product reviews and ratings, and other material on your Web sites has three great benefits:

1. It engages your customers emotionally and stimulates a stronger, deeper relationship with you and your brand. Even negative postings can serve a positive purpose by opening up a customer-service conversation that solves the initial problem and leaves the customers happier than they'd have been if no problem had occurred in the first place.

2. On e-commerce Web sites, customer-supplied reviews and ratings are given more credibility than any claims your company can make.

3. Customer-generated content is a triple boon from a search-engine perspective. You'll have customers creating new and often highly ranked "spider food" while you sleep. Their postings will rank well for the misspellings, slang, and informality that you would never use—as well as the superlatives you might never give yourself permission to use. And finally, customer-supplied content can attract valuable links from blogs and other external sites.

If your company is conducting e-commerce, that is, selling products online, introducing customer-supplied ratings and reviews is a no-brainer. Many e-commerce platforms now come with reviews modules built in, and third-party tools like PowerReviews and Bazaarvoice can be readily integrated with most sites.

Customer-supplied reviews are also a staple for restaurants, movies, in the travel and tourism business, and elsewhere.

In a survey of 1,000 online shoppers,[16] the E-tailing Group found that 63 percent of shoppers consistently read product or service reviews before making a buying decision. Asked to name their top sources of online reviews, here is how they responded; see Table 3.1 below.

Table 3.1   Online shoppers' top sources of product recommendations

Retailers' Web sites	65%
Manufacturers' Web sites	58%
Amazon.com	53%
Reviews Web sites	37%
Specialty Web sites	15%
Social media	6%

Gardener's Supply Company, a leader in equipment, supplies, and specialized tools for gardeners, partnered with PowerReviews to support customer ratings and reviews on its site, http://www.Gardeners.com. More than 70,000 reviews have been submitted to date, a testimony both to the size and fervor of Gardener's audience and the company's diligence about asking for reviews; a couple weeks after any order, Gardener's pushes product-specific e-mails, requesting feedback and linking directly back to the product page where a review can be submitted. Amazon does much the same—it is now best practice to solicit post-purchase ratings and reviews; without asking directly for reviews via e-mail, the growth of on-site reviews is painfully slow to nonexistent. And nothing kills an incipient customer-ratings program faster than page after page after page exhorting visitors "Be the first to write a review!"

Gardener's uses review stars all over the Web site—product pages, category views, search results, and in the e-mail program. Customer testimonials also show up prominently, paired to the specific product they describe—or, in the case of testimonials referring, say, to a beloved Mother's Day gift, to any timely holiday or occasion.

"These reviews are completely authentic," says Harris, "and they are completely perfect for the product or the occasion."[17]

Case studies on the positive impact of reviews and ratings are compelling:

- 77 percent of online shoppers use reviews and ratings when purchasing (JupiterResearch, August 2006).
- The conversion rate nearly doubled, from 0.44 percent to 1.04 percent, after the same product displayed its five-star rating (*Marketing Experiments Journal*).
- Shoppers who browsed the Bass Pro Shops "Top Rated Products" page had a 59 percent higher conversion rate than the site average and spent 16 percent more per order.
- Shoppers who browsed the "Top Rated Products" page at PETCO had a 49 percent higher conversion rate and 63 percent larger AOV.

Bazaarvoice's "Social Commerce Report 2007" found that user-submitted product reviews and ratings boosted site traffic, sales conversion rates, and average order values. Among e-commerce retailers in the United States and Europe who deployed reviews and ratings tools, 77 percent reported upticks in traffic, 56 percent reported improved conversion, and 42 percent reported higher AOV. Only 5 percent to 9 percent reported that ratings and reviews tools impacted their performance negatively—presumably because of the presence of negative feedback.

For online stores, ratings and reviews are the ideal user-generated content (UGC). Reviews can be a boon for your search-engine optimization efforts. Every time a customer rates one of your products, they create a new Web page linking to your product—enhancing your search-engine visibility even while you sleep. By the nature of user-created content, user reviews are conversational, informal, rich in the keywords searchers actually use, and often full of the kind of misspellings, slang, and colloquialisms that you as a brand-conscious marketer would never use—but which search-engine spiders gobble right up.

You can choose to syndicate your new product reviews out to RSS feeds and comparative shopping platforms like PowerReviews' Buzzillions, giving you additional exposure to Web shoppers. Expect to see a lot of additional convergence between user-submitted reviews and comparative shopping. Both are growing fast and will drive an increasing share of your traffic.

Another emerging syndication platform for your product reviews is the new "rich snippets" functionality now being supported by Google. Rich snippets are a way to mark up the source code of your Web site to tell the search engines more about your products, reviews, and other fielded data. Starred ratings and reviews already are beginning to appear on the Google search-engine results pages.

Currently, rich snippets Web standards exist for products, recipes, reviews, videos, people, and events. Clearly, many of these are perfect fodder for user-generated content. Already, Yelp, LinkedIn, TripAdvisor, UrbanSpoon, Rotten Tomatoes, and many other top UGC Web sites are using rich snippets.

"We're convinced that structured data makes the Web better, and we've worked hard to expand Rich Snippets to more search results," says Google.

Google's Matt Cutts, the head of the search-quality and anti-spam team, is a big fan of the concept: "This one is destined to be a favorite for Webmasters. Essentially, you use open standards (RDFs and microformats in the initial launch) to add additional markup to your Web pages . . . Then when Google thinks it will help users, we show a 'rich snippet' that has more information than a typical search snippet."[18] Examples include star ratings, prices for products, serving sizes, and nutritional info for recipes—all called out right on the search results pages and potentially harvested and syndicated elsewhere on the Web.

"I like that rich snippets relies on open standards, that the markup is simple, and that the data is out on the Web," says Cutts. "It's not locked up by Google in any way."

It's a new feature, so it's not clear precisely how it will impact your results. Already, you've probably seen star ratings now showing up on search results pages. It's speculation, but over time I expect several benefits:

- Your star-rated items could enjoy higher click-through.
- Your marked-up products could essentially be uploaded to Google Shopping every time your product pages are spidered.
- Because rich snippets are a new, open Web standard, comparison-shopping and review sites could harvest marked-up data and give your items greater exposure across the Web.

So here's your chance to be at the cutting edge of search-engine optimization, social-media style!

But wait, you say. What if my customers say negative or flat-out wrong things about my products or me? Three things:

1. The overwhelming majority of user comments—80 percent according to Bazaarvoice—are positive: four stars or better.
2. The world is full of folks with chips on their shoulder, and the online world amplifies it. Users know that. A negative review or two, among otherwise stellar ratings, will be discounted by most customers. Your willingness to display the good, the bad, and the ugly galvanizes your reputation as a trustworthy merchant.
3. Online review tools give you, the administrator, the ability to approve, disapprove, or edit submissions. Routinely you'll delete postings that are duplicate, incomplete, profane, or incoherent.

Regarding that last point, use your editorial power wisely! Legitimate gripes that you deep-six from your site will inevitably bob up elsewhere on the Web—BizRate, Epinions, TripAdvisor, or all over the blogosphere—and in more virulent form. Use this customer-feedback loop not just as a feel-good pretense to tout your stuff. More powerfully, it's an avenue to connect with your customers, understanding not just what they love, but what may be frustrating or misleading to them. In my opinion, it's fully ethical to take each rotten review as a customer-service call to action;

quickly solve the customer's problem. If you do, the customer will likely volunteer to retract or edit the nasty review.

And as the old chestnut of the customer-service industry goes, the customer who has a bad experience that you resolve wonderfully becomes a more loyal customer than the one who doesn't have a problem in the first place!

Conversion rates are higher on products with less-than-perfect reviews (fewer than five stars) than those without reviews at all, indicating that the customer feels that the product has been properly reviewed by other customers.

This isn't just about the product pages of your Web site. You should also leverage the value of customer-created ratings and reviews by:

- Using them in your e-mail campaigns.
- Syndicating them as RSS feeds.
- Syndicating them to shopping portals (the third-party ratings-and-review tools are already cutting deals with comparative shopping sites, and you can expect more to come).

When using star-ratings and reviews in its e-mails, pet-supply retailer PETCO realized a five times increase in click-through rates.

In A/B tests by Golfsmith, promotional e-mails that featured the star ratings and reviews of top products drove revenues 46 percent higher per campaign.

The takeaway is that customers trust and respond well to the voices of their fellow consumers. By transforming your marketing into a Web 2.0 customer-to-customer communication, you can tap into that trust, and your results will benefit.

Chapter 4

Taking It to the Next Level

You've crafted your general mission statement, done some listening and learning, staffed up your social-media team, and started posting and creating connections on the major social-media platforms. Perhaps you're publishing your company blog. You've built a core group of subscribers, fans, and followers—a fledgling online community. Now what?

The next step is to leverage your online community into something big and meaningful. Like a loyalty program, social media can help you strengthen your bond with your best customers. And like PR or prospecting, social media can help you get the attention of new customers.

We'll recommend you lay some additional groundwork: a more formal social-media business plan, and also a web-analytics program that lets you more formally track your social-media metrics and their effects on your overall business.

Taking your program to the next level will probably involve coordinated campaigns to get more attention, build buzz, support a worthy cause, stage an event, and conduct a major contest or giveaway.

To get more exposure on the social Web, we'll look at some of the specialty and second-tier social media platforms you should consider. We'll also look at using online advertising—both on the social networks and on the Web at large—to attract new fans and followers.

One of the most powerful aspects of online social media is when your online community transcends the digital and makes meaningful things happen in the physical world. So we'll close this chapter with a look at the phenomena of meetups and tweetups—and how you can put them to work for your business.

WHAT SHAPE IS YOUR FUNNEL?

First question: Is your online community comprised of a small subset of your existing customers? Or is it a big group of enthusiasts who may not even be your customers yet? Is it the wide mouth of the funnel or the narrow spout?

If your social-media community is made up of your most devoted customers, your social-media program will more resemble a loyalty program. If your community is mostly enthusiasts, your social-media efforts are more like introducing yourself and prospecting for new customers.

Most of the companies I work with are business-to-consumer companies doing lots of online business and usually pursuing some traditional direct marketing (catalog mailings, broadcast radio or TV ads, etc.). They're also active in online marketing, sending e-mails and paying for search-engine ads.

Their interest in social media has come about only recently, and so their fans and followers in social media tend to be a smaller and more committed core of customers than the larger consumer base represented, say, by the catalog mailing list.

Subscribers to the e-mail list are a subset of that, because not everyone opts in, not everyone orders online, and some longtime catalog customers may even predate the e-mail program.

This pattern, which I've seen in countless companies, calls to mind a funnel; see Table 4.1 below.

I've seen the pattern often enough that I think of it as a rule of thumb, but it describes only an old school of direct-response company that has just recently begun targeting the social media—and has targeted it principally by promoting their blog, their Facebook page, and their Twitter feed to their existing customer base. They display social-media logos on the Web site and in the e-mail program. They may even display them in the print catalog. Inevitably, since you're promoting to your existing audience, you're getting a subset of the same old faces.

But there are a number of innovative companies that have turned the funnel on its head. Often these are brand-new companies that don't have a

Table 4.1   Funnel pattern

1,000,000	customers on the catalog mailing list
500,000	customers on the e-mail list
5,000	fans on Facebook
500	followers on Twitter

big installed base of catalog and e-mail names. Maybe they are celebrities or a *cause célèbre*, or maybe it is a single blogger, speaker, or pundit.

Their funnel attracts scads of new friends, fans, and followers at the social-media level, *then* attempts to lure those online community members onto the company's Web site or retail stores, usually through contests, giveaways, and discount offers.

These sorts of companies enjoy huge, sometimes million-plus social-media fan bases. But the segment of that group that they can get to sign up for an e-mail newsletter or print catalog, or to visit and buy from their Web site will be a fraction of the whole.

In other words, is your social-media audience a *core group* of people already familiar with your brand? If so, your social-media program will be more of a loyalty and customer-service channel. Or is your social-media program followed mostly by people new to your company? Therefore your program will serve, at least in part, as an educative and customer-acquisition channel.

As I say, in my experience it's unusual for a social-media program to attract hordes of newcomers to the brand—but for inherently entertaining programs (or for those like T.G.I. Friday's, driven by the promise of a million free hamburgers), social media really can drive new customer acquisition.

SETTING GOALS FOR YOUR SOCIAL-MEDIA PROGRAM

For most everything they do, marketers have a particular goal enshrined as the driving purpose of their campaigns, the key metric to be tracked for purposes of measuring return-on-investment. For direct-response campaigns, the metric will be sales or qualified sales leads. For PR people, the key stats will be media mentions, reach, or impressions, and perhaps the paid-ad cost equivalent of free ink. Brand marketers will measure their impact by tracking market share, brand recognition, and brand attitudes.

But pity the poor social-media manager. She can rightly expect her efforts to pay off in any and all of those areas, but unpredictably, fleetingly, and probably without leaving clear footprints.

And yet while most organizations are happy to indulge in some exploratory tire-kicking of a new frontier like social media, before any serious investment of time and money is made, top management will expect there to be some tangible goals and measurement of progress toward those goals.

As Dale Nitschke, former president of Target.com, puts it, "You cannot move resources to this new channel unless you can measure some of the results."[1]

Let me say right away that too shortsighted a focus on metrics—or too ambitious a goal—will doom a promising social-media program to a premature death. Just because you won't vacuum up as much revenue as Dell doesn't mean it's not worth doing. What's the value of being where your most Web-savvy and interconnected customers are? What's the value of listening to what matters to them, of interacting with them directly and being a part of their online social circle? "Initially, it's very qualitative," points out Best Buy's Mark Mosiniak. "Does it *mean* something to the customer? That's very hard to measure."[2]

What Metrics to Watch

You can track key performance metrics yourself through your analytics package, and you can augment your own tracking by enlisting specialized social-media tools like Trendrr, TruCast, Radian6, or any of the several others cropping up daily.

Most external social-media tracking tools focus mainly on sentiment tracking—what's being said about your brand. They may employ spidering and screen-scraping technologies to find references to your brand or products, or those of specified competitors, across the blogosphere and social mediascape. These services are not unlike Google Alerts, which find references to your keywords in news releases, but they typically overlay trending over time, charting options, and other tools.

But don't overthink things, either. The simplest approach may just be to issue unique discount or promotion codes any time you promote offers on a social network. "If you have a specific promo code you use on Facebook and Twitter, that's the simplest form of tracking."

Here are touchpoints on your Web site to watch:

- Visits from social-media sites
- Leads, inquiries, and catalog requests from social-media sites
- Newsletter signups from social-media sites
- Orders and revenue from social-media sites

Note: since these stats measure what someone does on your site after visiting your site, use caution, and remember that "correlation does not prove causation." Many people may bop back and forth from your e-commerce site to your blog to your Facebook page and back again before making a purchase. Don't be too quick to say "Ha! Facebook caused a sale!" If you're not doing multichannel tracking, you'll never know whether that customer really came in the door in response to your trusty direct-mail catalog.

Other metrics track your social networks and your impact on the blogosphere, Twittersphere, and the Web at large:

- On Facebook fan pages, Page Insights is a section page authors can track that measures post quality; the post quality rating is a measure of the percentage of users that have interacted with your page ("liking," commenting, etc.). The star rating shows how your level of interaction compares your page with others with similar-sized fan bases.
- Track fans, followers, connections, or other measures of your network size. It's easy and provides a useful indicator of your footprint on social media—but I wouldn't read much into the data.
- Track mentions of your brand name and key products using Google Alerts, Tweetmeme, and other social-media "listening" tools.

Gatorade's Social-Media Command Center

What you watch is important. But until I learned about Gatorade's social-media "Mission Control" room, I didn't realize how important it is *how you watch*.

Gatorade Mission Control is a slick, glass-walled room glowing with the light of six huge, wall-mounted monitors. Other monitors and workstations cover a single curved desk, where as many as five marketing staffers keep their eyes glued to Gatorade's place in the social-media conversation, in real-time. One monitor charts tweets referencing the Gatorade brand and trending topics. Another shows several line charts tracking blog mentions of Gatorade as well as three rival brands.

The displays, custom designed for Gatorade parent company PepsiCo by IBM and Radian6, are visually impressive. But are they helping the company manage?

Gatorade's Carla Hassan, senior marketing director for consumer and shopper engagement, answers an emphatic yes.[3] For instance, in monitoring responses to its Gatorade Has Evolved campaign, Mission Control quickly saw heavy social-media buzz developing around a song by rap artist David Banner. Within 24 hours, the company had worked with Banner to release a full-length version of the song and distribute it to Gatorade followers and fans on Twitter and Facebook.

Gatorade's tools are being used to tailor Web sites and landing pages to its top-performing topics and videos, based on social-media conversations. As a result, the company increased engagement with its videos by 250 percent and reduced its landing-page exit rate from 25 percent to 9 percent.

I'd also suggest that merely establishing a command center highlights the importance of social media within a business—making it more fun, more engrossing, and more likely to percolate into the culture of the company as a whole.

Hassan says the goal of Mission Control is to "take the largest sports brand in the world and turn it into the largest participatory brand in the world."

To that end, Gatorade isn't just monitoring the conversation, but participating in it as well. The company hosts events on Ustream and Facebook in which a sports nutritionist answers questions from fans. During the 2010 Super Bowl, Gatorade invited fans to interact with some of its NFL stars through Ustream as they tested the new Gatorade G Series Pro drink.

If successful, the Mission Control strategy is likely to spread to other businesses within PepsiCo, according to Bonin Bough, director of global social media at the company. "We believe what we're building here is an example of a sandbox of tools and processes we can use across the organization."

To get a glimpse of the social-media command center in action, go to YouTube and search "Gatorade Mission Control."

WRITING A SOCIAL-MEDIA BUSINESS PLAN

You've already spent a lot of time on social media at this point, and now you're getting ready to spend more money. What exactly are you going to achieve by being active in social media? And how are you going to achieve it?

Just as you would write a business plan for a new entrepreneurial venture, or craft a marketing plan for a major new product or category launch, you now need to write your social-media business plan.

You're not trying to qualify for a bank loan, so don't knock yourself out. Take the exercise seriously, but try to keep the document to five to 10 pages. The purpose of planning is fourfold:

- Force yourself to think broadly and take the long view about your project and its objectives.
- Create a roadmap to follow with tangible goals.
- Sell the project internally to whoever must approve funding.
- Give yourself a framework to return to and revise as the project goes along.

The key ingredients for a good social-media business plan:

Executive summary: Summarize why participating in social media is so important to your company, what your broad strategy is, and what goals you'll achieve.

Mission statement: Restate the company's mission in light of the unique opportunities and nature of social media.

Competitive and market analysis: Since about 80 percent of the online public is using social media, calculating the size of the market is a waste of time, although impressive. The main question: What are your chief rivals already doing on the social-media networks? How many fans and followers do they have, what campaigns are they running, are they driving PR, revenue, search traffic, etc.?

Marketing plan: Describe what platforms you'll participate in right away, and show a rough time line for expansion into new platforms and opportunities.

Operations plan: Show how you'll staff the effort and what the team's responsibilities and deliverables will be. Describe your posting frequency, customer-service approach (CRM), and brief rules of engagement. Address how you'll put safeguards in place so that social media won't be a source of legal or brand-image problems. This is also the place to mention software, consultants, domain names, and other things you'll need to buy.

Goals and objectives: Unlike a typical business plan, whose upside is forecast in the financials, your social-media business plan will need to describe a number of important and quantifiable goals that are nonmonetary. See the section above on analytics for ideas. Project the number of new e-mail sign-ups and calculate their value, do the same for fans and followers, or external links for search-engine value, dollars trackable to social-media campaigns, PR placements, or brand mentions. Try to separate the goals of outreach (to prospects and the media) from the goals of loyalty and retention (of existing customers). A good social-media program will yield fruit in both regards.

Financials: These will be fairly simple. You'll need to have budget numbers on the expense side and some quantifiable goals—that may or may not include sales—on the ROI side. Charts forecasting traffic, fans, media mentions, or revenue are helpful tools both to sell the concept and to give you structure to run the program month by month.

SUPPORTING MULTIPLE SMALLER NETWORKS

We're still at the stage in social media where businesses are getting a great deal of attention for building very large networks on Facebook and for attracting 1 million-plus fans on Twitter. But there's an exciting, and potentially even more powerful, possibility: building lots and lots of smaller networks.

Dunbar's Number is a theoretical limit to the number of people with whom we can maintain stable, positive social relationships. It's named after the British anthropologist Robin Dunbar, who first proposed it based on his studies of primate groups, primitive human tribes, and historical records of medieval villages.

These are groups in which everyone knows everyone else and has a general sense of their communal identity. Such groups are stable and cohesive, with little need of formal rules or restrictions. While no precise number has been settled on, 150 is a commonly cited estimate, and one mentioned in Malcolm Gladwell's best-selling book *The Tipping Point*, which brought Dunbar's concept to millions.

So, for a group to function as a strong, cohesive community—in which all the members recognize one another and share a sense of group identity and solidarity—it needs to stay relatively small. Dunbar's number was an observation of groups in the physical world, but I think it has meaningful implications in the online social-media world. Two factors are at work here:

One, in a very large social-media group, each member knows relatively few other members; while there are no upper limits to how many people can "like" Shakira on Facebook, there is a real limit to how many relationships any member can maintain with his or her fellow Shakira fans. As Phil Terry said in chapter 2, these groups function more like mailing lists than true communities.

Two, with most social-media groups brought together by a company or organization, the bigger they get, the harder it is to "message" the members with relevant content. In the Shakira group, sure, everybody loves Shakira, and messaging is always going to be easy. But for any organization serving multiple markets and different demographics with several different products, it becomes harder.

Now let's think about the power and cohesion of smaller social-media groups dedicated to very specific communities.

I spoke with a marketing director of a bicycle and walking-tour company who talked of an emerging practice in his industry: They create dozens and dozens of Facebook groups a year, dedicated to each destination *and* its specific dates. So as soon as they've booked a tour, travelers are invited to a Facebook network created just for them—the June 12-19 Tuscany bicycle tour group, say, or the February 2-9 Machu Picchu Inca Trail trek. In the weeks or months prior to their departure, they get to know their tour leaders and their fellow travelers-to-be. They ask questions about what to pack, or how to train, recommend travel books to read, talk about past vacations, and upload pictures of themselves.

By the time they assemble on their first day in Tuscany or Peru, they already feel like old friends, hugging and having a grand time. Group dynamics can sometimes be awkward in the first couple days of a tour, but now the Facebook effect seems to erase that tension. The marketing director told me that customer satisfaction has been off the charts since they kicked off the social-media program.

Envision these same travelers after their trip, posting their fond memories and uploading their vacation photos, hearing from the tour leaders, staying in touch, and perhaps planning future trips together. I can imagine "graduating" the members of this Facebook group into a destination-specific "alumni" group—say all the company's former Tuscany travelers, and messaging them about upcoming tours to that and other destinations.

Any cohesive and focused group on Facebook can also be mirrored by a specific Twitter feed, so for example you could develop dozens of Twitter feeds based on information germane to each specific bike tour. Perhaps it would be of interest to the friends and family back home to hear several daily tweets about the weather and riding conditions, the lunch at the vineyard, the cozy Tuscan villa—these feeds could spread the word across a small but tight network and would probably inspire some future customers.

Building out several mini-communities is a daunting task, but the payoff could be huge. It's an especially attractive approach for camps, retreats, classes, and schools. My alma mater, Middlebury College, has built Facebook pages for each and every graduating class. That's a highly effective way to keep classmates connected and thinking fondly of their school, posting updates for the alumni magazine, being aware of alumni events and reunions—and, no doubt, responding to fund-raising appeals.

CAUSES, CONTESTS, AND GOING VIRAL

The California Travel and Tourism Commission launched a trivia game, promoted on its social-media pages, whose winners receive free airfares on Southwest or even a California vacation package. To sweeten the pot, California Tourism gave players extra points if they e-mailed a link to their friends via Facebook Connect.

I've mentioned a number of times the importance of hitching your social-media wagon to a "big idea," a larger cause or lifestyle interest that goes beyond merely hawking your wares.

With its Chase Community Giving program, Chase uses its Facebook page to collect votes for which 200 charities will receive grants ranging from $20,000 to $250,000.

These examples get at a simple fact of social-media marketing: Your reach multiplies exponentially when you tap the power of the crowd. Giving fans something to "like" generates strong growth. But giving fans something to win, something to vote for, explicitly rewarding them for spreading the word—that's what generates viral growth.

Text to Win on the Scoreboard. Fans attending Chicago Bears games at Soldier Field responded to scoreboard prompts to text to a short code to win six free wings at Chicago area Buffalo Wild Wings locations. The text message included a mobile Web site with store locations and promotion info. Big venues are a fantastic place for launching scoreboard text-message promotions to extend sponsorships. Add a third dimension to in-arena promotions using SMS and the mobile Web. If you have a billboard at any arena, it is a perfect place to reach a captive audience with a text promotion to drive post-game or in-game retail traffic. You also have the opportunity to deliver ongoing product messaging to consumers who opt in for your offer.

Sin to Win. Mobile users are now turning to their phones to confess their worst sins. Virgin Mobile in 2004 introduced Sin to Win, in which customers were invited to send in their sins in order to relieve themselves of a guilty secret for a chance to win prizes for the best confessions. More than 10,000 people sent in their SMS confessions!

Budweiser donates money to Keep America Beautiful every time someone texts "RECYCLE" to "BEERS" (23377)—up to a total of $50,000. The effort, part of the company's Budweiser's Better World initiative, spreads socially and draws attention to Anheuser-Busch's conservation efforts. Currently the company recycles 99 percent of its solid waste, making it one of the world's biggest recyclers of aluminum at 800 million pounds a year. While production has grown, its water use has declined—and renewable fuels are powering more of the brewing process. The company also keeps alive its tradition begun by Adolphus Busch in the late 1800s of recycling the brewer's spent grains into cattle feed.

Bud's environmental text-messaging campaign, managed on the MsgMe platform from Waterfall Mobile, is just one of many uses Anheuser-Busch has found for SMS messaging. For instance, Bud relied on text voting to pick 32 winners worldwide to be sent to watch the FIFA World Cup soccer matches in South Africa and live in Bud House, a deluxe Cape Town villa. After the voting, the campaign was integrated with an online reality show anchored on a custom YouTube channel, and each of the 32 "cast members" had their own dedicated Facebook fan page and Twitter stream. A-B even developed a Facebook app that let people "paint their faces" in their national team colors and apply the look to their Facebook profile picture.

In a major Facebook campaign, Bud used Facebook ads to urge people to vote for which of three commercials it should run for Super Bowl 2010. Those who clicked had to become fans of Bud before they could vote. The campaign also asked voters whether they wanted to post their vote to their wall—a great technique to spread visibility of the campaign to all the friends of fans. Bud's Facebook page currently has over 350,000 fans.

And in a campaign that may seem a touch at odds with the abovementioned environmental campaign, Bud ran a text-to-win sweepstakes for customers in Virginia and the Carolinas to win free gas for a year.

OTHER NETWORKS AND SOCIAL APPLICATIONS WORTH A LOOK

We could fill an encyclopedia with all the large and small social-media sites and networks. Many platforms that were yesterday's media darlings— and are still massive by any measure—have slipped out of the spotlight and lost market share to their rivals. Remember Friendster? Even MySpace, which at about 100 million users ranks third among the social networks, has taken on the aura of an also-ran (although the platform is showing signs of new life lately). But even second-tier platforms offer millions of devoted users. Third-tier platforms, if they serve a well-defined demographic or special interest that's important to your business, should also play a role in your social-media program. Most of these platforms are looking for revenue sources, so there's a wide variety of advertising opportunities to test.

Warning: Don't spread yourself too thin. You're better off doing an excellent job on the few leading networks than dabbling ineffectively in every little network you can think of.

Flickr

If you serve a visual market, try uploading your images to Flickr, the Yahoo-owned photo-sharing site. Of course, Flickr is a must for photographers and other visual artists, as well as models—it's a great place for an online portfolio, and the network of millions could be a promising audience. Travel businesses and tourism bureaus should be uploading sumptuous photos of their destinations. Fashion companies like Urban Outfitters have been active on the site for a long time.

There's very little statistical or case-study evidence on the effectiveness of Flickr for business, but it costs nothing to get on, upload a number of images, join several groups focused on your market or area of specialty, friend others, and see where it goes. One happy side effect of joining Flickr could be that your images start ranking for certain image-related searches on Google.

Beware, though: Although Flickr has filters and policies in place to try to keep pornographic and inappropriate content under wraps, it is evidently a big portion of what goes on at Flickr, and it can emerge somewhat without warning when you are connecting with new people and groups on the site.

Explore Chicago has a photo pool on Flickr of more than 11,000 images of the city, its people, and its happenings.

Urban Outfitters has been using Flickr for years for posting and spreading images of its clothes, models, and customers wearing UO and to otherwise support its brand image. While the UO Flickr group is a loosely organized assemblage of professional and amateur photographers, as well as ordinary customers, the administrator's guidelines are clear: "Please post only UO store design/window dressing, items purchased from the store, posing in UO clothing, catalogs/advertising campaigns, and photo shoots."

The Nikon Digital Learning Center on Flickr is a great example of perfect alignment between a brand, its audience, and the social-media platform. Here, Nikon connects on the world's biggest photo-sharing service with the world's passionate photographers. Its primary purpose is not to sell cameras, but to share information, build a user community, and promote image sharing around the emerging art and science of digital photography.

Unlike most Flickr communities, where user comments focus solely on the images, Nikon's community supports many active discussions on topics like "Has anybody used an aftermarket flash like Nissin on a d90?" By providing a home for conversations like these, Nikon makes itself a leader and a trusted brand in the space, helps enlarge the market for serious digital photography—and eventually, indirectly, boosts its business.

Foursquare

Especially if you operate bricks-and-mortar retail locations, local search results served up on mobile devices are your most exciting and fastest-developing opportunity. And like everything else, local search is getting social.

Foursquare is a popular mobile app that lets users "check into" physical locations like hotels, restaurants, and even doctors' offices. Users can search Foursquare for local businesses within a given radius of their location. Built into the application are social-networking elements called friend finder and social city guide.

Thanks to these social-media features, whether she's in a hair salon, an autobody shop, or a diner, a Foursquare user can post status updates about the place, which are broadcast across Foursquare and also integrated with her Twitter or Facebook feed. Similar to Yelp or TripAdvisor, she can share her ratings and reviews of the business, ask questions about it, and see whether other members of their social network recommend the place.

Foursquare incentivizes individual users to explore their surroundings and post their findings for all to share and it uses what it calls "game mechanics" (including the awarding of virtual "mayor" titles!) to incentivize people: "Our users earn points, win mayorships, and unlock badges for trying new places and revisiting old favorites."

"One of the main reasons it's gaining so much buzz is because those who 'check in' to places can instantly share these updates on Twitter and Facebook," says Chad Capellman of the Boston-based agency Genuine Interactive. "This, in turn, means literally millions of people are receiving these updates. The latest numbers, extrapolated by Mashable, show that the service is approaching one million check-ins per day."[4]

In turn, business owners can use Foursquare to reach their mobile customers by offering Foursquare discounts and prizes. The application offers owners "venue analytics," like how often their business profile or their specials are accessed.

Establishing a presence on Foursquare is free and easy, and the benefits are likely to grow along with the importance of smartphones and PDFs in our daily lives. Capellman offers step-by-step advice on how businesses can get the most out of Foursquare:

1. Claim your business location and verify you're the owner.
2. Describe the benefits of your business (e.g., free parking, vegetarian menu, Spanish-speaking . . .) in the form of tags.
3. Write additional content about your business (descriptions of your services, customer-service philosophy, etc.) in the form of tips. Reviews of your business submitted by Foursquare users will also appear among your tips.
4. Get connected to other users. "Search all of the businesses within a mile or two of your practice, and make friend connections with people who have checked into those businesses," advises Capellman. "In my own experience and in conversations with others, people seem more likely to reciprocate connections through Foursquare than they would through LinkedIn, Facebook, or even Twitter."

5. Whenever you get to work, "check in" via Foursquare. Like a status update on other networks, checking in puts you and your business onto the radar screen of everyone in your extended Foursquare network. As the mobile Web, the Foursquare app, and your personal network all grow, checking into your location will remind scores or even hundreds of your neighbors about your business—and it will no doubt nudge a few nearby fans to stop in.

The potential of Foursquare goes well beyond promotions by individual businesses. In getting people to follow the steps of Ferris Bueller and relive their favorite scenes from the classic teen movie, Chicago's tourism office generated lots of buzz and fun while introducing Chicagoans and tourists alike to many of the city's treasured places.

Recently the Chicago tourism office employed Foursquare to promote an On Location badge, which challenges local users to trace the steps of Ferris Bueller from the movie *Ferris Bueller's Day Off.*

Then in a Foursquare contest, the city gave away two Southwest Airlines tickets, a hotel stay, and passes to the renowned Art Institute of Chicago, where one of Bueller's famous scenes takes place. The Explore Chicago giveaway was posted on Foursquare Facebook page earlier that day, asking users to leave a comment with the scene they'd like to recreate from the movie for a chance to win the prize.

Explore Chicago does a great job keeping its Twitter feed fresh and exciting, with frequent posts about cool happenings in the Windy City—and also direct-messaging its thousands of followers, answering tourist questions, and otherwise interacting with its online community. With a slew of podcasts, YouTube videos, an RSS feed, a presence on Facebook, a great photo pool on Flickr, and its channel on YouTube, Explore Chicago is hitting on all cylinders and using all media to get out the message about the city.

Groupon

Groupon is a new group-buying concept, focused on local retail stores and attractions. Groupon members are offered big discounts—but only if a minimum number of other members sign on too.

Gap's 50%-discount offered on the Groupon in August 2010 rang up a reported $11 million in sales, and in the process demonstrated some best practices for e-commerce in this new, more social Web 2.0 era.

According to Groupon spokesperson Julie Mossler, the Gap offer was the most successful Groupon promotion to date, ringing up as many as 532 transactions per minute during its busiest periods Thursday morning. Traffic was so intense that Groupon had to manage the load by directing visitors to alternate landing pages in order to avert a server crash.

What I find impressive about the Gap campaign is the sheer number of coordinated moving parts cross-promoting a single offer:

- 15 million Gap and Groupon **e-mail subscribers** receive the offer, starting at midnight and in staggered fashion throughout the day
- The offer is tweeted to the 180,000+ followers of **Twitter's @earlybird** promoted tweet stream
- Gap **tweets** the offer to its 30,000+ followers
- Groupon manually tweets and **Facebook** posts on its pages dedicated to each of the 85 geographical markets where Gap's offer is valid
- Gap posts the offer to its 606,000 fans on **Facebook**
- Groupon's 1,500 **affiliate partners** post Gap's offer on their Web sites
- A sponsored post appears above the fold on **Digg**

All in all, it was a big win for Gap, and impressive evidence of how online promotion and social shopping, courtesy of Groupon, can drive sales to bricks-and-mortar stores.

"Our customers had been asking us to feature a national retailer, and the Gap deal was a perfect fit for Back-To-School and even pre-holiday shopping," Mossler explained. "Gap even has stores where Groupon hasn't launched yet; so, it's a perfect way to reach new and existing Groupon fans with a deal they won't find anywhere else."[5]

iLike

iLike is a "social music discovery service" that was bought by MySpace in 2009. With more than 60 million users, it's a destination in itself, but more importantly it's the leading music application on Facebook, Google, Orkut, hi5, and Bebo. If you're a musician, iLike is a great distribution channel. If you serve a market that is into music, you can add interest to your Web site or your social-media pages by integrating with iLike's developer tools.

Meetup.org

Meetup is the world's biggest online network devoted to helping people organize in-person get-togethers of local community groups.

Since I think the bridge between online social media and offline action is powerful, we'll talk about it in depth later in this chapter. We'll look at how Meetup works and how your business can use it to make more powerful, in-person connections with the people in your online social network.

MocoSpace

MocoSpace is a social network accessed primarily via mobile phones. It reaches a younger audience, particularly the 18- to 24-year-old demographic. Organizations wanting to reach a multicultural audience would do well to look at MocoSpace. The platform has 11 million members, and roughly a third are Hispanic, a third are African American, and the remaining third are white, Asian, and other.

MySpace

MySpace was the hottest and biggest social-media platform on the planet, circa 2006, when it was on everyone's lips for its blistering growth rate and its millions of members, most of them in the 16- to 34-year-old demographic. Since then, MySpace has been eclipsed by Facebook and Twitter. Yet there is still a lot to like about MySpace—chiefly its now 100 million members, an audience share of 80 percent of the total online audience, and MySpace's long-standing special focus on music, games, movies, and other entertainment.

MySpace offers a wealth of tools for tricking-out your company or personal page, with a unique graphic look, blog posts, friends, and, for recording artists, an array of online music previewing and buying apps.

Simply stated, if you're an entertainment company or a band, you need to be on MySpace. More broadly, any company catering to younger audiences could do well to participate in MySpace with a company page, friend relationships, and possibly advertising.

"MySpace is moving back to its original DNA: appealing to self-expressive, creative under-35-year-olds who are into games, music, and movies," wrote Jon Swartz in *USA Today* in 2010. "More than half of MySpace's estimated 100 million users are 25 and younger, according to market researcher ComScore. The 13-to-34-year-old demographic spends 84 percent of all user time on the service."[6]

Second Life

No doubt about it, Second Life is an innovator. The technology of this virtual world/online multiplayer game is incredible. What is unclear is what, exactly, are the opportunities for businesses and organizations.

Second Life has moved out of the spotlight since, around 2006, big-name brands like Coke, Reebok, and Scion were building their own elaborate in-world virtual locations—or islands—to interact with the denizens of Second Life. Unfortunately, nobody came. A reported 85 percent of avatars created by would-be Second Lifers are abandoned. Of the 18 million registered users, Linden Lab, creator of Second Life, admits just under a million are active. In June 2010, Linden laid off 30 percent of its staff.

The focus for businesses has changed. While big business islands have been a bust, a number of entrepreneurial ventures selling virtual goods and services usable within the game have flourished. Meanwhile, Linden's 3D technology has been put to use serving businesses, schools, and nonprofits with online conferencing, collaboration, and prototyping.

IBM held two major meetings virtually using Linden's technologies in 2009, estimating it saved some $320,000 it would've spent had it held the events in a traditional bricks-and-mortar venue. "The meeting in Second Life was everything that you could do at a traditional conference—and more," says Joanne Martin, president of the IBM Academy of Technology, "at one-fifth the cost and without a single case of jetlag."

Now, Linden aims to remake itself as less of a virtual-world game and more of a social network.

"If you think about what the experience, and the product, and the platform actually enable, they enable people to communicate, express themselves, and connect in a rich, immersive, shared context. That's fundamentally what it's about," says Tom Hale, chief product officer for Linden. "People talk about Second Life as a place where you go and look at things, but I think it's actually more of a place where you go and communicate with people."[7]

SlideShare

Old PowerPoints never die—they just crawl off to SlideShare. Yes, there's a social-media site for *everything*, and SlideShare is devoted to storing presentations, Word docs, and PDFs. If you're a public speaker, consultant, analyst, academic, or a businessperson who crafts a lot of PowerPoint and other presentations, try uploading your work to SlideShare.

"Individuals and organizations upload documents to SlideShare to share ideas, connect with others, and generate leads for their businesses," says the company. With some 25 million monthly visitors, these docs tend to be seen, shared on LinkedIn, and quoted in the blogosphere and mainstream media.

Spoke

Spoke lags well behind the leading business-networking site, LinkedIn, but it is worth a look, especially if you're in business-to-business. The site is a business directory of 60 million people compiled by a Web spider that crawls and parses countless articles and other Web pages about business-people. As with the similar ZoomInfo Web site, it can be a good idea to "claim" your profile and make sure it is up-to-date and has current contact info if you're interested in lead generation.

Squidoo

At its best, Squidoo is a passionate and sizable network. Founded by Seth Godin, the world's best-recognized business blogger and author, it's a publishing platform, something of a second-generation blog network with a social twist. Its growth has tapered off some since 2009, when it was one of the top 10 fastest growing domains in terms of organic traffic. Today Squidoo ranks among the top 250 most visited sites in the United States. The strength of Squidoo is that creating a graphically attractive and interesting page (or "lens" in Squidoo parlance) is a piece of cake. Lenses can be effortlessly linked to other sources of information and further reading and can be linked to your accounts on other social-media sites, including your blog, Flickr, Google Maps, eBay, Twitter, and YouTube.

It takes just five minutes to build your first lens, according to Squidoo—and although you'll no doubt spend more time than that on building your page and making it unique and of high quality, it's still a real snap.

What's attractive about Squidoo is that it's a low-effort, potentially high-reward publishing platform, and at the very least establishes yet another home on the Web where people may find you—typically through organic searches. In the past, Squidoo has been derided by some as being a magnet for SEO spam—pages designed solely either to attract search traffic themselves or, through a multitude of spam links, boost the page rank of other target sites. In 2007, Google's search algorithm punished the site for such content, sending Squidoo's overall traffic down 30 percent by excluding spam pages from its search results.

"We have been working on this spam issue for months," said Seth Godin back in 2007. "We found that there were several dozen people that were dramatically exploiting the systems within Squidoo that were previously only used for good. People using the site for nefarious ends will come to an end. That's what we're doing without Google's input."

Since then, the Squidoo neighborhood has been a dramatically cleaned-up place.

Lensmasters on Squidoo can connect with one another and gain reputations within the community and the most prolific of them can produce literally thousands of lenses dedicated to topics as diverse as tantric yoga, zebra mussels, and cheats for Grand Theft Auto. Because the pages support advertising—in which the lensmaster gets a share—Squidoo can make its best Lensmasters (aka "Giant Squids") some decent money.

Notably, Squidoo also encourages and supports giving some or all of the ad revenues to the charities of your choice—so over the years, the platform and its lensmasters have given away hundreds of millions of dollars to more than 90 charities.

EARNED MEDIA VERSUS PAID MEDIA

The term "earned media" has long been used in PR circles to describe the "free" press and broadcast coverage generated by public relations campaigns, word-of-mouth, or just plain good luck. But the emphasis is on *earning* attention in a noisy and attention-deficient world—earning notice by being new, noteworthy, different, weird, revolutionary, and/or remarkable.

Paid media, on the other hand, is just what it sounds like: paying for attention via advertising.

The emerging social-media scene is doing radical things to both earned media and to paid media. For one thing, earned media buzz is easier than ever to generate and pass along, on a viral growth curve, through whatever online community you've built.

Paid media opportunities have now moved on to the major social-media platforms in fits and starts and it hasn't always been pretty. The first wave of paid advertising was distributed paid search text ads of Google AdWords and the other major search networks.

Eager to wring some revenue from their millions of members and their page views, the social networks have now rolled out various ad options and doubtless more are to come. The possibilities range from traditional banner advertising "run-of-network" ads (broad exposure and low click rates) to "hypertargeted" ad distribution based on the stated interests, hobbies, college, and other attributes of the members.

ADVERTISING IN SOCIAL MEDIA

When they first came along, "Web logs," or blogs as they came to be known, were non-commercial, highly personal affairs. Then, as now, the reputation of the blogger for personal integrity and trustworthiness was paramount.

But daily publishing of high-quality writing is a time-consuming job. For the best bloggers to be able to commit to it—and eventually in the case of top sites, quit their day jobs—they needed a revenue source. That arrived in 2003 when Google launched its AdSense program, the network of Web site owners ("publishers" in the parlance of Google and the rest of the ad-network world) that is the distribution channel for paid AdWords ads distributed on the Google Content Network.

No, AdWords ads don't appear exclusively on blogs—they appear on hundreds of thousands of Web sites on every topic imaginable. But they are the single leading revenue source for most blogs today (affiliate sales revenue share, product sales, and other ad sales are other sources of money).

When ads began appearing all over the blogosphere, it rankled many, both by cheapening the appearance of some sites, giving the appearance of potential editorial conflict of interest, and also providing incentive for SEOers to create and optimize Web sites that served no end in themselves but were merely platforms to serve tons of AdWords in the hope of collecting paid clicks. For sites like these, the derogatory term "MFA spam sites"—for "Made for AdSense"—was coined.

Of course, some bloggers are valued less for their objectivity and freedom from bias as for their pure entertainment value. The whole notion of advertising on social-media platforms is anathema to many folks, especially the pioneers and purists who were blogging when the whole "social" scene was being born.

Is it a new and enlightened way to do business—or is it just old-fashioned greed camouflaged in modern clothing?

But more pernicious than AdSense (which has also, it must be said, really has cleaned up its act in recent years) was another development aimed squarely at bloggers: paid mentions.

Another temptation waved before the eyes of bloggers and other site owners is text link advertising. These programs pay bloggers to insert "keyword rich links" to paying clients. I recommend steering clear from schemes like these. Google has made clear that link buying and selling for the purposes of SEO violates its webmasters' guidelines; Google will at the least disregard the "juice" passed by such links—and at worst, penalize participating sites. Furthermore, embedding spammy links in your posts just cheapens the image of your blog.

Clickable is an advertising tracking and analysis platform that is now investing heavily in social-media metrics. Max Kalehoff is vice president of marketing at the company and he writes the weekly "Online Spin" column for MediaPost. In early 2010, Clickable launched a forum for its customers to sound off on what social-media tracking tools they wanted to see added to the Clickable platform. "We took a social approach to how to approach social," notes Kalehoff.[8]

Kalehoff has been in the space a long time. He was on the founding management team of Buzzmetrics, which he describes as "the first social media monitoring and analysis firm." When it was sold to Nielsen in 2006, it validated in the eyes of many that social media metrics would be an important discipline for the future.

Kalehoff has seen a clear evolution in social-media participation by businesses, and now in social-media advertising. "In the early days of social media catching on," he says, "it was almost exclusively brand marketers investing and experimenting. It was the agencies who were last to the party. Now it's mainstream—everybody's involved in it."

Clickable's first innovations have been to incorporate Facebook advertising metrics into its dashboard, where it can be viewed and managed alongside a company's other online campaigns, such as paid search and e-mail. The result is "common metrics across any ad platform."

"What we want to do is put your ability to manage your social advertising on the same dashboard you use to manage your paid search," explains Kalehoff.

Complicating matters, because the social-media landscape is still changing so fast, especially for businesses, it's not obvious what the best techniques will prove to be. Your biggest choice in advertising on social media is whether to click away from the platform or stay within it. That is, will your Facebook ad pitch products or services that have to be bought from your Web site, off Facebook, or will you focus your Facebook ads on driving people to your Facebook fan page?

Strategy: Jump to External Sites

Ever since the dawn of banner advertising, right through to the explosion of Google AdWords text ads, when you've seen an ad, clicking on it takes you away to a new Web site. It may launch in a separate browser window, but the effect is to go to a different site where you can transact whatever business the ad is promoting.

The pluses of this strategy are obvious: You pay to bring somebody else's visitors over to your site to see and buy your stuff. The process is essentially one step. With Web analytics in place, you can measure precisely how effective your advertising was.

Strategy: Stay on the Social Platform

The "jump to external site" model has a couple major flaws when applied to social media. First, let's remember that the lion's share of online advertising up to this point was search-engine advertising. Triggered by the search query and serving ad pitches tailored to that specific search query, these ads are highly targeted to a customer's needs—and such searchers have no qualms about clicking away from the search engine and exploring other sites for their needs; that's what a search engine is for!

Social networks, on the other hand, are closed systems, addictive entertainments, chat rooms and ongoing conversations, via wall posts, that are very hard to leave. Indeed, on May 4, 2010, Nielsen reported that the average time per person spent globally on social-media sites soared 100 percent. The average person spent more than six hours per month on social-media sites—an increase of 100 percent from the previous year.

In "Facebook and Twitter Post Large Year over Year Gains in Unique Users," Nielsen found that in the United States, Facebook posted a 69 percent increase while Twitter had a 45 percent increase.

So the platforms' sheer entertainment value is one major barrier to clicking away. Another, on Facebook, is a warning page that advises visitors—who have already clicked on an ad—that they are leaving Facebook, and that they should never enter their Facebook password on a non-Facebook site. Reluctance to leave a fun Web site and discomfort with this creepy warning screen are both sizable deterrents to clicking through to a third-party (read: your company's) Web site.

Saddled with those challenges, many advertisers have explored keeping ad-clickers within the social network but driving to their fan page to either "like"/ become a fan, or perhaps to enter a contest or do something interactive. Another option is to construct an online store right in the Facebook framework.

FACEBOOK ADVERTISING

WrestlingGear.com is one of the nation's leading sellers of shoes, singlets, and equipment for college, high school, and younger wrestlers. Owner Jeff Pape has made excellent use of Facebook ads—on a very modest total budget and spending an average of 20 cents a click—to attract new fans to his Facebook fan page. Once there, his fans are kept up-to-date on new products, including popular and limited-edition wrestling shoes that create a lot of buzz in the sport and drive much of WrestlingGear's sales. We'll look more closely at Pape's experience in the next chapter.

As Pape discovered, the bigger you get, the less able you are, under Facebook rules, to send messages to your fans. Most businesses are prohibited from e-mailing event invitations or other communications en masse. Facebook has many limitations on the frequency of use of their features. Overuse can and will result in the feature being blocked and/or your account being deactivated. You can add an e-mail sign-up form to your fan page so that you can manage a fan e-mail list outside of Facebook.

Facebook's cost-per-click advertising is currently very low-cost and provides some terrific targeting options. Niche companies can use it to great advantage to attract fans, contest signups, and customers.

Terry Bicycles, a pioneering maker of women's-specific bike frames and a leading seller of women's cycling clothing, has had great success using Facebook advertising to target its key demographic: women aged 30 and up, in the U.S. and Canada, who name bicycling as one of their interests. Terry advertised on Facebook to drum up entrants to its $500 cycling wardrobe giveaway. In the process, Terry added several hundred new names in its mailing list, and over time drove tens of thousands of dollars of sales from customers it found through Facebook.

Dartmouth Coop is a business ideally suited to one of the "hypertargeting" selects in Facebook: your college. This purveyor of Dartmouth College sweatshirts, pennants, mugs, and other paraphernalia began advertising to self-identified Dartmouth students and alums on Facebook in 2009.

Wine of the Month Club advertised for new fans among the hundreds of thousands of self-described wine enthusiasts on Facebook. The pitch wasn't a commercial one: There was no effort to sign them up to the club, just to get them to join the fan community. That effort paid off. Today, Wine of the Month Club's Facebook fanbase is over 44,000 people. When you reach that level, every day's posts elicit dozens of "likes" and "comments," which are broadcast across the friend networks of all members. As a result, fan pages like WOMC get several hundred new fans a day organically.

According to the social-media analytics software Sysomos, 77 percent of all Facebook fan pages have fewer than 1,000 fans. Some 35 percent of fan pages are languishing with fewer than 100 fans—hardly a number worth bothering to create and update a page for.

What types of organizations create Facebook fan pages? As the Sysomos data shows us, the distribution is very uniform; see Table 4.2.

What's not at all uniform, though, is how many fans these pages attract. Music and celebrities rule the roost. Small wonder, when the biggest celebrity page, for Michael Jackson, counts 10.4 million fans. President Obama is at 6.9 million. Starbuck's is the reigning product page, with 5.1 percent.

Table 4.2   Distribution of Facebook fan pages as per Sysomos data

Nonprofits	7.5%
Music	7.4%
Organizations	7.4%
Places	7.4%
Web sites	7.4%
Products	7.3%
Restaurants	7.3%
Services	7.3%
Stores	7.3%
Celebrities	7.0%
Bars and clubs	6.9%
Movies	4.6%
Sports teams	4.4%
Politicians	4.0%
TV shows	3.4%
Games	3.2%

Among the behemoths, pages with more than 1 million fans, see Table 4.3 for category breakdown.

In addition to the many "hypertargeting" options on Facebook, advertisers can also display their ads to friends-of-friends, that is, to friends of their brand fans.

The Friends of Connections targeting feature allows you to expand your reach by delivering your ads to the friends of people already connected with your fan page. It's logical to think that the appeal of your brand runs strong among circles of friends or a given demographic. "In addition to harnessing the social graph by targeting your connections' friends," says Facebook, "every 'Friends of Connection' targeted ad promoting a page or event includes social content about a friend's interaction with your business, amplifying the relevancy of your ad." And since the average Facebook user has over 100 friends, your potential audience balloons whenever you use this option.

FACEBOOK STORES

On the cutting edge of the commercial/social network are Facebook stores or "shoplets." 1-800-Flowers, Best Buy, and Avon were among the early adopters, and all are tight-lipped about their results. Perhaps, as with setting up a virtual brand "island" on Second Life, this is a speculative bet

Table 4.3   Category breakdown of pages with more than 1 million fans

Music	16.7%
Celebrities	16.0%
Products	11.9%
TV shows	8.5%
Movies	3.4%
Games	1.4%

where the advantage may not be to the first-mover, but to the second, who learns from the mistakes and successes of the first-movers and comes along when more critical mass of demand has been reached.

"The challenge with shopping on Facebook is you're training users to do something different than they've done in the past," says Andy Lloyd, CEO of Fluid, Inc.,[9] which offers a Facebook fan shop. "People really haven't shopped within Facebook." But that seems to be changing.

It's pretty easy to get started with a third-party Facebook store app like Payvment, BigCommerce, or SortPrice. SortPrice claims to have built more than 1,000 Facebook stores to date. More ambitious stores, like those from Alvenda or Fluid's Fan Shop, could cost $20,000 to $25,000 to build.

Yoga apparel and product company Gaiam recently went live with a Facebook store built by Alvenda. Gaiam made an introductory $20-off offer to encourage people to try it. "We spent a lot of energy cultivating a loyal fan base on Facebook," says Kristin Fox, Gaiam's new business development manager. "This is another way for [consumers] to engage with the brand on Facebook. They can spread the word within their friend groups. If they have an upcoming birthday, they can shop on Gaiam and put things in their registry and wish lists that can be shared on Facebook."[10]

Sharing "likes" and wish lists across Facebook and integrating Facebook functionality on your own Web site via its social plug-ins toolset like Gaiam does are smart tactics to interconnect the social and the shopping experience.

Avon and 1-800-Flowers have also built e-commerce capabilities into the news feed, which can be a good strategy because many Facebook users never stray far from their home pages. "The reality is, hardly anyone goes to fan pages of companies on Facebook," says Wade Gerten, CEO of Alvenda. "Most users stay on their own Facebook homepage and pay attention to the news stream."[11] As a result, says Gerten, e-commerce-enabled wall posts are 18 percent more effective than a "shop" tab.

It is not assured that visitors to a social network like Facebook will ever really care to shop there in addition to socializing there. But the pace of change is blistering and will continue to be. Take these encouraging examples:

- Rachel Roy, a division of Jones Apparel, launched a store selling Facebook-only merchandise. It sold out in the first six hours, the brand added 1.5 new fans a minute, and the company's fan base increased 35 percent, according to Fluid.[12]
- When Pampers recently offered its new line of Pampers Cruisers through a storefront on its Facebook fan page, the limited supply of 1,000 packages for $9.99 apiece sold out in less than an hour.[13]

The takeaway? Betting against social commerce is probably a bad wager.

MYSPACE ADVERTISING

MySpace also offers advertising opportunities ranging from small text ads to highly interactive banners and widgets. You can get started with pay-per-click ads with budgets as low as five bucks a day. Big advertisers on MySpace include 20th Century Fox and Skittles, and BestBuy advertises new music there.

Although the program, dubbed MyAds, supports text ads, the emphasis is on moving even small companies beyond text to more eye-catching display ads. Channel Targeting is an option to display ads on specific topics across 1,000 Web sites in the MySpace network; ads are displayed not just on the pages of MySpace, but also syndicated onto relevant pages of AOL, Yahoo, Car and Driver, BabyCenter, and NBC.com.

Channel targeting allows you to show ads on a group of Web pages with related content. For example, if you sell a financial product or service, you can target the finance channel and your ad will appear alongside financial and investing articles and related content. Channels include auto, gaming, health, shopping, news, sports, technology, women's interest, and many others.

Audience targeting allows you to target the type of people you want to see your ads. Audience targeting options include age, gender, education level, relationship status, occupation, and parental status; target by location (city, state, and zip, plus radius); and targeting by hobbies and interests. The latter, thanks to the strength of profile information, lets you aim your ads only at people who've expressed interest in sports, fashion, movies, specific music, politics, and more than 1,000 other interests.

MySpace also offers what's called remarketing—you drop a cookie on visitors to your Web site, and then in the future, whenever they visit a site on the MySpace network, they'll see display ads promoting your business. Remarketing is a powerful way to extend your brand across a vast swath of the Web and ensure that you're always on the radar screens of your customers and visitors.

TWITTER ADVERTISING: PROMOTED TWEETS

"One of Twitter's key benefits is that it gives you the chance to communicate casually with customers on their terms, creating friendly relationships along the way—tough for corporations to do in most other mediums." So says Twitter in its best-practices advice for businesses.

Before Twitter devised how to monetize its platform, enterprising third parties found their own ways. Firms like SponsoredTweets, Ad.ly, Assetize, Magpie, Izea, and 140 Proof assembled networks of celebrity, specialist, and ordinary-folks tweeters willing to incorporate sponsored messages into their Twitter stream. Or they inserted sponsored messages into the streams displayed on third-party Twitter clients like Tweetdeck, TweetUp, and Echofon.[14]

Now, Twitter has entered the fray with its own Promoted Tweets service. In a blog post describing the move, Twitter pointed out that it had moved slowly and with such deliberation, that pundits like comedian Stephen Colbert were scoring laughs with lines like, "So, I assume that 'Biz' in 'Biz Stone' does not stand for 'business model.'"

Under the Promoted Tweets system, businesses will bid to promote their own tweets into conversations on particular topics. Say you're promoting Kim Kardashian's line of cosmetics. You might create a tweet triggered by her name, her reality show, or other relevant terms. Your tweet then appears atop Kim-related conversations (identified by the label "Promoted Tweet").

Among the first companies sponsoring tweets in the phase one version of the program were Starbucks and Virgin Airways.

Shortly after launching its Promoted Tweets system, Twitter banished those precursor third-party ad networks. "We will not allow any third party to inject paid tweets into a time line on any service that leverages the Twitter API," said Twitter COO Dick Costolo on the company blog.

The company also announced its own official Twitter apps for the iPhone and Blackberry, killing the entrepreneurial hopes of third-party mobile developers.

While the move is meant to block third parties from advertising as tweets (or tweeting as ads, however you choose to look at it), Costolo did not lay claim to all monetization schemes that might grow up around Twitter. Indeed, while Twitter seems to own the tweet-stream ad channel, Costolo's blog post described a variety of ways third parties might still make money "in the vicinity" of the tweetstream—and it also supported a privacy and "owner-ship" stance that contrasts a bit with Facebook's notoriously lax view:

1. We don't seek to control what users tweet. And users own their own tweets.

2. We believe there are opportunities to sell ads, build vertical applications, provide breakthrough analytics, and more. Companies are selling real-time display ads or other kinds of mobile ads around the time lines on many Twitter clients, and we derive no explicit value from those ads. That's fine. We imagine there will be all sorts of other third-party monetization engines that crop up in the vicinity of the time line.

3. We don't believe we always need to participate in the myriad ways in which other companies monetize the network.[15]

One such third-party monetization effort is PostUp, formerly TweetUp, a destination Twitter search engine founded by serial entrepreneur Bill Gross (billionaire creator of Overture, Picasa, CarsDirect, and the tech incubator IdeaLab). PostUp has a ranking algorithm it says will float the best, most relevant tweets to the top for a given keyword search. Meanwhile, any tweeter can bid for higher rankings in the tweetstream as displayed on PostUp.

"I think that PostUp's business will come from the whole spectrum of Tweeters, ranging from the individual to the company to the big brands," Gross told *Venture Beat*. "We are not requiring people to bid to be included. We want to get all the best people coming and listing their keywords at PostUp, whether they bid or not."[16]

Twitter has devised a quality-scoring system similar to that of Google AdWords: If your promoted tweet is frequently clicked, retweeted, or favorited, it will remain highly listed for its key terms. If not, it will sink into obscurity.

The important thing here, as with any social-media advertising, is to recognize that these environments were designed to be social, personal, and honest. They are not designed for traditional advertising. Blatantly commercial messages served up as promoted tweets will surely backfire—turning off the receivers, and turning them against the platform. To be warmly received and passed along to friends, family, and business contacts, a sponsored tweet will need all the ingredients of a winning "natural" tweet:

- Be hilarious, offbeat, fascinating, heartwarming, or remarkable, or
- Make a powerful offer (a deep discount, cool contest, or giveaway), or
- Appeal to people's instincts for social good or other strongly held causes, or
- Fit a tangible need for specialized information (recipes, how-to, breaking news, events, and top-10 lists)

At this time, Twitter seems to be the social-media platform least conducive to advertising. That's due in part to the always-scrolling nature of the news feed, and also to the one-size-fits-all design of Twitter. Generally, the user-interfaces of Facebook, MySpace, and LinkedIn make it clear what's an ad and what's a person's wall post. (Yes, they're blurring the picture somewhat with commercial posts!) But of all the major social platforms, Twitter seems least able to segregate ads from the newsfeed and still display ads in a way that will get any attention.

Web strategist Jeremiah Owyang, who experimented only once with inserting an ad into his Twitter stream (using the Ad.ly model), advises caution. "I asked my community what it thought, and people didn't like it. Some people unfollowed me. It broke trust," he said. "There are ways it can be done right. But it has to be something that you are expecting from that person."[17]

Before promoted tweets crashed the party, Ad.ly had 26,000 paid Twitterers, including celebs and personalities like Kim Kardashian and Mark Cuban. Advertisers included Microsoft, NBC, and Universal Pictures.

Another former Ad.ly Twitterer is Megan Calhoun, the 38-year-old Californian and mother of two who created TwitterMoms. She was stunned she could make as much as $1,500 a pop to plug products on Twitter. But the day she made her first paid tweet, plugging a movie, she was met with deafening silence.

"I thought I would hear something," she said. But instead, the Twitter ad "just adds to the noise, really. People see it and don't pay attention. It's almost like getting junk mail. You just kind of ignore it or you have a negative reaction."[18]

But it would be unfair to judge the effectiveness of Twitter's Promoted Tweets on the experience of Ad.ly—or at this early point in the game. Twitter has a history of smart innovation and a culture well attuned to its users' likes and dislikes. I expect Twitter will develop advertising and sponsorship opportunities that work both for businesses and the 190-million-strong Twitter audience.

ADVERTISING ON LINKEDIN

The employment advertising and recruiting services are the lion's share of LinkedIn's revenues, and if you are a hiring manager or recruiter, LinkedIn must be among your choices for employment advertising. Complementing Monster, CareerBuilder, Dice, and other job sites, since it is a professional network rather than solely a job site, LinkedIn may give employers better access to the *currently employed* who might just be open to other opportunities. One of the nice aspects of LinkedIn is that it lets members identify themselves as to what sort of offers or opportunities they're interested in.

If you have professional services to offer, software, or other B2B staples, LinkedIn ads could be a good platform to test. While the site offers custom ad packages for firms willing to spend $25,000-plus, most companies will dip their toes in the water with LinkedIn DirectAds. These are mostly text-based ads, but they can contain a small image, say your company logo or a person's profile photo. They can be bought either on a cost-per-click or cost-per-impression basis, and budgets can be set as low as $10 a day.

Such ads can be run across the entire LinkedIn network or are targeted by up to seven criteria: company size, job function, industry, seniority, gender, age, and geography.

Such "hypertargeting" is typical for social-network advertising—after all, these platforms know a *lot* about their members—and it could be a real boon for reaching the specific types of businesspeople you want. Imagine you are preparing for an industry conference, launching a B2B consulting practice, or selling an industry-specific software system. Just take a gander at the industry selections you can make to target your ad distribution. If you're a niche business or have an ounce of direct-marketing DNA in you, you'll start to see the possibilities.

The downside is that when you start slicing up the audience into segments, that 66 million dwindles pretty markedly. For instance, if you want to reach buyers, the audience drops to 275,000; refine it to fashion and apparel buyers and you're down to a wee 5,637 people. And yet many business-to-business advertisers are finding LinkedIn advertising successful.

"Fifty percent of our paid inbound leads come from LinkedIn," says Matt Johnston, vice president of marketing at uTest. "LinkedIn is our most cost-effective online marketing channel."

The Boca Raton, Florida-based online marketing firm MoreVisibility has used LinkedIn ads for its business-to-business clients. "We achieved a conversion rate for our client that was almost three times that of the overall Web site average by targeting the professional audience on LinkedIn," says Danielle Leitch, executive vice president of client strategy at MoreVisibility.[19]

PROMOTING YOUR SOCIAL MEDIA ACROSS THE WEB

Thus far we've addressed using the new ad-serving options on the social-media platforms to reach their members—either to drive fans to your SM pages or to drive traffic to your main site.

Another emerging opportunity is to advertise on the Web's best-established ad-serving networks, with search-engine ads to drive traffic to your fan pages, blog, or other community sites.

The leading platform for such advertising would be Google and the Bing/Yahoo partnership—search engines reaching essentially 100 percent of the online audience and capable of serving up highly targeted, trackable, and budget-controlled cost-per-click ads, usually in response to specific search terms.

Most terms that imply a "shopping intent" (searches for items you can buy) have been bid up to serious money. Examples might include "knitting needles," "hiking boots," or "Festool portable drills." Meanwhile, generic terms associated with hobbies and interests, as well as searches modified with words like "information" or "photos," have shown to convert poorly into customers, so they're relatively inexpensive to buy in paid search. Examples: "knitting," "hiking," or "woodworking." Other high-volume searches that may be more oriented to community than commerce are news-related and current-event searches.

It's quite possible you can use paid search ads to attract thousands of fans to your community pages on a relatively small budget (under $1 per fan, I would think), and if you conduct an engaging and compelling enough social-media program, you'll later convert some of them into paying customers for your goods and services.

Currently, AARP places search-engine ads prompted by searches for lifestyle activities like knitting. The Humane Society buys "Save the Whales" ads in response to searches for "whales." Budweiser promoted its YouTube FIFA World Cup soccer ads in responses to searches for "World Cup." In all those cases, these socially oriented advertisers had the Google real estate largely to themselves. There's not a high profit margin to attract crowds of commercial advertisers—and Google's quality-score algorithm suppresses ads that aren't relevant enough to attract sufficient clicks. That could mean that a well-executed and well-targeted social-media campaign could generate tons of traffic from the highest-profile pages on the Web—and inexpensively at that.

Another ad-serving option is called **remarketing** or retargeting. With remarketing, you pay large ad networks like Dotomi, FetchBack, Acerno, and others, to show your banner ads and other display ads to visitors shown (by a cookie) to have visited you in the past. The effect is to remind your customers, fans, and prospects about you wherever they go on the Web. It's an effective way to bring people back to your site—and it also gives the impression that your company, small though it might be, has a pervasive ad presence throughout the biggest and best-known sites on the web. Google now also offers retargeting as an option for its content network of Web sites.

MOBILE

The Web experience—and the social-media experience—is moving off the desktop and into your pocket.

The story of the past five years has been social-networking Web sites growing to millions and millions of members and consuming an ever-larger slice of our online time. But the story of the *next* five years is not about social Web sites, but social applications—people-powered apps for mobile devices and Web-enabled gadgets.

Phones are getting smarter, and Web-enabled gadgets are popping up everywhere.

In October 2009, a group called the Wi-Fi Alliance, made up of Apple, Intel, Cisco, and 300 other Wi-Fi equipment makers, announced plans to sell wireless Web-access technology that will effectively turn household gadgets into mini Wi-Fi devices. From a range of 300 feet, these gadgets will automatically scan for existing hotspots as well as any other Wi-Fi equipped devices, including smartphones, computers, video game consoles, and Web-enabled TVs.

This new wave of always-connected gizmos will change our lives in profound ways—and a social-networking layer will overlay all of it.

NETWORKS WITHIN NETWORKS: REACHING SPECIAL MARKETS WITH SOCIAL MEDIA

The National Basketball Association is trying to boost its appeal across a wider demographic, both with an ambitious international exhibition game schedule, Noche Latina stadium promotions, and now a Spanish-language campaign targeted at U.S. Hispanics. The campaign, Éne-Bé-A (the Spanish pronunciation of NBA), is anchored by accounts on Facebook, Twitter, MySpace, You Tube, and the Spanish-language social networks Quepasa and Sonico, as well as the Mi Página ("My Page") social network of Univision.

ComScore Media Metrix found that while Facebook and Twitter may be the top general-market social-media properties, MySpace leads among Hispanics in the United States. The NBA's effort is also supported by television ads on Telemundo, Univision, ESPN Desportes, Fox Sports, and MTV's Spanish-language channels.

As we mentioned in the last chapter, the mobile social-media platform MocoSpace is a good bet for reaching a young, racially diverse audience.

Saskia Sorrosa, senior director of U.S. Hispanic marketing at the NBA, says the league has been specifically targeting the Hispanic market since 2000. "We have been using in-language assets for several years, including game broadcasts. What we are doing this year is bringing it all under a new brand umbrella."[20]

The Éne-Bé-A Web site includes social features, webisodes featuring Latino NBA players, news, and photo galleries. It also highlights in-arena promotions and special events for Hispanic fans, like Noche Latina. The associated Facebook/enebea page has almost a quarter of a million fans.

ADD SOCIAL FEATURES TO YOUR WEB SITE

While you're busy establishing and growing your presence on the important social-media networks out there, don't neglect your home base. Your own Web site needs to come into the Web 2.0 era and harvest the same social power that is working to the advantage of these sites.

Most powerful (but also most difficult) is to support custom profiles for your users and the ability for them to establish friend networks with other users. Ning and the major blog engines provide this kind of functionality, but it is lacking from most e-commerce software. However, applications like Google OpenSocial and Facebook Connect let you build social features into your Web site.

Supporting customer-generated content is pretty easy—it's baked into blog software, forum and chat software, survey tools, and ratings and reviews. All of these things can be readily plugged into your Web site.

You can develop widgets that use JavaScript, Flash, and other technologies to display your cool stuff on the Web sites, desktops, and profile pages of your audience. Widgets can be integrated with MySpace, Facebook, Twitter, Ning, and elsewhere. Anything you produce that is timely, fun, entertaining, or otherwise I-demand can be a candidate for a widget. Amazon's best-seller lists, Weather.com's local weather forecast, the Food Channel's recipes, Weight Watchers' calorie-counter, Sports Illustrated's swimsuit models, Motley Fool's stock picks—all this popular content is now available in the form of widgets and is now spreading virally and being shared among online networks. Just like paid advertising, the spread of these widgets brings in ever more prospects.

COMMUNITY BUILDING AND CUSTOMER ENGAGEMENT

Gardener's Supply e-commerce director Max Harris touts his company's non-promotional, research and development-focused "Help Us Build It Better" e-mails. The purpose of these requests is not to ring the cash register, but to reach out to recent buyers, on a product-specific basis, to tap them for feedback and constructive criticism that might make the product they bought even better.

It takes a bold and confident company—and an open-minded one—to ask ordinary customers for their honest opinions. You may get an earful. But again and again, we've seen that companies that ask customer opinion hear great things, and what criticism they hear is in the spirit of improving their company's products or services.

"Gardeners are just passionate about sharing," says Harris. "They *want* you to ask them what they think, how they feel about your products, what new products they want to see from you."[21]

Earlier in this book, I've argued against the idea of throwing a party at your own house (i.e., building an ambitious company blog or your own custom-built community Web site) as opposed to going out to the big, existing blogs and social networks where the party is already hopping.

While step one is surely exposing yourself to and participating in the social-media party already underway, building your own can be a smart next step. Especially if you serve a hobby, special-interest, or movement that has unique needs not easily met on the existing software platforms, you may need to create your own platform to truly tap into the enthusiasm of your market—or to more directly control the online experience, rules for interaction, or to maintain access to community members and integration of their community experience into other aspects of your site, such as e-commerce, order history, preferences, etc. When T.G.I. Friday's, for instance, built its million-plus member community on Facebook, it was explicitly bound by

Facebook's limitations of how the company could interact with its members. Had it built its community on Ning or on its own software platform, T.G.I. Friday's could, for instance, e-mail new coupons, offers, surveys, and other messages to all its million members—which can't be done on Facebook. Not that that's necessarily a bad thing; Facebook members are generally attuned to the culture of Facebook, what's permissible for fan-page sponsors and what's not. But know that when you build a big community on the public platforms, you're giving up a significant measure of control and flexibility.

Custom communities like that of BodyBuilding.com provide a wealth of custom features that are vital to the success and appeal of the site—in the case of BodyBuilding.com's BodySpace, we're talking shared workout plans and results, diet and supplement plans, uploaded photos—and feedback and encouragement between members. Yes, you can develop custom apps for Facebook and other platforms. But the process is still inherently less wide open than owning your own platform.

Sears designed and built MySearsCommunity to host customer-to-customer forums, display customer reviews and ratings, solicit customer suggestions in the MySears idea forum, promote discounts for particular products, and more. More than 466,000 users have registered, and Rob Harles, Sears vice president of social media and community, says the customer feedback has been all-important: "We find out things on there that we would never have known."[22] When a customer suggested Sears offer "new, trendy styles for younger shoppers," Sears reached out to that community member for more specific thoughts and passed the input directly to Sears product designers.

CROWDSOURCING FROM YOUR ONLINE COMMUNITY

Bubbleroom is an innovative fashion Web site based in Sweden that crowdsources both its product development and, in large measure, its sales and promotion. Bubbleroom has allied itself with hundreds of influential but very grassroots fashion blogs in order to (1) identify nascent fashion trends just as they are emerging and (2) build an engaged community of avant-garde fashionistas to inspire new products and guide their production, then help promote and sell the items once they're produced.

What's amazing about Bubbleroom is that their decentralized, people-powered approach has helped them outcompete many of the best funded and most established fashion designers on the planet. Their time to market is remarkable—Bubbleroom can bring a new product to market in a matter of weeks, while traditional design firms typically take several months to bring a new apparel item or accessory to market. In fashion, speed is everything—and Bubbleroom's crowdsourcing approach is a disruptive technology that's changing the playing field.

YouGoods is another excellent example of social product development. YouGoods is an initiative of UncommonGoods, the quirky and stylish house-wares and gift company. The mandate of the program couldn't be clearer: "Product development of the people, by the people, and for the people."

"We started our YouGoods program as a way of finding unique product ideas that weren't already available in the marketplace, something very important for our brand," says Brian Hashemi, director of marketing for Uncommon Goods. "So we just put the challenge out there to the crowd—send us your product ideas and the winner receives a cash prize, gets to have their product produced by us, and receives a cut of any sales we make. The winners would be determined by popular vote amongst our social media followers, as tallied by Facebook 'likes.'"

The YouGoods program has brought to life some remarkable and unique items: chalkboard pillows, basswood "multiblocks" building blocks, a chair upholstered with a webbing of reclaimed seatbelts. Not only are the products cool, but the *process*—which played out in social media—was all-important.

"The response was overwhelming—over 250 submissions and thousands of votes for the finalists," says Hashemi. "The biggest success, I believe, was leveraging the viral nature of Facebook to encourage voting. It was just so easy to get new people to share an experience with our brand. Our Facebook fan base grew by 26 percent in one week, and more than 50 percent over the course of the first contest. That's thousands of people who had never heard of us before and are now getting our updates, and who now have some sort of idea of what UncommonGoods is all about."[23]

BRAND AMBASSADORS

One secret to building a strong online community is to cultivate a small, core group of influential evangelists, and then let them help you spread the word to a larger audience.

Constructive Playthings, a leading retailer of educational and hands-on toys, has anointed a dozen brand ambassadors, all of whom are moms and are also well-known bloggers. Jonathan Freiden, company CEO, runs this third-generation family business along with his brother Seth. Jonathan told me about their blog ambassador program, which is a great, grassroots way to further Constructive Toys' mission—of promoting high-quality, nonviolent toys "inspiring creativity, learning, and family fun."

The 12 mom bloggers are collectively dubbed the Constructive Moms. They're hired to write honest reviews on Constructive Playthings toys and spread the word on the company's new toys and games. In addition to reviews, each blog offers a 15 percent discount for purchases made from Constructive Playthings.

These "blog ambassadors" are similar in concept to the world-renowned mountaineers, surfers, and other outdoor extreme-sport enthusiasts sponsored by Patagonia. And as we'll see in the next chapter, scissor-maker Fiskars has experienced great success building a scrapbooking community thanks to the efforts of a handful of carefully chosen brand ambassadors called Fiskateers.

Ambassadors are a great way to build strong and mutually beneficial relationships with the most influential figures in your marketplace or specialty. They can give your brand and products a "halo effect" and help you rapidly grow an online community without sacrificing the strength of its connections.

MEETUPS AND TWEETUPS

A real value of these online networks is to build and support strong, real-world communities, the kind that commune at a conference, club meeting, fundraiser, or other get-together. In the Web 2.0 world, events engendered, organized, and promoted online but taking place in the offline world have a name: meetups. (Those springing specifically from Twitter, naturally, are tweetups.)

Meetup is the world's largest network of local groups—promoting local action, everywhere, facilitated by an online social network at Meetup.org. The Meetup Web site makes it easy to join one of the thousands of local groups already meeting up face-to-face: African drum circles, singles groups, mountain-bikers, Spanish-conversation groups, book discussions, mom-and-toddler playgroups, wine tastings, gay and lesbian groups, salsa dancers, Harley riders, the local atheists' club, medieval battle reenactors, environmental activists, off-roaders, and on and on.

Can't find the group you have in mind? You can organize and promote a new one. According to Meetup, more than 2,000 groups get together in local communities each day, each with the goal of improving themselves or their communities.

Meetup was cofounded by Scott Herfernan, who in the wake of 9/11 in Manhattan felt a surging sense of neighborliness and social cohesion. That post-9/11 feeling didn't last very long, but it got Herfernan thinking. "It was important," he says, "to find ways for local community to emerge."

"So, me and four guys, we locked ourselves in a 200-square-foot room at Lafayette and Spring for a few months beginning in 2002 with a design goal of 'How can we make it easy for people to self-organize local community, local meetings, about anything, anywhere?'"[24]

From those humble beginnings has emerged a genuine social and Internet phenomenon. The five initial developers have been joined by a staff of about 60, based in New York. Today, Meetup.org's numbers are staggering:

- Meetup.org has 6 million members, and gets about 6 million visits a month.
- The site hosts 68,000 groups meeting in 45,000 cities across the planet.
- Every month, 180,000 local meetups are organized, and more than 2 million members RSVP to attend them.

Meetup's mission, it says, is to "Revitalize local community and help people around the world self-organize. Meetup believes that people can change their personal world, or the whole world, by organizing themselves into groups that are powerful enough to make a difference."

How Can Meetups Work for Business?

So how can a business like yours participate, if meetups are organized—as most of them seem to be—around recreation and leisure interests, and community, social, and political issues?

To that I have two answers: First, as I've said earlier in this book, it's critical that you associate your company's social-media program not just with your company and its products, but with the larger market, activities, and social interests that you serve.

Thus, Patagonia, REI, LL Bean, and Orvis are not merely selling outdoor gear. They are:

1. Promoting and associating themselves with hiking, biking, paddling, fly fishing, climbing, surfing, and the other outdoor activities their customers enjoy, and
2. Taking a principled social stand on conservation, global warming, the health of oceans and streams, and other issues that affect wilderness and the environment.

The social-media posts of these companies are not dominated by efforts to sell more hiking boots. What more powerfully engages their social network is, for example, promotion of National Bike to Work Week, or a video of Patagonia's "surf ambassadors" catching waves in northern Sumatra.

My second answer is especially for all of us businesspeople whose marketplaces are not quite as broad or inherently sexy as these outdoor-adventure companies I've just mentioned: There is a Meetup group for everyone.

No matter how small your niche or how dry your industry, there are ways to reach out, in person, to small but potentially influential groups in your market. There are groups whose members raise llamas, groups that talk about insurance, and groups devoted to any topic you can imagine. You can find them, participate, meet people, learn, and connect in ways that benefit your business.

WEBS, "America's Yarn Store," nicely bridges the online and offline world. Sure, their Web site, http://www.Yarn.com, is one of the leading online sellers of knitting and weaving yarns, patterns, and supplies. But owners Steve and Cathy Elkins also maintain a bricks-and-mortar store-front and host knitting classes and events like bringing renowned knitters and designers to their store to speak to their fans. They conduct a local talk-radio show devoted to knitting—which is also available as a podcast.

The people behind Yarn.com are knitters and weavers just like their customers—and they make a point to get together in person to have fun, learn, and promote and grow the hobby they all love.

Sponsoring Local Meetup Groups

Says Herfernan, "A smart philosophy for any organization, any business, any community is to really pay attention to how people are naturally using" the system. Meetup noticed more and more groups were getting local business sponsors on their own. "Plus," says Herfernan, "we were getting lots of business, big companies contacting us and saying 'Hey, we want to sponsor lots of meetups.'"

While local groups and sponsors were in many cases finding each other on their own, the system was inefficient and not living up to its real potential. That has since changed, and Meetup today has a formal sponsor-matching system that enables scalable, win-win relationships between sponsors and meetup groups.

"If we can help someone like Columbia sportswear sponsor hundreds of hiking meetups around the country," says Herfernan, "then that would be helping the meetups, especially if we gave them a big chunk of the money. So we are hooking them up with these sponsors, and they're getting paid."

Even more exciting, says Herfernan, "We launched the ability . . . to make it easier for them to manage their own sponsors." He calls it one of Meetup's most quickly adopted features, noting that already, more than 25,000 sponsor businesses are in the Meetup system. If your company is a potential sponsor, go to Meetup.org and sign up. "It's just creating a real explosion. The meetups, which are self-organized communities, are having their members fan out," in search of sponsor businesses. If your business can help meet the modest sponsorship needs of these local groups, you can really establish an enduring bond with their members, do terrific things for the reach and image of your brand, and help worthy groups in the process. You could do well by doing good.

"That's like the heart and soul of what's exciting about Meetup, and frankly what's exciting about this era we are heading into together, which is people being powerful together in new ways, in easier ways than ever, because the internet is the world's best organizing tool."[25]

Local bike shops can be sponsoring their local cycling groups. Wine shops—or national winemakers—can sponsor wine-tasting meetups—extend special discounts for members.

Tips for a Successful Meetup

While Meetup.org certainly sparked a cultural trend and coined a term, the Meetup platform does not have an exclusive lock on the concept. Any physical get-together of an otherwise digitally organized network is a meetup. Many social-media platforms now promote the concept.

Need an example of just how interwoven these networks have become? A large San Francisco Bay-area LinkedIn group dedicated to social-media marketing on Facebook and Twitter uses Meetup to organize its monthly get-togethers. It makes your head spin!

Megan Casey, Squidoo's editor-in-chief, is a big advocate of meetups. The publishing network promotes an annual, worldwide meetup day to encourage its members (or "lensmasters," as Squidoo calls them) to get together in person.

"Over the last few years, I've gotten to meet a handful of illustrious lensmasters for tea and fun conversation," says Casey. "Sometimes I'm surprised by the enthusiasm or concerns they voice to me in person, face to face, that they were too shy, too polite (or sometimes, too truculent or too cynical) to talk about virtually. Other times I find special insight into what makes that person tick, and I always get new ideas for ways to run the community just a little bit better. And I can promise you that for the most part, the person behind the lenses is far more interesting than you'd ever guess!"[26]

Casey offers a number of practical suggestions for making a meetup fun and successful. She recommends meeting in a coffee shop, local bookstore, Irish pub, or maybe even having a picnic or just going to see a movie together (the latter she suggests somewhat as a safe option for introverts coming out of their shells). Other options, she suggests: "A local museum, a greenhouse, a teahouse, a magic shop, a retro diner, a bakery, at a landmark, at a playground (if you want to bring your kids along)."

Wherever you meet, you can be assured of a few things:

- Being connected to one another online, and involved in the same marketplace, topic, or effort, is a built-in recipe for finding common cause and enjoying each other's company in person.
- The element of discovery, of meeting the real, multi-dimensional human being behind the online profile, is a powerful, positive—and fundamentally human—experience.
- It's helpful to build a specific cause, purpose, or topic into your meetups. Sure, it's fun just to get together with digital friends and socialize in person. But you'll find that over time, meetups are stronger and better if there's a particular reason for gathering. As Meetup.org puts it in its mission statement: "Do something. Learn something. Share something. Change something."

FLASH MOBS

Flash mobs are a cool and powerful cultural trend. What are they? Carefully preplanned, coordinated, and choreographed, they're public performance-art pieces. Performers—initially undistinguishable from the rest of the crowd in an urban square, college quad, department store, or mass-transit station—emerge and come together in a mass dance, a coordinated stop-motion "freeze," or some other attention-grabbing performance.

When the performance is done, they melt back into the crowd and disperse as mysteriously as they came together.

Why include flash mobs in a book on social-media marketing? Because flash mobs are so inherently Web 2.0 in spirit and execution. Operationally, they rely on people's social and artistic coordination through Internet technology. Private or public social networks are now the key coordination tools to mobilize and direct a flash mob.

Or as Wikipedia puts it: "The term flash mob is generally applied only to gatherings organized via telecommunications, social media, or viral e-mails."

And thanks to Web 2.0, these ephemeral, seemingly spontaneous events are not lost, but can *last*. Once a flash mob is conducted, and inevitably caught on the cell phones and cameras of both insiders and spectators alike, the event spreads virally through the Web thanks to YouTube, e-mail, Twitter, etc. Popular flash mob videos attract literally millions of views on YouTube.

But let's back up. How might a flash mob help draw attention to your product or service? Remember, the first flash mobs were art for art's sake— performance art events organized to occur at Manhattan department stores, the London Underground, etc. A pillow fight was staged simultaneously in 25 cities worldwide. New York's Improv Anywhere troupe has organized scores of "missions," including a mock-synchronized swim in the Washington Square Park fountain and its annual No Pants Subway Ride.

Flash mobs have also been used to raise awareness of causes and social issues: Earth Day dancers in Jacksonville; costumed maids and janitors vacuuming trees and dusting park benches for Keep Austin Beautiful; pregnant women break-dancing in London to raise awareness of Oxfam's campaigns for safe childbirth in the Third World.

So obviously, flash mobs can work well when they're simply unusual, attention-getting stunts. And they can work to draw attention to a worthy social cause.

However, their pure novelty, energy, and impact made it inevitable that groups with buzz to kindle and stuff to sell would latch onto flash mobs for commercial purposes. Here are some examples of flash mobs whose purpose was, essentially, business promotion:

- **Jamie Oliver's Food Revolution**: April 2010, Chef Jamie Oliver and students from Marshall University staged a culinary-inspired flash mob in Huntington, West Virginia, to raise awareness for healthy eating.
- **Kettle Corn**: August 2009, a song and dance routine broke out at City Museum of St. Louis.
- **ElfYourself**: November 2009, OfficeMax drew attention to its ElfYourself viral holiday cards by assembling several hundred choreographed dancers, all in elf costumes, in New York's Union Square.
- **Oprah Black Eyed Peas**: September 2009, to kick off a new season of Oprah, 20,000 dancers took over Chicago's Michigan Avenue, dancing to "I Gotta Feeling." It was the largest single-city flash mob to date.

- **Georgia Lottery Powerball**: March 2010, costumed Powerball mascots visited Atlanta airport. Music broke out and the mascots were joined by over 100 synchronized dancers.

All these examples managed to attract positive attention and burnish their organizers' reputations without any embarrassing or damaging problems. But this is a touchy area, so tread lightly and with sensitivity. Associating your product or brand name with a flash mob can backfire in myriad ways. A cool and flashy event might do more harm than good if tied to a dull or irrelevant product. A small or badly organized mob can make you look stupid. A mob subbed-out to a fancy outside marketing firm could make your company seem like old-school stuffed shirts, out-of-touch and impersonal— exactly the opposite effect you want from your social-media efforts.

Remember: If your social-media plan isn't authentic, honest, personal, and sustainable, it isn't worth doing, period.

Finally, I'd be remiss not to mention that when it comes to flash mobs, some people are distinctly *not amused*.

The *London Evening Standard* quoted a disgruntled commuter after a dance rave staged in the Underground on May 4, 2007: "I was trying to get my train home but the whole concourse was filled with students dancing and I couldn't get through. The last thing I wanted after a hard day at work was to miss my train because of the idiots."

When an artsy collective is behind a stunt like that, it's no big deal if a few people fail to see the humor. But when your company's reputation (and potentially its legal liability) is involved, be careful.

Not all flash mobs are organized around sweet dance moves, either. Lately, rowdy teenagers have been implicated in flash mobs in Philadelphia, Kansas City, and elsewhere that have sparked vandalism or violence.

For further reading, see *Smart Mobs: The Next Social Revolution* by Howard Rheingold. The book describes global social and political changes brought about by text messaging, cell phones, Twitter, and the wireless Web.

MOB AND MEETUP PROMOTION, 2.0

Whether your group or organization is avant-garde enough to stage a flash mob, or you just want to bring together key industry folks for a cocktail party, use Web 2.0 tools to pull it off:[27]

- **Facebook**: Create a Facebook event with all the details and invite everyone you know. Encourage them to pass along the invitation to their own Facebook friends.

- **Craigslist**: Advertise the event on Craigslist and other relevant boards, forums, and networks. Posting your event on more platforms means more reach.
- **Foursquare**: Create an event for users of this local-oriented mobile app.
- **Eventbrite**: Online events software like Evite or Eventbrite can help you manage RSVPs or limit attendance if space is an issue.
- **AdWords**: If you have any promotional budget, consider advertising on Google, prompted by relevant search phrases and targeted to a specific location.
- **Twitter**: Write a series of tweets about your event, linking to your Web site, Facebook event, or your Craigslist ad. Ask for retweets.
- **LinkedIn**: If it's a business event, promote it in your status update and profile page.
- **YouTube, Flickr, Facebook**: When all is said and done, post a video or photos of your mob or meeting on YouTube, Flickr, Facebook, and elsewhere. This is a great way to create a permanent testimony to a fleeting event—plus, thanks to the power of embedding, linking, and "liking," the reach of the event will be multiplied.

Truly, the opportunities to take your social-media program to the next level are limited only by your imagination. You can harness some of the new social-advertising platforms and explore special-interest or second-tier networks. You can even tap the power and potential of your digital network by organizing them and turning them out for a memorable event in the physical world.

Chapter 5

Success Stories

This is an exciting time to be launching or growing a social-media program for business because so many companies of all sorts and all sizes are getting into the act and providing inspirational examples.

In the case studies I touch on in this chapter, I've tried to assemble a broad variety of businesses. Some are big, multinational brands whose social-media efforts are devoted to increasing brand awareness and positive vibes. Others are tiny niche players whose efforts are more targeted and have direct sales at least in the back of their minds.

What they all have in common is this:

- They're authentically personal in the connections they've established with their online community.
- They serve some larger purpose—it's not just about selling something, but about making something better or at least more colorful and fun.
- They're innovative and creative in their approach and make a memorable impact on the community they target.

DELL

Dell is famous for being an early adopter of corporate Twittering and for being able to attribute revenues—and significant revenues—to the Twitter channel. Powered by the almost 1.6 million devoted followers of the discount-driven @DellOutlet Twitter stream and the other special-focus

Twitter accounts, Dell has racked up millions of dollars in sales. In 2009, it reported that a total of $3 million had been driven by its Twitter posts since it first launched the program in 2007. Some $2 million had been driven directly through links in individual Dell tweets, while about $1 million came from visitors clicking from Dell's Twitter profile.

Direct2Dell.com is one of the world's most visited corporate blogs. Dell's YouTube channel, which specializes mostly in new-product demos and how-to videos, has garnered 2 million views. On Facebook, the main Dell page has about a quarter of a million fans and it supplements the product-oriented wall posts with messages about its environmental efforts like its Green Servers initiative and its donations to the Conservation Fund to plant 43,000 trees. As with its Twitter accounts, Dell maintains separate Facebook pages for business, home computing, Dell India, etc.

All the Dell social-media properties share a fanatical devotion to support, through the customer forums, links to drivers and downloads, documentation, and more.

But you don't need to visit Twitter, Facebook, or YouTube to see Dell's commitment to social media and its drive to foster customer interaction. Prominently displayed on all Dell Web sites are robust community features: the company blog, of course, but also its very active support forums.

Dell is quick to point out that its social-media efforts are not aimed principally at ringing the cash register, but at improving communication with its customers and providing the best customer service.

Marissa Tarleton, Dell's global head of online merchandising for small and medium businesses, puts customer care and responsiveness at center stage: "I spend the first half hour of my day having coffee and going through customer feedback."[1]

"We have two billion conversations with customers a year. The Dell philosophy is very much to listen. We have a really robust process to filter those conversations and that feedback and get it back into the organization to learn from it and respond and improve."

Highlighting the importance Dell places on customer insights, Tarleton points to the company's embrace of IdeaStorm, an online crowdsourcing and collaboration platform used by Dell to solicit customer ideas, comments, and suggestions. IdeaStorm enjoys prominent positioning on the Dell Web site alongside the other community features. Since putting IdeaStorm into practice, Dell has received 11,500 customer ideas and has already implemented hundreds of them. "It's a very good way to keep your finger on the pulse of the customer, and a very good way to make the customer feel more involved."

One of the beauties of crowdsourcing from your customers is that it empowers a person-to-person network of helpful advice and tips, which can nicely complement and expand on the reach and effectiveness of your company tech-support staff. "We have started to move from a place of Dell talking to its customers to a place of customers also talking with each other."

HEWLETT-PACKARD

Rival computer maker HP has also shown adeptness with social media, but has taken a different approach than Dell. Although like Dell, HP maintains the requisite Twitter feeds and Facebook fan page, the real activity is more targeted and campaign oriented—most impressively with the social-media efforts surrounding its annual technology forum.

HP uses Twitter, Facebook, LinkedIn, podcasts, and blogs, as well as its own HP Connect online community, to promote the HP technology forum and its important sessions and to integrate the physical-world event with the digital community around it. Another key goal in its "Get connected. Stay connected" campaign was to maintain the social-media conversation and technical learning after the tech forum was over.

"We were trying to find ways we could use social media to enhance the experience of attendees at the event and reach out to those in our audience who were not able to make it to the show," says Rebecca Taylor, HP social-media manager. "We wanted to provide people an opportunity to engage with during the event and after it was over."[2]

HP hosted a tweetup at the event to bring its online community together and also to encourage viral retweets. Twitter followers also had the inside track on entering to win backstage passes to meet the Beach Boys, who played the closing party. Session feedback was also solicited and delivered via Twitter.

HP's Twitter and Facebook efforts also focus a great deal on events— tech events like sponsored webinars, the HP Innovations in Education Worldwide Summit, and other targeted events where HP can connect with well-defined groups to whom it has something specific to offer. The Facebook page is also a hub for support as part of HP's Total Care initiative.

The strategy is paying off. Leading up to the show, HP tracked 877 mentions of the event in social media. During the show, there were some 1,200 tweets about the event, and on the first day, the event-specific hashtag #hptf made it to the top-100 tags on Twitter. By the show's end, HP had doubled its Twitter followers.

HP continues the dialogue with its online community about products, how-to tips, and next year's event. "Once we create that audience," notes Taylor, "we don't want to lose it."

SIGNING TIME

Signing Time is a for-profit business, but it's really one mother's labor of love, born out of Rachel Coleman's desire to create a community that could communicate with her deaf daughter, Leah. Leah, who was born in 1996, taught the whole Coleman family the challenges of raising a hearing-impaired child—and introduced them gradually to the powerful impact that sign language training tools, adopted at the very earliest age, had not only on Leah but also on their second child, Alex, who had normal hearing and who quickly learned sign language to communicate with his big sister.

Two Little Hands Productions, co-founded by sisters Rachel Coleman and Emilie Brown in 2002, produces and distributes the Signing Time product line, aimed at bringing sign language instruction to kids, infants, and their parents.

When the Coleman's third child, Lucy, was born with spina bifida, they despaired that she would ever be able to communicate. But as Signing Time puts it, "The Coleman family experienced a miracle of their own making: after two years of no communication, Lucy began to sign along with Signing Time, despite her physical challenges. Shortly thereafter, Lucy started talking. At age five, Lucy began attending mainstream kindergarten, something Rachel never imagined possible."

The benefits of the Signing Time program to families with hearing-impaired kids are clear. The benefits to those with normal hearing are now being realized by parents wanting to communicate with their infants before they can talk—or to increase their child's reading and language abilities.

Some studies have pointed to a variety of advantages for children with normal hearing who learn to sign, suggesting they:

- Have higher IQ scores
- Are better adjusted
- Read at an earlier age

From its beginnings, Signing Time looked more like a community, a network of like-minded parents, than a typical for-profit business. Today, the company puts its community front and center, and has impressively leveraged that community through social media. On its Web site, the company gives pride of place in the middle of its top nav to a community tab. They had a thriving online community before it was cool.

I spoke with e-commerce Michael Lyman, VP of business development, about what makes the Signing Time online community so special and what other organizations can learn from the example.[3]

How would you describe the market you serve? What makes them a bona-fide community?

Signing Time serves young children ages 0–8 and their caregivers. This includes parents, grandparents, educators, and professionals such as doctors, speech language pathologists, occupational therapists, day care providers, preschools, and elementary education.

Our community comes together to promote Two Little Hands Production's vision, which is:

> "A world in which all children—regardless of their abilities—are endowed with the precious gift of communication, are valued and cherished, and have a clear knowledge of their inestimable worth."

Through this vision we use our products, our services, our instructors, and our online communication channels to help children reach their full potential.

Can you share any anecdotes about what is happening in the different channels (chat, Twitter, etc.)? Are some representing more of a "sweet spot" than others, or do they all work together?

We have a variety of online communities within Signing Time. The main communities are:

1. **Rachel Coleman's blog**—The co-creator of Signing Time and host of the Signing Time series has a personal blog where she promotes her philosophies and life experiences raising two children with disabilities.
2. **Signing Time blog**—The main company blog where we have announcements, news, stories, testimonials, and our sign-of-the-week program.
3. **Signing Time chat room**—A weekly chat room held to discuss with fans and communities members their thoughts and questions related to parenting, children, and Signing Time products and services.
4. **Signing Time forums**—The forums have a huge variety of subforums with topics related to children with special needs, parenting, and

general sign language help. The community is self-sustained and moderated by community members and employees.

5. **Facebook fan page**—Facebook provides a perfect social community for fans of Signing Time to get news quickly and easily and post up their thoughts, comments, and testimonials.

6. **Twitter**—We run two Twitter accounts, one for Signing Time and another for Rachel Coleman. Both are successful, but Rachel Coleman has a huge following on Twitter.

Were you an online community before it was cool? Have you always given the community such prominent real estate on your Web site?

We have been running a Signing Time forum, Rachel's blog, and a chat room for over five years. Previous to that we had a Yahoo group for interacting with our community. We attribute some of our growth and success of our company to the willingness of our owners to be very accessible to the consumer and parents and interact with them through social media since the beginning.

Reaching out to your community for instructors for the Signing Time Academy is very interesting—obviously there is not much of a dividing line between you and your community, your customers, and your virtual staff. How is that program working?

The Signing Time Academy is new, and it is growing fast and furious! We've had over 100 instructors in five countries certify within the first 90 days of the program. The growth has continued and is picking up steam as we head into the spring season. The great thing about having a core group of instructors is the ability to take the community of Signing Time, right to the home and the town where people live. Having a live representative who is certified and trained by our staff and who can represent our products and brand direct to consumers is a huge bonus. We recently announced that 10 associate directors have been trained and installed to help build and continue to grow the Signing Time Academy.

Do you measure the impact of social networking in your Web analytics? What does it tell you?

Google Analytics tell us the following comparing 2009 to 2008:

- Facebook—Visits up 921 percent and revenue up 550 percent.
- Twitter—Visits up 90 percent and revenue up 320 percent.
- Blogs—Official blog visits are up 98 percent.
- Forums are down 12 percent and chat room is down 55 percent.

This is a little telling that people in our community are migrating to the more social interactive mediums that have quicker and easier responses and don't have a scheduled time like our chat room.

Is there anything you'd do differently?

We were a little late moving to Facebook and Twitter. We should have been a bit more proactive in our social marketing. We were comfortable with our existing social-media program and didn't take advantage of the new social networks as soon as we could have. Actually, it was our fans and consumers who helped move us to Twitter and Facebook.

Do you have any advice for other businesses starting out in social media?

Be real, be honest, and take the time to talk and interact with and build a community. I think many companies are creating social media because that's what everyone is doing. Our approach is to use social media to help build the relationship and provide a positive approach to parenting and raising children.

AVATAR

It wasn't just flashy 3-D effects that propelled James Cameron's sci-fi epic *Avatar* to become the highest-grossing movie of all time. Avatar also mounted a multi-front social media and guerilla marketing campaign like no other blockbuster before or since.[4]

It is no surprise that *Avatar* developed its own microsite, plus Facebook, MySpace, and Twitter pages. That's standard practice these days. The nearly 31,000-follower Twitter account was used to spread news about the coming film, which was retweeted with viral effect. The Facebook page boasts over 2 million fans. *Avatar*'s Facebook page was also the home of a groundbreaking live webcast.

Avatar debuted its online trailer on Apple iTunes and announced it on Twitter. The trailer was so hotly anticipated that Apple's servers struggled under the load. A second trailer was rolled out a month later. These web-only trailers gained added buzz when fans remixed them and created mash-ups with other movies.

A special interactive trailer was presented as a downloadable Adobe Air application. With it, *Avatar* fans could view featured content and could read the latest social-media updates about the movie from within the trailer. "The stunt got press coverage and word-of-mouth buzz," notes Samuel Axon, digital entertainment reporter at Mashable.

The "*Avatar* Live" webcast really kicked things into high gear. MTV produced this Facebook-hosted, LG-sponsored webcast. In it, director James Cameron, producer Jon Landau, and stars Sam Worthington and Zoe Saldana were all asked questions that had been submitted by rank-and-file fans via social media in the days leading up to the webcast.

"The 30-minute interview might have been the most glamorous webcast to date," says Axon. "You just don't see that many huge Hollywood names sit down to take questions from Internet fans."

The *Avatar* premiere was broadcast live to Web audiences on the video streaming Web site Ustream, as well as directly on the *Avatar* MySpace page.

Hollywood is of course peerless when it comes to creating tie-ins, licensing deals, and other partnerships, and *Avatar* kicked it up several notches. With McDonalds, *Avatar* created a number of Web-based games and promotions: Pandora Quest, an augmented-reality experience, and Pandora ROVR.

Between these tie-ins, all the buildup in the months prior to the movie's opening, and all the high-profile webcasts, it's clear that *Avatar* powerfully leveraged social media to raise the energy level of fans and critics alike.

Interestingly, the action on *Avatar*'s social-media pages is ongoing. They've touted the film's winnings at the Oscars and other movie awards. They've encouraged fans to upload to Facebook their drawings and other visual art inspired by the movie. In reference to the spiritual/natural center depicted in the movie, they've urged fans in each region to "adopt" a digital "home tree." The *Avatar* social-media pages even served as a platform for director James Cameron to pitch his strategies for stopping the BP oil spill!

Doubtlessly, Cameron and the others behind *Avatar*'s smash success know that, whether there's an *Avatar II* or not, there's a big benefit in maintaining a low-cost, 2-million-fan online community.

GARRETT WADE

How can a small- to medium-sized business compete for "share of mind" of its target market—and reach prospects amid the din of competing messages? How can you get noticed in a noisy world?

The answer for one New York-based tool company seems to be just do your thing, specialize in a niche that attracts passionate followers, commit yourself to uniqueness and high quality—and the PR, links, and online community will follow.

For a small company, Garrett Wade woodworking tools gets a lot of ink and a lot of links. I suspect the reasons are threefold:

1. Unique, top-shelf, and hard-to-find products
2. A passionate audience of woodworkers and lovers of fine tools who like to spread the word
3. An eagerness to engage with these woodworkers one-to-one in social media

Bear in mind, Garrett Wade doesn't even do PR campaigns. For the most part, their mentions in the media and on woodworking and tool blogs are popping up spontaneously.

For instance, their key-shaped pocketknife made the wish list at *Men's Journal*, the "Things We're Coveting this Month" in April 2010. Designed to fit right onto your key ring, it's a convenient little blade you'll always have with you. It is the kind of offbeat item that tool fanciers love, and love to read about and tell friends about.

The *New York Times* featured another Garrett Wade item in a humorous piece about getting your "man cave" ready for winter.

Men's Journal and the *Times* are general-interest publications. Where Garrett Wade has also been showing up is in the thriving crop of special-interest Web sites, publications, blogs, and community Web sites devoted to tools, DIY, and woodworking, like Woodworking Illustrated, the Wood Whisperer, and This Old House. Hobbies and interests like these inspire tons of user responses, reviews, comments, and tips. Some of the mentions are direct outgrowths of the company's founder and other staff being active members of the social networks devoted to these hobbies.

The Hardware Aisle section of the This Old House blog has featured a number of noteworthy Garrett Wade tools, including heavy-duty metal scrapers, hardwood-handled multitools, and unusual ceramic birdhouses. The Gear Culture blog has celebrated items like the wind-and-waterproof match case. Specialty blogs like these can be great, long-term friends for a niche business.

A long thread in the forums of the American Long Rifles Web site chronicles the design outreach that Garrett Wade's president made to an individual (and very well-connected) hobbyist named Jerry Crawford, of Alfred, Maine. Crawford had blogged about a favorite swiveling vise, the Versa Vise, which had gone out of production in the 1970s.

The post caught the attention of Garrett Wade's president Gary Chin, who began corresponding with Crawford. Chin determined to bring back a new and improved vise and relied on Crawford for input and guidance. Two years later, the resulting Versatile Vise appeared in Garrett Wade's catalog—and Chin credited Crawford personally in the catalog and on the Web site.

Crawford proudly posted the story on the American Long Rifles forum and shared with fellow members this letter from Garrett Wade's president:

Dear Jerry Crawford:

Knowing how superbly functional the old USA-made Versa Vise was when it was last available in the 1970s, I like you was frustrated by the limited utility that the Grizzly copy provided. So I am delighted that Garrett Wade's enhanced model will finally appear in our April 2010 catalog. Your generosity was critical to the success of our effort as it allowed us to quickly present a manufacturing solution to the China maker.

In retrospect, I wish I had remembered to give you personal credit in the April catalog copy; this unfortunately slipped between the cracks over the holidays (when the March catalog was being put together). But I have made a note to fix that in May and to make the change in the Web copy right away. You will also be credited in the technical usage note that will go out with all vise shipments. All of this is well deserved and, again, your generous willingness to assist in this project has been greatly appreciated by me.

The thread had been read a couple thousand times and elicited scores of comments, including this one: "Good deal. Nice to hear of a company that does the right thing. Too often the desire to turn a profit overrides everything else."

Not long ago, Garrett Wade also kicked off a Facebook page that today counts a few hundred fans and a Twitter feed with a couple hundred followers. These are tiny numbers compared to the million-fan pages of celebrities and some mass-market brands, but the focus on a small, niche market pays its own dividends. Garrett Wade has established itself as a leader in a small and personal niche community, and that can only benefit its brand—and, indirectly, its sales.

When Garrett Wade product-buyers journeyed to the Swedish countryside to visit the factory where Wetterlings has crafted hand-axes for over 100 years, they made sure to take lots of photos. Those photos, uploaded to the Facebook page, further bolstered their image as bona-fide tool guys—and fired up the appreciation of their fans and customers.

You don't need a massive PR machine to reach relevant customers and prospects and gain useful press and inbound links. You just have to reach the right people by tirelessly making your business and its products remarkable to your core audience and participating in an authentic and sincere way, as a fellow hobbyist, on the blogs, social-media platforms, and other sites devoted to the hobby.

1-800-FLOWERS

The gift business 1-800-Flowers has been pioneering new territory for decades. In fact, 1-800-Flowers has the distinction of serving the very first e-commerce transaction on AOL, in 1995; then 15 years later, in 2009, they tallied the first-ever transaction on a Facebook store. In between, they were one of the first e-commerce companies to launch a transactional mobile Web site.

So it's not a surprise that 1-800-Flowers should be out at the forefront of social media.

"Mobile and social media really fit into our core competency as a business, which is make gifting easy," says David Siegel, senior vice president of 1-800-Flowers.[5]

Their approach to social media doesn't shy away from the company's core commercial mission, which is selling gifts. But their social-media program is a nice hybrid of business and relationship-building, as well as good, old-fashioned customer service.

"We think of it as social commerce—it's a blending of selling and relationship," says Siegel.

WRESTLINGGEAR.COM

Jeff Pape, owner and president of WrestlingGear.com, is a leading specialty retailer of equipment for high school and college wrestlers. He is no stranger to reaching out to the wider community he serves, not just to sell them stuff but just to spread the word and be a wrestling booster. After all, he is part of the community, too—a former high school wrestler himself who went on to wrestle varsity at the University of Illinois. He is always interacting with fellow wrestlers and coaches, promoting local and national meets, and raising money for the National Wrestling Hall of Fame.

Because his eldest son Jackson was born with a cleft lip, Jeff has also made fund-raising for the Smile Train one of his public charitable works—part of his company's social mission and the inspiration behind the nonprofit Pape Foundation. WrestlingGear.com is a great example of a family business with very little division between his business and personal life, profit motive and charitable impulse, and customers and fellow community members. It is perfect for the Web 2.0 social-media world in which we now live.

Wrestling Gear is executing a number of integrated social-networking efforts: sharing wrestling photos on Flickr and videos on YouTube and developing and spreading widgets for IllinoisWrestling.com and the WrestlingGear.com blog. The widget is a RSS reader that you can put almost anywhere—your desktop, MySpace, Facebook, your personal blog or profile pages, and more—to stay up-to-date on wrestling events as well as newly released wrestling shoes and equipment. For wrestlers, their families, and fans, this kind of information is of huge interest, so it benefits WrestlingGear.com to remain at the forefront of their audience's Web experience, wherever it takes them.

They're building their own social network (on the Ning platform), http://www.WrestlingGear.net. Their efforts on Facebook have been impressive and have been accomplished on a modest budget.

First, they established a Facebook fan page. When they realized they needed at least 100 fans to qualify for a personalized Facebook URL, they went for it—e-mailing and cajoling friends throughout the wrestling scene. Soon they blew past 100 members, collecting the http://www.facebook.com/wrestlinggear URL in the process. (The minimum Facebook fan base to qualify for a custom URL has since been decreased to 25.)

They experimented with Facebook's "hypertargeted" ad platform, aiming ads only at Facebook members who named wrestling or mixed martial arts as one of their hobbies and interests. The ads are displayed only in the United States to Facebook members under the age of 65 and only to people who aren't already fans of WrestlingGear.com. If age 65 seems high, Jeff Pape has a ready explanation: "Most of our customers are high school age or younger, so they often have to get approval—and maybe a credit card—from their parents or grandparents before buying a new pair of wrestling shoes or whatever. So we found we have to involve the parents and grandparents. That also influences when we serve our ads, both on Facebook and on Google AdWords. It turns out the dinner hour and later in the evening is a really good time for us to be displaying our ads—and that's a time of day when some of our competitors' ads have stopped running due to daily budget caps."[6]

Their ads don't make a hard sell. The first test said merely, "Are you a wrestler? Visit our page and become a fan of WrestlingGear.com." For about 20 cents a click, Jeff was driving thousands of visitors to his page—and most of them were becoming fans.

WrestlingGear.com's next generation of Facebook ads expanded the message to detail what was actually going on on the page: "Merchandise giveaways, prizes, top new gear updates. Become a fan of the #1 wrestling gear fan page on Facebook."

Phase three plays to one of WrestlingGear.com's strengths: its knowledge of the market and ability to get new, hot, and limited-edition items: "Approaching 12,000 fans. Visit our page and become a fan. Nike, Adidas, Asics, Matman, Cliff Keen, and Brute fans, this is a must see."

The results were powerful. Today, WrestlingGear.com's Facebook page has more than 15,000 fans. Jeff's Facebook ad spending to date has been around $2,000. Is Jeff getting return on his investment, are those fans spreading the word, visiting his Web site, joining his e-mail list, buying his products?

The indication is yes. In response to the survey question, "Has this fan page increased the likelihood you'd buy from us in the future?" about 77 percent responded positively.

WrestlingGear.com gives back to the wrestling community in several ways, including hosting team Web sites on the blog http://www.wrestlinggear .net.

Pape is also SMS texting the latest product news to the cell phones of his loyal subscribers—demonstrating his core customers are eager to give him access so they can get the inside scoop on limited-quantity shoes like the Nike Inflicts in royal blue or the Asics Dan Gable Ultimates. Whatever market you serve, no doubt there are similar "hot-button" products or topics.

FISKARS

You might not think Web 2.0 social media would be a natural environment for a venerable company celebrating its 360th birthday. And no, that's no typo—the Finnish company Fiskars, known mainly for its iconic orange-handled scissors, has been in business since 1649. Fiskars is the world's number-one scissor brand.

Fiskars is also a leading maker of premium gardening tools and has a focus on eco-friendliness, a new line of modernistic push mowers, rain barrels, and more.

In fact, the company's focus on the home and garden market is one main thrust of both its social-media program and its ambitious social mission and grant-making efforts.

"Fiskars Orange," their signature color, is an important part of the Fiskars identity. Orange-handled scissors are a registered trademark of Fiskars Corporation. The orange color came about partly by chance when the iconic scissors were designed in 1967. The prototype handle was created using leftover orange resin used to produce an orange juicer. Fiskars staffers put the question of color to a vote, and orange defeated black by nine votes to seven.

The rest is history: In the 40-plus years since, Fiskars has sold more than 1 billion orange-handled scissors. In the process, they have built not just an iconic and global brand image, but a thriving online community.

It's not unusual for a large global company, serving lots of overlapping markets, to maintain separate niche communities, and Fiskars does this—for instance, its Fiskateers network is oriented toward the scrapbooking hobby (a thriving pastime that, indeed, buys a lot of scissors!). Meanwhile, thanks to its garden tools, eco-friendly lawnmowers, and rain barrels, it also supports a green, environmentally conscious community whose primary home is the Fiskars Facebook page and Twitter feeds, as well as the corporate site's section dedicated to Project Orange Thumb.

The heart of any social-media effort is *people*, and Fiskars excels at reaching people, emotionally and personally, online and in person.

Project Orange Thumb

Project Orange Thumb, begun in 2002, is the company's charitable effort that reaches out to communities worldwide with projects and grants to green-up and revitalize the planet one garden at a time. The grant program provides community garden groups with the tools and materials they need to reach their goals for neighborhood beautification and horticulture education. Recently, Fiskars selected 25 grant recipients from the more than 1,300 applications received from four countries. All of the grant winners are making a difference in their communities through their unique community-garden initiatives.

During its inaugural year, Fiskars provided tools, materials, and support to three community gardens in Chicago. Eight years later, Project Orange Thumb had provided more than 115 community groups with nearly $1 million to create and develop their own community gardens, neighborhood beautification projects, sustainable agriculture, or horticultural education.

The program also performs garden makeovers in communities all over the world. Working closely with neighbors, business leaders, volunteers, and community partners, Fiskars volunteers roll up their sleeves and transform abandoned spaces into thriving gardens—in a single day. Recent garden makeovers in the United States and Canada were completed in Vancouver, Orlando, Toronto, Baltimore, Chicago, San Francisco, Atlanta,

Columbus, and Portland. Similar projects happen throughout Europe, Australia, and New Zealand.

Project Orange Thumb makes good use of blogs, Facebook, and Twitter to spread the word, attract new grant requests, and tell the stories of the successful community-garden projects. Each grant is relatively modest—$1,000 worth of Fiskars garden tools, $1,000 of seeds and materials, plus a supply of Project Orange Thumb T-shirts. But the manageable scope of each project means that Fiskars is able to perform more of them, touching more people in more communities, and spreading its good work farther.

Fiskateers

As I mentioned, Fiskars has been making scissors for 360 years. When they performed a opinion survey asking consumers what they thought about Fiskars, respondents answered that if Fiskars were a drink it would be milk. If it were a snack? Crackers. Not especially a hip or trendy image![7]

But Fiskars market researchers found that many customers use their scissors for scrapbooking and crafts—and around these two activities there's an abundance of passion. Fiskars needed to find a way to become part of this passion.

Social media was the answer.

With the help of their branding agency, Brains on Fire, the company surveyed scrapbookers and crafters. They identified leaders and superstars within the hobby and viewed them as candidates to help launch and run a new Fiskars-sponsored online community. The Fiskars team flew to major cities and interviewed bloggers and performed events in craft stores. They told scrapbookers, "Bring your craft, show us what you do, and show us your life."

The search resulted in the hiring of four part-time paid community leaders—dubbed "Fiskateers." The women were brought to Fiskars U.S. headquarters in Madison, Wisconsin, and trained about Fiskars history and products. They met company engineers and project designers and got to play with all the newest and coolest trimmers, scissors, stickers, paper, and materials. They were reminded their job was not to pitch Fiskars scissors, but to build a bona fide and lasting online community dedicated to the hobby.

The Fiskars fan community is centered around a fun and funky social-network site, http://www.Fiskateers.com. The original leads have been joined by a fifth. These brand ambassadors (Cheryl, Andrea, Kelly Jo, Wendy Jo, and Rebecca) are paid for 15 hours a week of work—but it is clearly more than just a part-time job. The Fiskateer leads are energy behind the online community, a social space where scrapbookers can discuss and share their craft, upload pictures of their creations, share tips, and more.

The lead Fiskateers attend trade shows and lead classes in scrapbooking at stores in their regions and beyond. They build relationships with storeowners. They blog, they're active on message boards, and they plan contests and events. They conduct online chats with Fiskars product developers, transmitting excitement and passion for products they love—and urging changes in products with which they weren't fully satisfied.

"This truly is a movement of devoted crafters just wanting to have fun and share their love," says Stephanie, a Fiskateer.

Unlike mainstream communities that are built to scale massively, the Fiskateers community requires new members to connect with one of the leads and be personally welcomed into the group. "Angela tweeted to me that she'd seen my request, so the leads really do answer these registrations personally," says one member. "What a great way of immediately creating a personal relationship between the scrapbooker and the community!"

Once you join up you receive your very own Fiskateer scissors (one handle is green, the other orange) with your personal Fiskateer number engraved on the blades. Needless to say, these are highly prized. They are also great conversation pieces at crafting get-togethers, which spreads word-of-mouth and encourages more people to join.

Andy Sernovitz, an 18-year veteran of the interactive marketing business, teaches word-of-mouth marketing at Northwestern University. GasPedal, his consulting company, advises brands like TiVo, Dell, Ralph Lauren, Sprint, and Kimberly-Clark. The Fiskars community deserves special credit in his eyes.

Says Sernovitz: "The Fiskars fan community has significantly reduced Fiskars' advertising expenses, generates 13 new product ideas a month, and increased sales 300 percent—all for a 360-year-old brand. It's simply one of the best fan communities ever created."[8]

"It was our goal to create a long-term, sustainable movement," says Spike Jones of Brains on Fire. "And I'm happy to say that's what is happening."

Among the positive outcomes:

- Branded mentions of Fiskars products are up more than 600 percent.
- Mentions of the Fiskateer blog and Web site are up 400 percent.
- There were more than 7,000 Fiskateers as of March 2010. That's up from 1,200 members in 2007.

- The site regularly attracts visitors from 50-plus countries.
- 1,000 certified volunteer Fiskars demonstrators teach classes in retail stores.
- Retail stores visited by Fiskateers have more than doubled their sales.

Jones shares the strategies behind how Brains on Fire worked with Fiskars to create this amazing community.[9] A few of his chief lessons:

- It's not about campaigns, it's about movements. Movements have a beginning and no end. While campaigns are an on-off switch, movements are volume dials with no zero. The Fiskars fan community is a movement.
- Find the passion conversation. Help fans talk about their passion, not about your products. For Fiskars, it's not about scissors, it's about what you do with scissors.
- Movements have inspiring, passionate leaders. When looking for the fans that would lead this community, Brains on Fire didn't look for the people with the most followers on Twitter, they looked for the people who were most passionate about crafting. Passion can't be created, but influence can.

LEGO

LEGO, the iconic building toy company, latched onto social media in a big way with its Click! Campaign, celebrating those "aha!" moments when everything clicks—or as the company puts it, "those unpredictable but powerful light-bulb moments in life when things just CL!CK."[10]

In 2009, LEGO took a gamble with digital and social media, and in targeting not kids, but adults who grew up with the brand and still held a strong, if untapped affinity for it. Company research pointed to a group of grownups, mostly young, creative professionals who had been avid LEGOs fans as kids. "We figured this group already had an affinity to the brand and would be easy to reactivate if we found a way to engage them," says Mike McNally, brand relations director at LEGO. "This audience harbors a sense of nostalgia for these little bricks that can turn nothing into something."[11]

Already on YouTube there was ample testimony to the appeal of these colorful building bricks. Some 300,000 user-generated videos feature LEGOs, often making clever use of stop-action animation. LEGO World Cup soccer games, scenes from *Star Wars*, and a depiction of classic 1980s video arcade games are just some of the artsy undertakings that have attracted millions of views and tens of thousands of comments.

First, to tie into the CL!CK theme of inspiration, LEGO used social media and traditional PR to build buzz around the creation of "the world's largest light bulb"—entirely of LEGO bricks—at the Smithsonian's National Museum of American History during an August weekend in 2009. Museum-goers created an eight-foot-tall bulb of more than 300,000 LEGOs.

Then, in December 2009, posters appeared all over New York City depicting portraits rendered by mosaics of LEGO bricks. These Andy Warhol-esque images bore simply the LEGO logo and the address of the new http://www.legoclick.com microsite.

The site is really a social network in its own right. The hashtag #legoclick trended to the sky at Twitter. Legoclick.com takes a live Twitter feed of any-thing tagged "lego," while the site also encourages photo and video upload-ing. Basically it is a very cool and interactive 3-D video sandbox for playing with virtual LEGOs and connecting with other enthusiasts. The theme for sharing is, as mentioned, those rare and special inspirational moments.

The campaign next launched an iPhone app, which let users upload their own photos and turn them into LEGO mosaics. The resulting images could be e-mailed to friends, printed, tweeted, or uploaded to Facebook and other social networks.

LEGO also commissioned a three-minute short film called "LEGO Click." That video went on to be shown on the LEGO site, YouTube, and other social-media sites. It was even screened at the elite TED conference in early February and won a bronze award at the One Show, an ad industry awards event.

The company also launched http://www.legoclick.com, a richly involv-ing blog featuring uploaded photos and videos of the LEGO creations from the community. It's also a platform for stories and reflections from LEGO designers and company insiders.

The campaign was mostly digital and social in nature, with viewers sharing and spreading the video and contributing their own examples of moments where their creativity, inspiration, and ideas just "clicked." Some of the key performance metrics achieved by the campaign included:

- The LEGO iPhone app had almost 2 million unique downloads and more than 8 million sessions during its launch month alone.
- The three-minute "LEGO Click" film amassed more than 1.6 million views and enjoyed two consecutive weeks in the top 10 of Ad Age's weekly Viral Video Chart.

• By the end of February, LEGO had almost 900,000 fans on Facebook, and the average time spent on the Click site was just under four minutes, per Google.

PEPSI REFRESH PROJECT

Among marketers and business leaders, there are still plenty of skeptics who doubt social media will, in any meaningful measure, replace traditional advertising. But skeptics and true believers alike took notice in 2009, when Pepsi opted against its annual Super Bowl ad in favor of a novel campaign driven largely by social media: the Pepsi Refresh Project.

The Super Bowl is the biggest, most mainstream, and mass-market advertising buy that can be made in America. It's a venue where advertisers can reach more than 100 million viewers—and they will drop more than $3 million for just 30 seconds to do it. And that's just for the ad buy, not including all the ad creative and production costs.

Pepsi's Refresh Project, on the other hand, is probably the most ambitious campaign yet in the short history of corporate social media.

Pepsi chose not to invest the millions it takes to stage a Super Bowl ad, but instead will give away millions—an expected $22 million in year one—to worthy causes and innovative ideas that will make the world a better place. Under the banner "Every Pepsi refreshes the world," the program is truly broad in scope, aiming to benefit individuals, non-profits, and even businesses, with grants as small as $5,000 and as big as $250,000.

The breadth of the project extends to the areas Pepsi will fund: it makes grants for projects in health, arts and culture, food and shelter, the planet, neighborhoods, and education. Each of these six areas is led by an "ambassador." A map of the United States sprouts pushpins whenever new grants are awarded; thus far the recipients have included Care packages for troops, potlucks on wheels, school gardens, and even wind turbines.

"We're looking for people, businesses, and non-profits with ideas that will have a positive impact," says Pepsi of its campaign. "Look around your community and think about how you want to change it."

There's a lot of logic to the effort. In addition to the inherent good done by all the sponsored causes, one wonders—with the cold calculations of a businessperson—where one's money is best spent, where a given dollar creates the most positive associations with your product and ultimately stimulates the most sales. Is it 30 seconds of TV time beamed into millions of living rooms? Or might it be cash grants to worthy groups all over the nation, big and small?

If the Pepsi Refresh Project makes a positive impact for PepsiCo, in the 2008 presidential election, the Obama and McCain campaigns spent a combined total of $1.7 billion. Based on the number of votes cast, they spent about $6 or $7 for each vote.

A good cause is a good engine for social media. Indeed, one of the refreshing things about the booming popularity of social-media Web sites is that some companies, in wanting to be part of the revolution, have opted to make not selling but *doing good* the focus of their efforts. The Pepsi Refresh Project is probably today's biggest and most notable example.

Companies with overt social missions have a clear path in social media—green businesses like Seventh Generation and Patagonia have an easier time than the typical widget-seller to connect with people online and stimulate conversation and word-of-mouth pass-along of their message.

"It doesn't matter that you have followers, fans, or a community. Those are assets, not returns," says Forrester Research analyst Augie Ray. "It is how you use those assets that matters. In Pepsi's case, they've clearly found a way to gain new followers and fans, but that's not the objective of the program; instead, the brand is putting social media to work for a higher goal—making the world a better place and associating the brand with that vision."[12]

One powerful asset of the Pepsi Refresh Project is that it truly works as a self-sustaining and self-promoting viral community. Money, of course, injects great energy into the community—and serves as a magnet for the many underfunded organizations across the country. The application and voting process is a natural amplifier, because once they've applied, groups are motivated to spread the word as broadly as they can—to their members and their community, friends, family, and the media—so that their entry might attract enough votes to be moved up the "leader board" and be granted funding.

Because Pepsi is giving away more than $1 million every single month, and then starting the application and voting process all over again, the Refresh Project is guaranteed to stay on the radar screen.

In general, contests are terrific for generating buzz in social media—and community voting is a superb way to decide contests.

Add several million dollars, and the appeal of not just one but a huge spectrum of social causes, and it's clear that Pepsi has put together something powerful.

"Social media changes everything," says Forrester's Ray. "Social media alters the playing field for everyone within the enterprise; formerly successful strategies and tactics are being challenged, while old and tired methodologies are getting new legs. For example, Best Buy is using social media to improve its customer support in new ways; Starbucks is embracing consumers' ideas and driving innovation and loyalty; and, as we see, Pepsi is using social media to give new energy to cause marketing."

It's too early to know whether Pepsi's big gamble to forgo Super Bowl advertising in favor of social media will pay off. What the bean-counters and shareholders of the beverage giant will measure, in the end, is not whether Pepsi made the world a better place, but whether its sales and profits grew and it made market-share gains against Coke.

Meanwhile, PepsiCo has garnered a lot of great press and stimulated a lot of positive feelings. Articles about the Pepsi Refresh Project and the decision to ditch the Super Bowl ad ran prominently on CNN, ABC, the *Wall Street Journal*, National Public Radio, and the Reuters and AP news services.

Pepsi's Other Social-Media Tactics

Before it grabbed headlines for ditching its Super Bowl ad, PepsiCo rolled out its concept, smaller scale, as a contest on-site at the South by Southwest (SXSW) conference in Austin, Texas,

PepsiCo clearly knows that in embracing the social-media channels, it has two constituencies to reach:

1. Its customers and prospects, presumably the same people who work for, vote for, and benefit from the groups receiving Pepsi Refresh grants, and

2. The media—and the tech-savvy opinion-makers who attend events like SXSW, Internet Week in New York, and other techie pilgrimages.

Pepsi Zeitgeist is a social-media powered site with status updates, tweets, and posts from Twitter, Flickr, stickybits, and Foursquare.

Not all of its forays into the social-media sphere are about philanthropy. Pepsi launched a mobile customer-loyalty application for the iPhone. The Pepsi Loot program uses geo-targeting so that iPhone users can search for nearby restaurants that serve Pepsi. When the customer visits those locations—say it's a Taco Bell, an Arby's, or a Pizza Hut—the customer "checks in" to the app and is automatically given credit for Pepsi Loot, which she can exchange for free music downloads and other prizes.

PepsiCo has also partnered with the local-mobile app Foursquare for a similar promotion with retailers.

Writing in *DMNews* on May 17, 2010, Dianna Dilworth said, "The mobile loyalty app is the latest example of how PepsiCo is taking a more social approach to its marketing efforts."

PepsiCo's Nicole Bradley told *DMNews* that the goal of these programs is to "further develop our two-way conversation with consumers."

Pepsi's commitment to social media and new technology does not appear to be a fleeting, trendy interest. For instance, it recently announced a tech incubator program called PepsiCo10, in which start-up technology and media companies compete for funding for new social-media, mobile, video, and gaming ideas.

In the summer of 2010, the company's Mountain Dew brand staged a 30-day, 69-city grassroots promotion tour called "DEWmocracy: The Flavor Campaign" whose purpose was to elect the winning flavor among three candidates (called White Out, Typhoon, and Distortion) to be rolled out nationally.[13]

What was unique about the tour was that its destinations, activities, and venues were largely determined not by PepsiCo, but by fans using social media.

Three mobile teams consisting of marketing staff and hard-core Mountain Dew fans went cross-country to engage people in the flavor competition and voting through live events. The teams first used online and social media to spread the word about the tour and its sampling opportunities at skateboarding competitions, art exhibits, concerts, and sporting events.

Matt Statman, founder of Motive, the lead creative agency for the tour, estimates that about 60 percent of tour decisions were made by consumers. Fans gave input via Twitter and a dedicated microsite to influence which cities, activities, and venues were visited. They rallied friends and families to participate, they posted photos and videos online, and, of course, voted for their favorite flavor.

Among the guerilla marketing done by the fans on the ground:

- Teams attended several concerts, armed with glow sticks, beach balls, and ample soda samples.
- The teams sponsored skateboarding competitions in Orlando, Philadelphia, and Kansas City.
- Fans generated local television coverage, got testimonials from small-town mayors—even staged Mountain Dew-themed weddings in Oregon, Michigan, and Tennessee.
- Other happenings included a graffiti art event, samplings at various pro and regional sporting events, and the Indy 500.

When all was said and done, the teams distributed about 60,000 samples of the Dew flavors, made direct, in-person contact with more than 100,000 consumers, and generated more than 1.5 million total impressions in person, online, and through social media, according to Statman. White Out flavor won the competition, with 44 percent of votes versus 40 percent for Typhoon and 16 percent for Distortion. The campaign drew more than 2 million votes in all and increased Mountain Dew's Facebook fan base by nearly 800,000.

"I've been doing event marketing for 20 years," says Statman. "This experience was a game-changer, from my perspective. Tapping the 'collective intelligence' by turning decisions over to consumers resulted in far more opportunistic and meaningful engagement. The loyalty- and community-building results were huge. I'll definitely be thinking about using the core concept for future campaigns."

GARDENER'S SUPPLY COMPANY

Gardener's Supply has made a huge priority of connecting directly with its customers and being an advocate and champion of gardening. Its Garden Crusaders award spotlights gardeners whose efforts improve the world.

Its annual garden survey asks the question, "Why do you garden?" and scores of other more specific questions. The survey has generated a whopping 100,000 responses over the past five years. In addition to giving Gardener's Supply valuable insights into the demographics of its customers and what makes them tick, Gardener's benefits by sponsoring an annual research even of genuine interest to its audience. They post excerpts from the results on the company blog and Facebook page.

Because Gardener's thanks participants with a free shipping offer from its store, the initiative even drives revenue, but in a decidedly public-spirited, non-mercenary way. As Harris puts it, quoting from part of the company's mission statement, "We honestly believe that gardening makes the world a better place."[14]

GAP ADVENTURES

To celebrate its twentieth year in business, the adventure travel operator Gap Adventures held a global Create Your Own Adventure contest.

"We loved the idea of creating your own adventure, so we built an interactive site where consumers could come and create their own dream itinerary," explains Greg Hayes, online marketing manager at Gap Adventures.[15]

The promotion, which ran about three months, was aimed at engaging its existing consumers in the United States, the UK, and Australia, and also growing its database of prospective travelers.

First, Gap Adventures used e-mail to tell its list of subscribers about the contest and to spur them to share the news with their friends. The company used its Facebook fan page and Twitter account to spread the word and made media buys in travel ad networks. Offline, Gap handed out postcards at industry events and at coffee shops.

Ten judges from the travel industry helped determine which of the 7,000 entries would make it to the final round of 20. Judges included Gap Adventures founder Bruce Poon Tip; Tony Wheeler, cofounder of Lonely Planet; and Céline Cousteau, granddaughter of Jacques Cousteau. These respected and well-connected judges were encouraged to talk about the contest during interviews and public appearances, and spread the buzz in their own social and professional networks.

Social media also played a role in deciding the vote, with 50 percent of the final score being determined by popular voting on Facebook (the judges accounted for the other half).

The results were very tangible and impressive: Thanks to all the buzz and promotion, the contest Web site received 200,000 visits and more than a million page views. Some 30,000 new e-mail addresses were added to Gap Adventures' file.

VICTORIA'S SECRET

Victoria's Secret came up with a cheeky (sorry!) promotion with Facebook: a pair of bikini panties bearing the Facebook thumbs-up icon and the slogan "You Like This" across the seat. The panties were free with any purchase from VS. Customers had to "like" the VS Facebook page before they could download the requisite coupon.

Just in the months I've written this book, Victoria's Secret's Facebook fanbase has more than doubled from 3.4 million to over 7.5 million people. No doubt by the time you read this, there will be millions more. The company does a ton of clever and innovative things using social media—for example, using its Facebook and Twitter presence to invite fans to attend New York in-store events like a 2010 Meet the Models, and uploading their sexy ads and photo-shoot videos to YouTube.

But for me, the "You Like This" panties are especially memorable. It's the conversion of a social-media icon and the biggest name in lingerie. Need we any more proof that social media has become sexy?

HIPS AND CURVES

Speaking of lingerie, the Los Angeles-based Hips and Curves, which specializes in plus size lingerie, has done great outreach to what it calls its Curvy Community.

"Our Facebook fans and Twitter followers have become our most loyal customers at Hips and Curves," says president and CEO Rebecca Jennings. "This whole social-media wave has become a great way to attract new people to Hips and Curves, and also to build a stronger connection and loyalty with our existing buyers."[16]

Hips and Curves has a more important mission than merely selling bras, corsets, stockings, and bustiers—there is a real undercurrent of celebrating all women, especially the "big, beautiful women" who are the Hips and Curves customer and who often struggle in a culture that sends women so many negative messages about body image, ideal weight, and self esteem. The Curvy Community, as evidenced by the Hips and Curves blog, is an affirmative and spicy place.

The company recently produced a steamy short film on YouTube and some "behind the scenes" lingerie photo shoot videos, each of which has attracted ten thousand views, and drawn appreciative comments like this one: "Thanks for showing such a tasteful depiction of plus-size sexuality!"

SKECHERS

Skechers is a billion-dollar footwear company with more than 2,500 different styles. Founded in 1992 in Malibu, California, the company's earliest offerings were hip, anti-fashion boots and suede skateboarding shoes. In the almost 20 years since, Skechers has grown at a torrid pace, launched several new categories, and reinvented itself. Skechers appeals to girls thanks to endorsement contracts with female pop stars and celebs from Christina Aguilera to Vanessa Hudgens.

Most recently, the company has carved out an enormous swath of the market for orthopedic footwear thanks to its Shape-Ups line of cushioned fitness shoes that appeal especially to people suffering foot pain and the complications of being overweight.

Skechers says Shape-Ups tone muscles, and make it easier to lose weight and get in shape—and to underscore the point, the shoes come with an exercise DVD.

Skechers is a great example of a brand coordinating messaging across traditional advertising (how much more traditional a media buy can you make than a Superbowl ad?) as well as social media and other nontraditional campaigns. Skechers took its show on the road with a person-to-person event dubbed the Skechers Shape-Up America Tour that hit six cities in the fall of 2009. At each stop, the brightly painted tour bus— emblazoned with the slogan "Get in shape without ever setting foot in a gym"—invited people to try the shoes on for a test-walk and encouraged them to enter a drawing for a free pair. The tour was coordinated with PR, retail store events, and other marketing.

Like any good Web 2.0-minded e-commerce company, Skechers is also harnessing the power of customer-written reviews and ratings of products on the Skechers.com online store.

Skechers is active on Facebook, Twitter, YouTube, MySpace, and even the lesser-known Bebo network. Bebo, with an estimated 3 million members in the United States, skews toward girls. The dominant age group, about 40 percent of members, are 17 and under, and about 60 percent of members are female.

Skechers bills its Shape-Up shoes as designed to help their wearers lose weight, tone muscles, and improve posture.

The Shape-Ups are being marketed for both men and women, with Skechers using Hall of Fame quarterback Joe Montana as a spokesman in its marketing campaign.

Thanks in good measure to Shape-Ups, Skechers sales soared 44 percent in the first quarter of 2010.

Some of the tactics are so simple it's almost painful. Mere posts of "Tweet if you love Shape-Ups!" elicit the expected response from Skechers' 2,500 followers. And when anyone tweets about Skechers or its products, @SkechersUSA does a good job of retweeting those messages.

The company launched a MySpace page, but with only 1,200 fans, they've essentially abandoned it for the more vibrant and fast-growing Facebook audience. Well over 80,000 people "like" Skechers on Facebook.

One novel thing that Skechers is doing is coordinating its Facebook page, public-relations campaigns, and its interactive Shape-Up America bus tour. Fitness guru Denise Austin was part of the tour, and she told the *Huffington Post,* "The Skechers Shape-Up America Tour has been a great experience traveling around the country and meeting people. We've literally seen thousands of people as we travel from city to city who are now getting out to walk in their Skechers Shape-Ups."

Skechers has given the community a name, "Team Shape-Ups," and launched a microsite, http://www.myshapeups.com, centered around the shoes and Joe Montana, their pitchman. The "Share your story and win" campaign invited people to upload videos, slideshows, or record audio testimonials about the shoes. Like many successful social-media campaigns, the Skechers program enlists community members to vote for the winners. Entries will be narrowed down to 10 finalists and the My Shape-Ups community will vote for the person they want to succeed. Ten finalists will receive Shape-Ups gear—and one winner will become "the new face of Shape-Ups" in advertising and promotional campaigns. The winner will also receive a spa relaxation retreat. Hundreds of consumers have publicly rhapsodized about the shoes and their fitness, weight loss, and comfort benefits.

Where all the action seems to be is the Skechers fan page on Facebook. It's an impressive clamor of praise and enthusiasm for the shoes—hordes of fans extolling the shoes and sharing anecdotes about their beneficial impact.

Sandie Mainwal-Price of Vero Beach, Florida, is typical: "I have minor back problems and I play lots of tennis," she posted. "I bought my first pair of Sketchers to see if they might help. They feel like I'm walking on a cloud. They are so much fun. People in the stores stop me to ask about them. I am like a walking commercial for Skechers."[17]

ZAPPOS

Speaking of shoes, Zappos is a brand that has embraced social media from the outset. The Zappos YouTube channel has about 2,000 subscribers. The videos are a mix of video testimonies on the unique Zappos workplace culture and philosophy (which Zappos customers seem to eat right up), as well as offbeat and silly stuff just aiming for a laugh. The company also maintains a separate ZapposHowTo channel devoted exclusively to how-to videos, from how to measure your calves for boots to how to pluck your eyebrows.

The Zappos Facebook page is liked by over 70,000 fans, although it receives almost no real estate on the Zappos Web site.

But Twitter is where Zappos really shines, especially because Zappos' CEO Tony Hsieh is one of the longest-standing and most prolific of all tweeters. Followed by a mind-blowing 1.7 million people, he was number 69 on the list of most-followed people on Twitter—a list dominated, it bears noting, by celebs like Ashton Kuchter, Kim Kardashian, Oprah Winfrey, Britney Spears, Ellen DeGeneres, and Lady Gaga.

Not surprisingly, news and entertainment outlets like the *New York Times*, E!, *People*, CNN, and the *Onion* also garner a couple million followers apiece. But the only other consumer product companies in the top 100 are Whole Foods Market and Dell Outlet.

LIPTON BRISK

Lipton Brisk iced tea (a brand of the Unilever food conglomerate) is energizing its brand with a combination of guerilla marketing, social media, and the hiring of young, Twitter-savvy brand ambassadors on college campuses nationwide.

The labels for Lipton Brisk's six flavors now bear the funky and colorful designs of young artists, winners of the first Brisk Emerging Artist contest. Putting their products' packaging into the hands of "the people" was just the start.

Unilever has hired scores of college students as Lipton Brisk Campus Reps. Their job? Get paid to look for new and emerging artists on their campus, host events, and hand out free bottles of Lipton Brisk around campus.

In its advertising for college reps, Unilever says, "We are seeking high-energy, motivated people who are heavily involved in campus activities and have a genuine appreciation for art and design. You will be tasked with hosting events to connect your fellow students with Lipton Brisk and recruit new and emerging artists on your campus."

Lipton Brisk campus reps work only about 20 to 25 hours per semester and receive a payment of $750 per semester. They can also receive internship credit and even college course credit in some cases. In a nod to the hope that many college reps might cherish, of finding a job with Unilever post-graduation, the company notes that there are "additional opportunities based on performance."

Campus reps at 30 schools, including Penn State, Temple University, the University of Oregon, Cornell University, and Boston University, recruited graphic artists for the Brisk Emerging Artist contest, with a $10,000 prize driven by voting from students at all the colleges, encouraged via social media.

The key to success for any campus rep is (1) to be outgoing, popular, and well connected, and (2) to have high energy and be fluent with social-networking sites, especially Facebook and Twitter, to build and connect with an online campus community, then post event announcements, photos, and event recaps online.

Meanwhile, Lipton Brisk is also giving summer jobs to dozens of "Urban Street Spotters" with a knack for digital photography and a strong familiarity with—you've got it—Twitter.

We are looking for high energy, motivated individuals with a real pulse of the city! You will be tasked with roaming around high traffic areas of the city looking for people that are expressing themselves in unique and different ways. This could be anything from street performers, to painters, to people with cool style . . . it's up to you!

Youth marketing particularly is an area where built-in social media is an absolute essential. The combination of brand ambassadors/campus reps, event marketing (think concerts and skateboarding or extreme sports events), plus a focused social-media campaign is becoming the recipe for reaching Generation Y and Millennials.

Brisk tea isn't alone. Campus rep programs are in full swing for brands as diverse as Red Bull energy drink, the 20th Century Fox movie studio, many ski areas and spring break destinations, Victoria's Secret PINK fashion line, and even the Firefox Web browser.

It's too early to know whether the Brisk campaign will catch on and be effective, but what I like about the campus rep angle and the street-level guerrilla marketing like the Brisk urban photographers is that we're seeing a big multinational brand trying to make a wider impact through a mere handful of well-connected, highly active individuals. That's taking it to the street.

WINE OF THE MONTH CLUB

Paul Kalemkiarian, owner of Wine of the Month Club—and son of the founder who in 1972 launched it as the first and original wine club—spoke alongside me onstage one bright and early morning at the Retail Marketing Conference in Orlando, Florida. Our job was to address attendees about social-media marketing. And if you're picturing some sedate PowerPoint exercise, think again. Paul is a born showman and zipped through tons of practical, high-energy, no-nonsense tips on using video, Facebook, Twitter, and other relationship building to connect with your customers.

The session, dubbed "Social Media Marketing: How Wine of the Month Club Uncorked the Power of Its Online Community," began with a splash: Paul K., brandishing a big serrated carving knife from the hotel kitchen, sabered off the top of a champagne bottle, *whack*! This before many conference-goers had gotten through their morning croissants.

Kalemkiarian is a big, garrulous personality, which makes him the perfect spokesman for a company social-media program. The Wine of the Month Club is the original and only trademarked wine of the month club. Every week, Paul tastes 400 wines (that is *not* a typo!) to choose the dozen he will offer each month as his featured selections. The club is headquartered in Arcadia, California.

Kalemkiarian's message: If you want to build a following using social media, don't try to sell on Facebook and Twitter—just be yourself.

Initially, he took the well-established route of being a wine expert and a wine educator to enthusiasts. But in the process, he wasn't letting his personality shine through on Facebook, Twitter, his blogs, and his video channels.

Yet it was his personality, honesty, and fanatical devotion to customer service that had always driven the club. These were the qualities that made successful wine tastings and restaurant partnerships and had helped Kalemkiarian sell tens of thousands of dollars of wine at California state fairs. These, in fact, were some of the qualities the club was born on, back in Paul senior's day, in the early 1970s, when California wines first knocked the socks off French judges in a blind tasting made famous in the movie *Bottle Shock*.

Today, Kalemkiarian infuses all his social-media posts and all his e-mail messages with his unique voice. Sure, he'll tweet Wine of the Month Club discounts and specials, but he considers social media to be a place to build bona-fide relationships that could lead to sales down the road. Social media also lets your customers see that you're human, and not just a salesman with a pitch.

"My competition is trying to sell products on Facebook, and I hope he keeps doing that," Kalemkiarian said, pointing out that the much better use of social-media platforms is in building *relationships*. Relationships just might help you sell more stuff, down the road, but that's not the first priority of a social-media effort. "These fringe relationships are helping me sell more wine than I did when I was using Facebook to sell wine."[18]

One relationship Kalemkiarian developed on Twitter turned out to be a quite profitable one. After Kalemkiarian started exchanging tweets with a follower, he sent her two free bottles of wine to try.

That relationship turned into a $100,000 sale, Kalemkiarian said, thanks to what he later learned was the contact's involvement in a major wine-club comparison Web site. And the cost to build that relationship, besides the Twitter time, was $6.

When a new member joins the club, Kalemkiarian sends that customer a personal e-mail with a custom video greeting, which he films at his desk and uploads to Vimeo, in which he welcomes the customer to the club and calls him by name. It takes a few minutes per customer—and many a company owner would scoff at the notion of spending the time. But if you're in the relationship business (and thanks to Web 2.0, we're all in the relationship business), can you afford not to?

In another video, Kalemkiarian answers the oft-heard question, "What do you do with the wines you don't like?" The video, available on YouTube, shows him in the back parking lot, while a bunch of warehouse staffers watch from the loading bay, while he shatters 10 bottles with a nicely rolled bowling ball.

Though the video was just a lark, it too has yielded commercial benefits—some $1,000 of revenue came directly via the coupon code displayed at the end of the video.

In all of this, what is most special about the Wine of the Month Club's program is letting Kalemkiarian's unique voice shine through. Here's a sample of an e-mail to his house list urging them to join his Facebook fan page (you'll see it also enumerates a number of exclusive benefits only to Facebook fans—a worthy tactic to emulate):

> You know, I didn't get it for a long time. Each day I find myself on Facebook more and more and get excited about seeing what everyone is doing.
>
> I want you to be a fan. So many fun things are happening and Facebook has become a great way for members and non-members to share wine information, ideas, and to just "shoot the wine breeze."

- *Facebook fans get the first look at e-mail specials. I release the e-mail special wines to Facebook fans six hours before the general e-mail goes out.*
- *Facebook fans get a first look at each month's wine videos and all special feature videos.*
- *Facebook fans gain access to unique promo codes and freebies when I get excited about a special wine.*
- *Facebook fans get weekly highlights of special newsletter articles written by my father.*
- *Facebook fans get historical looks at special selections from the early days.*
- *Facebook fans get instant food and wine pairings.*
- *Facebook fans get instant info on upcoming events.*

> *And how about this: There will be a promo code for FB fans only by the end of the day today . . . just for jumping on board.*

And speaking of voice, have you ever heard of any company getting fan mail for its promotional e-mail program? Wine of the Month Club does:

I enjoy your wonderful e-mails. You sell the wine, tell a story about the source/region, add a trivial component, perhaps a recipe, a link to a podcast of you dancing or enjoying your selection. You are colorful, you are engaging. You captivate your audience, you don't just sell them wine. You are old school with a modern twist.

The message here is simple: In your social-media efforts, and in all communications from your company to your customer, seek to be remarkable—engaging, personal, and real. Send them useful and valuable information in a style and format that works for them. That's part of the new two-way conversation between business and consumer in the Web 2.0 world.

The challenge is that you have to *earn* your place in the in-box, in the status update box. But having earned it, that communication is infinitely more valuable than the tired and increasingly ineffective "interruption marketing" most direct-marketers grew up on.

YARN.COM

WEBS, "America's Yarn Store," is one of the country's biggest sellers of yarn and supplies for knitting and needlework. Founded in 1978, this second-generation family business, headquartered in Southampton, Massachusetts, has been growing at a 25 percent annual clip since 2002. How do they do it?

Owner Steve Elkins points to Ravelry.com, a niche social-networking site exclusively for knitters who share tips, upload photos of their latest projects, recommend new yarns and patterns to one another, and save a wish-list "stash" of yarns they want to buy—a digital equivalent of the real-life stashes of yarn that all knitters seem to hoard. ("One great thing about our business," Elkins notes wryly, "is that knitters buy a lot more yarn than they actually use.")

By being on Ravelry as an active participant and also doing a lot of advertising on the site, WEBS builds an ever-higher profile within the knitting community—and it also generates real sales. "Ravelry is our Facebook," Elkins says. "There are 500,000 knitters on Ravelry, and visits to our Web site from Ravelry account for 5.6 percent of our traffic."[19]

The lesson here: If you serve a niche market, don't necessarily be wooed by the big, mainstream social networks. There just may be a smaller, more-focused network that is a much better avenue for you to reach your true audience.

ICE.COM

Ice.com is a leading online jewelry store, with sales of more than $60 million a year and growing at a double-digit clip. Pinny Gniwisch, executive vice president and chief marketing officer at the Montreal-based jewelry retailer, gives some of the credit to the company's forays into social media.[20]

Gniwisch spoke at the Internet Retailer Conference in Chicago in 2010 at a workshop entitled "Coordinating Search Engine Optimization with a Social-Media Plan." He and Eric Papczun, vice president of SEO and feed for Performics, offered these tips for using social media to drive traffic, sales, and search-engine rank:

- Create Wikipedia pages for brands or key products.
- Upload pictures to Flickr, either of key products or to give a behind-the-scenes look at your company.
- Create your own channel on YouTube.
- Promote contests where consumers create videos that celebrate your brand or products.

Ice.com has long used its company blog to connect to customers and better its search-engine results. For the recent Oscar awards, Ice.com paid bloggers to write about the jewelry worn by celebrities; the retailer then offered similar items on its Web site.

Retailers should also blog about their brands and products and update those blogs frequently, Gniwisch says. Such efforts can produce news breaks and boost search-engine traffic, although sometimes in unpredictable ways. For instance, Ice.com posted an item about Tipper Gore's jewelry—then later saw traffic to its site increase after Al and Tipper Gore announced they would separate.

Gniwish is another strong proponent of using social media like Twitter and Facebook to listen closely to customers. After just four months on Facebook, Ice.com has some 30,000 fans. Up to 25 percent of their Facebook posts and replies concern customer service, says Gniwish. In a nice touch that I have not seen many other retailers doing, Ice celebrates a Fan of the Week with a photo and a testimonial.

On the subject of listening, Papczun suggests retailers monitor Twitter for negative tweets about their company name, brands, or products—especially since those messages can now end up among Google results mere minutes after being posted.

"Resolve problems *before* a massive Twitter conversation makes it to the search-engine results pages," advises Papczun.

Chapter 6

Fails and Fiascos

We've talked about some of the successful and inspiring ways companies are using social media. But it's not all pretty. The social-media landscape is still foreign to most of us, and there are myriad opportunities for your well-intentioned social-media efforts to blow up in your face.

I'm generally a big fan of Jim Tobin and Lisa Braziel's metaphor that social media is a cocktail party. But it's not all roses; social media is not always a festive gathering buzzing with warmth and welcome.

In fact, the social sphere can turn mean faster than a clique of teenage girls. And that cocktail party can start looking like the prom scene from *Carrie*.

Naturally, cliques of teenage girls, and boys, are part of the social-media landscape. So are rabid wing-nuts from either side of the political spectrum, staunch privacy advocates and anti-marketing zealots, and average people for whom the relative anonymity of the Web bestows a courage verging on road rage.

You *can* find your audience online and make real connections with grace and good humor. But there are people in the room rooting for you to fail.

The appeal of watching someone or some organization crash and burn online is so ingrained in Web culture that it has a name: fail. It's a noun, not a verb, as in, "Did you catch the Skittles fail?"

Fails especially worthy of the name are described in the superlative as *epic* fails.

Twitter, which not only *gets* social culture, but also drives it, managed to diffuse the occasional site slowdowns that have accompanied its skyrocketing growth by inventing its "fail whale" error graphic. Depicting a flock of Twitter birds laboring to keep a whale aloft, the fail whale nicely captures the challenges of a little start-up company coping with exponential traffic increases.

(FailBlog.org and EpicFail.com are good places to see images and videos of screw-ups and embarrassments across the entire range of human failure—from lame Web site error messages to accidentally hilarious road signs and slapstick real-life videos.)

While "fail" is not reserved for social-media blunders, it's definitely a minefield for would-be social-media strategists to avoid.

Let's take a closer look at two things: (1) prominent screw-ups that companies have made trying to establish their social media presence and (2) mistakes or embarrassments that were made elsewhere, but whose damage was spread virally thanks to the power of social media.

VIRAL EMBARRASSMENTS

The Web has always been a viral medium. It lacks the messaging "friction" of the bricks-and-mortar world, where prior to the Web, word-of-mouth was anchored in time and space in conversations around a watercooler and the passing around of physical media.

The amplification of any trend on the Web is now heightened by the sheer profusion of social-network sites, the increasing size of the average person's network, and the increasing ease of communicating with everyone on your social graph. Notably, tools like retweeting and "liking" make it effortless to signal your tastes and interests to everyone in your network. When word-of-mouth spread at the watercooler or by telephone, friction slowed its transmission. The Web (and e-mail) eliminated most of that friction. Today's social Web has eliminated it almost entirely.

Social networks turn the volume up to 11. Anything we think worthy of note can be effortlessly shared with all our friends. With a mere click of the mouse we can tell the world "Jane likes this,"—and the network effect takes over to spread the word along her social graph and all its connected networks.

A number of studies have lent credibility to the notion that we're all, everyone on the planet, connected by "six degrees of separation." A few isolated Amazon tribesmen may disprove the idea, but in general, it is borne out. Based on recent research, the average number of linkages between, say, Internet users, or users of instant-messaging services, is in the range of 6 or as much as 6.6. On any given network, unsurprisingly, the connectedness is tighter; everyone among the hundreds of millions on Twitter, for instance, is connected within five steps.

Table 6.1   The author's network statistics on LinkedIn

1	degree away: your trusted friends and colleagues	**409**
2	degrees away: friends of friends	**194,800+**
3	degrees away: members reachable through a friend and one of their friends	**7,726,400+**

Facebook reports that its average user has 130 friends. The average Twitter user has 127 followers. The average LinkedIn user has 63 connections. But these averages count the many inactive users who joined but never friended or followed anyone (50 percent of Twitter's total, or about 9 million people, according to *Harvard Business Review*). And we all know many super-users who have many times these numbers of connections.

Looking at the concept from the other side, it's the exponential or viral-growth characteristics of a network that cause its incredible worldwide reach.

Witness my own network statistics on the business network LinkedIn in Table 6.1 above.

Basically, thanks to the exponential nature of networks, I'm four degrees away from all 50 million of LinkedIn's members.

Suffice it to say, your good news travels faster than ever on the Web—and your bad news travels even faster.

When one of the top search-engine results for searches on your brand name is a slam from an alienated customer, your brand image is being tarnished every time a hopeful customer comes looking for you. For example, one of the page-one Google results for "Comcast" is an embarrassing YouTube video of a hapless Comcast technician, on hold with his company's own tech support, and fast asleep on the couch of a customer who filmed the whole thing and posted it. Not good! The video has been around for four years now, always enjoying high search-engine visibility, and garnering over 1.5 million views to date. That's one of the critical things about online mistakes and embarrassments. They can be fleeting, yet they leave an indelible mark.

The "Comcast technician sleeping on my couch" video galvanized a lot of anti-Comcast sentiment among consumers. But it also galvanized something else: Comcast's impressive, sensitive, and successful use of social media to connect with customers and solve their gripes. Comcast has had its troubles, but today they're a company that totally gets social media and uses it well.

With the advent of social media, it's easier than ever to step into a minefield. First, there's the sin of omission: failing to establish accounts on the major and even minor social networks, and thereby allowing squatters and pranksters to create high-profile accounts slamming your brand or making it look bad. That's not to say that your participation in online social networks should be aimed at taking individual consumers out of the equation! Far from it. One of the most powerful business forces of Web 2.0 social networking is to unleash consumers' honest and passionate tributes to, and reviews of, your products and services.

But you don't want to be in the position of Anheuser-Busch, and find that the MySpace username Budweiser—with some 16,000 friends—is a dubious yet somewhat official-looking tribute page reading: "Being a beer built on taste, qulity [sic] and most of all tradition, Budweiser encorporates [sic] all aspects of beer drinking needed to keep its drinkers happy, satisfifed [sic], and DRUNK."

That's also a great example of the importance of snatching up your company or brand name as a username. Budweiser failed to get its handle on MySpace, Twitter, and YouTube—the low-quality squatter accounts that are sitting on those valuable Budweiser social-media URLs are embarrassing. But the race is to the swift.

Critical voices about your business are also part of the online conversation. And should bad press and word-of-mouth ever reach crisis proportions, the golden rules for crisis response are truer than ever in Web 2.0—and they need to be deployed at the speed of light. Companies must understand both the positive and negative sides of viral growth on the Internet. When a potential crisis emerges, today's companies need to be completely upfront and immediately start to remedy a problem, be it a product recall, severing a controversial relationship, or what have you.

SOCIAL-MEDIA PITFALLS FOR EMPLOYERS

Social media is still a relatively new phenomenon, and although the Emily Post Society has offered etiquette guides for this unfamiliar landscape, many people are still making blunders, especially where business and personal lives converge.

The Federal Trade Commission recently established strict regulations governing employees' use of social media to talk about a product or service offered by their employers. Basically, businesses can be held liable for unsubstantiated claims made online by their employees.

As Delaware attorney Molly DiBianca puts it:

If an employee tweets about his employer's pizza being the best around, he must do so in compliance with the regulations. Failure to do so and both the employee and the employer are on the hook. Both can be held liable if the comment or statement is false or unsubstantiated. So, if the pizza really is the best in town and you've got the studies to show it, then there's no real risk of liability. But if an employee leaves a comment on a blog about a particular brand of laundry detergent that works wonders on grass stains, and another person reads the comment, buys the detergent, and isn't satisfied with its stain-fighting powers, there may be problems.[1]

What a tangled Web! Of course employers don't want their staff posting derogatory things online. But who would have thought, especially in an age when word-of-mouth and popular buzz are so sought after, that we could be hurt by our employees' *positive* postings? Says DiBianca: "The critical takeaway from the new FTC guides is this: Employers must have a social-media policy that addresses the ways employees talk about their employers."

DiBianca has also thought a good deal about the impact of social media on the hiring process. She notes that the Facebook, Twitter, YouTube, and other social-media profile pages of a job applicant are now commonly considered by HR as part of a background check. She counsels that employers must disclose their intention to review such pages and get the applicant's consent (as part of the background check consent form).

Meanwhile, younger workers who came of age in the social-media era may face a harsh wake-up call when they realize that online evidence of a wild and crazy personal life can stand in the way of their budding professional life.

Clearly, social media presents both opportunities and potential liabilities— for employers and employees alike.

JENNIFER LAYCOCK AND THE PORK BOARD

We all know the adage "pick on someone your own size"—but if you're a business, when it comes to the Web and social media, *don't pick on anyone.*

Jennifer Laycock, a mom and breast-feeding advocate who edits Search Engine Guide by day and the Lactivist blog by night, supports her breast-feeding site by selling funny T-shirts like "That's my baby's lunch you're staring at."

One day, Jennifer received a stern cease-and-desist letter from lawyers for the National Pork Board regarding a shirt emblazoned with the slogan "The Other White Milk." They were unamused by the shirt's similarity with their "The Other White Meat" trademark, and insisted she stop selling the shirt, destroy all unsold inventory of it, and take other measures.

Rather than roll over, Jennifer fought back, sharing the nasty letter—and her own indignant and hilarious take on the whole issue—with her blog readers. Almost immediately, the blogosphere turned up the heat: Jennifer's blog post was linked to, commented upon, and posted about by hundreds of readers and other bloggers. It was Dugg hundreds of times and tagged on del.icio.us and Reddit. Angry supporters rallied to her side, e-mailing and calling the Pork Board (whose executives' names and contact info Jennifer helpfully posted on her blog). The controversy made its way onto more mainstream venues like Salon.com and Brandweek.com.

Law firms volunteered to defend Jennifer pro bono against the board. Chief among them was the Electronic Freedom Foundation, which bills itself as "the leading civil liberties group defending your rights in the digital world." Jennifer's hosting company threw free bandwidth at the huge traffic increases to her site.

As with many viral campaigns on the Web, this one was a perfect storm: partly a moral crusade, and partly just plain laughable. "National Pork Board Stumbles into Hornet's Nest of Bloggers," posted *Information Week*, while Search Engine Roundtable put it more wryly: "Search Engine Industry Blogger, Jennifer Laycock, Ordered to Remove Her Shirt." It helped that she had two natural constituencies: tech-savvy search-engine geeks from her professional world, and the parenting and lactation community of her personal life.

Suddenly it no longer looked like such a straightforward trademark-infringement play from the corporate law 101 playbook. It was starting to look like the pork industry versus breastfeeding and motherhood.

For the record, the National Pork Board eventually did the right thing: It quickly dropped their attorney's threats, the CEO sent an apology to Jennifer, and individual board executives and staff even dug into their pockets to support the charity of Jennifer's choice, Mother's Milk Bank of Ohio.

No doubt the organization was mortified that a boilerplate letter from their outside law firm landed them on the wrong side of a powerful and emotional issue. Jennifer Laycock applauded them for their resolution of the affair. It's worth noting that any organization that maintains and invests in trademarks has not just an interest in, but a legal obligation to defend those marks. But the point is, any organization doing business today must recalibrate its interactions with the outside world.

No longer can you assume a spurned or dissatisfied customer will simply go away. They just may well be among the small but potent fraction of Web users who are energetic content creators: well-connected, active bloggers, evangelists, and gadflies whose causes and opinions grow virally across the Web.

Importantly, the pork industry group's black eye didn't fade when the PR crisis blew over. While bad broadcast news cycles are measured in days, and bad press coverage gets carried out with the recycling, unflattering Web pages are forever. Even today, four of the top 10 Google results for "National Pork Board" point to pages about the T-shirt controversy.

T&J TOWING

Justin Kurtz, a 21-year-old Western Michigan University student in Kalamazoo, Michigan, woke one morning to find that his Toyota Corolla had been towed from its legal parking spot at the parking lot of the apartment complex where he lived.

The towing company, T&J Towing, contended they had the right to tow the vehicle because its permit sticker wasn't visible. Kurtz argued the sticker had indeed been properly displayed—until T&J removed it. But the towing company refused to release the car until Kurtz ponied up $118.

That's when Kurtz, outraged, went to the Internet for revenge. He created a Facebook page called "Kalamazoo Residents Against T&J Towing." Within a couple of days, 800 people had joined the group, some posting comments about their own frustrating experiences with the company and alleging a history of shady practices.

Frankly, things might have petered out right there, but T&J threw gas on the fire, hiring a lawyer, claiming the site was hurting their business, and slapping Kurtz with a defamation suit seeking $750,000 in damages.

The story spread fast throughout the social-media landscape. Kurtz's Facebook page hit local Kalamazoo news outlets, then, thanks largely to social media, went national: ABC News, CNN, and the *New York Times* covered it. The Humanist Society, a nonprofit, sprang to Kutz's legal aid. He filed a countersuit, alleging the $750,000 damage claim was an attempt to harass and intimidate him and stifle his free-speech rights.

Meanwhile, his Facebook page was steadily gaining support, growing to 14,000 fans. Consumers spread the word that T&J had earned a grade of "F" from the Better Business Bureau due to its failure to answer any of the more than 20 consumer complaints about it that had been received by the BBB over three years. On YouTube, a local news video critical of the company received 2,000 views.

Kalamazoo businesses that had contracted with T&J, concerned by the public outcry, began deserting the company. Kurtz's apartment complex was one of them.

The Consumerist is a leading consumer-advocacy Web site and an effort of Consumer Media, publisher of *Consumer Reports*. The Consumerist reported: "T&J has lost half of its commercial towing accounts, including the apartment complex from which the creator of the Facebook page had his car towed in January."

Failing to see that the real damages to the company were self-inflicted, the lawyer for T&J Towing said of his client, "He has wrongly become a pariah in the eyes of many people in the community . . . He's lost upwards of 15 accounts because of the hostility this situation has created."

Not surprising, a Google search for "T&J Towing" today reveals lots of unflattering coverage of the lawsuit and resulting uproar. The "Kalamazoo Residents against T&J Towing" Facebook page ranks on the first page, surrounded by negative media reports and bad reviews on pages at Yelp, Yahoo, and the Better Business Bureau. T&J Towing doesn't even appear to have its own Web site.

"I didn't do anything wrong," says Kurtz, who recently finished his junior year. "The only thing I posted is what happened to me."[2]

The case was still at an impasse at the time I was writing this book—but from my perspective, every day the towing company persists with its suit is a day of self-inflicted injury.

"There's no reason I should have to shut up because some guy doesn't want his dirty laundry out," concludes Kurtz. "It's the power of the Internet, man."

Erik Qualman, author of *Socialnomics* and a professor at the Hult International Business School, likened T&J's lawsuit to "waving that red flag in front of a raging bull."[3]

"Whatever the verdict is, it is a lesson to companies that the consumer has more power than ever before," he said. "Folks want to be listened to, they want to be heard."

He said that research has shown that if companies can resolve an issue when a customer lodges a complaint, they will be five times more likely to become repeat customers.

But ignoring customer feedback can just fan the fire.

"People can be heard in ways that they never used to be," notes social-media guru Chris Brogan, coauthor of *Trust Agents: Using the Web to Build Influence, Improve Reputation, and Earn Trust*. Thanks especially to the new online networks, "people have the opportunity to be heard in a public forum and cry out when they feel wronged."[4]

DELL AND DELLA

We celebrated Dell's amazing Twitter successes in the previous chapter on success stories, but they also deserve mention here in our "fails" chapter. What's important here is that being nimble in social media doesn't magically insure you against screwing up.

Della was a microsite and social-media campaign targeted at women, and it was roundly mocked as seeming condescending—trivializing women as calorie counters, recipe-downloaders, and wide-eyed newbies to technology.

Dell's audience has historically been dominated by male technology geeks and businesspeople; understandably the firm wanted to extend its reach to women who might take less of a gadget-centric focus. True, there's evidence that male and female consumers approach high-tech purchases differently, so it's hard to fault Dell for seeking an approach that works better with women customers.

As Forbes put it, "Della is targeted at women. Tech has traditionally had a male-dominated client base, but with women now making 83 percent of all consumer purchases, they are no longer a sliver of the consumer market. Women are the market."[5]

But the execution of Della gave the impression that Dell was stereotyping and belittling female consumers, pitching them feminine-looking and colorful laptops that they could use to (wow, really?) manage their appointments, download recipes, and track their workouts with an app called Gyminee.

What ensued was a blogging firestorm of contempt for Della. Women all over the Web, on blogs, and Twitter bristled at the idea they need a separate Web site for them to understand computers, dumbed down or adorned with flowers or butterflies. The Jezebel blog called it "ugh-worthy." On GearLog, Nicole Price Fasig slammed Della's "patronizing language and cloying images of women with matching cardigans and netbooks."

The criticism went viral. From Twitter and the blogosphere, the story jumped to the mainstream national media, including MSNBC and the *New York Times*.

Dell tried to respond, adding a feedback section on Della, but what flooded in was mostly negative. As one tech-savvy woman said of Della, "This child can be thrown out with the bathwater."

Within three weeks, all links to Della were gone, directed instead to the gender-neutral Lifestyle section of the main Dell site.

And to its credit, Dell addressed the online community directly, apologizing for any offense, and laughing a little at itself: "We can do better and are already making changes based on what you're telling us. For example, we've made the 'tech tips' section, well, more technical. We'll be incorporating more business-oriented products and information. And there's less pink."

"We *are* listening," concluded Dell. "Thanks for the feedback. It's essential to how Dell does business."[6]

As we've learned, women are an extraordinarily powerful and interlinked force on the Web. Reach out to relevant communities of women, with sensitivity and real back-and-forth, and you can build a strong and lasting program. But pander to them, stereotype then, or rub them the wrong way, and you're in for trouble.

The Della fiasco reminds me of the Motrin Moms ad campaign of late 2008. It its eagerness to appeal to mothers, McNeil Healthcare, maker of Motrin, ran a series of ads appearing to mock the practice of parents "wearing" their babies in sling carriers and other contraptions. The ads suggested the strain of such 24/7 child-carrying might take a toll on your aching backs, moms of America, but in the words of one ad, it "totally makes me look like an official mom." And at least you can keep popping those Motrin.

Parents female and male alike took offense. The virtues of child carriers for both convenience and good child development are well established. And anybody gets their hackles up when their parenting is criticized or trivialized, as Motrin's ads seemed to do.

The backlash was swift, especially across Twitter and the blogosphere. "The maker of painkiller Motrin got a painful lesson in the power of online social networking," wrote *USA Today*. "McNeil Consumer Healthcare is yanking new Motrin ads after an outpouring of negative 'tweets,' or postings, via Twitter, video on YouTube, and postings on other social sites."[7]

McNeil sent apologies directly to prominent bloggers and Twitter users and posted a separate apology on Motrin.com. "We have heard your concerns about the ad," wrote Kathy Widmer, marketing vice president. "We are parents ourselves and take feedback from moms very seriously. We are in the process of removing this ad from all media."

TOO MUCH INFORMATION (REMEMBER PRIVACY?)

This chapter is rightly devoted to the examples of companies whose use of social media to reach their customers or make a PR splash blew up in their faces. But I want to touch on a couple of other cautionary examples of social-media minefields that affect everyone: companies ignoring privacy, and individuals assuming they *have* privacy.

Facebook's Brave New World

Facebook has charted new territory in our global culture—and more than 500 million users have voted for the appeal and usefulness of the site by using it.

But in the process, Facebook has become the poster child for disdain for privacy, continually launching new features and policies stretching the bounds of online privacy, making new assumptions of what personal information and content they own, and what they can do with it. Invariably— and it has now occurred with regularity—Facebook has rolled out new features with cavalier disregard for privacy concerns, taken a storm of backlash from users and the media, staunchly and arrogantly defended its actions, downplayed privacy, dug in, and finally relented after an extended period of bashing from the public.

It hasn't helped that young founder Marc Zuckerberg, who conceived and programmed Facebook as a Harvard sophomore in 2004, has so often taken a dismissive stance on privacy concerns and suggested that today's expectations of privacy have changed permanently.

In private instant messages from 2004, revealed by Silicon Alley Insider in May 2010,[8] a 19-year-old Zuckerberg is quoted shortly after he launched Facebook from his dorm room:

> Zuckerberg: Yeah so if you ever need info about anyone at Harvard.
> Zuckerberg: Just ask.
> Zuckerberg: I have over 4,000 e-mails, pictures, addresses, SNS.
> [Redacted Friend's Name]: What? How'd you manage that one?
> Zuckerberg: People just submitted it.
> Zuckerberg: I don't know why.
> Zuckerberg: They "trust me"
> Zuckerberg: Dumb f**ks.

Ironically, Zuckerberg's first project, called Facemash, was a hack he performed as a Harvard sophomore one drunken night, and which later drew official sanctions from the Harvard administration. Zuckerberg's Facemash site (similar to the site Hot or Not) compared profile photos of pairs of Harvard students, inviting users to rank which of the two was better looking. To launch the site, Zuckerberg hacked into protected areas of Harvard's computer network and downloaded student images used for dormitory IDs. *The Harvard Crimson* reported he was charged by the administration with breaching security, violating copyrights, and violating individual privacy. He faced expulsion, but ultimately the charges were dropped.[9]

(If it all sounds like high-tech meets high drama, that's probably why the early days of Facebook made it to the silver screen, in the Columbia Pictures film *The Social Network*. Tagline: you don't get to 500 million friends without making a few enemies.)

Early Facebook employee and Zuckerberg confidant Charlie Cheever said: "I feel Mark doesn't believe in privacy that much, or at least believes in privacy as a stepping stone. Maybe he's right, maybe he's wrong."[10]

As I'll discuss in the next chapter, Facebook and Zuckerberg may be correct that our collective view of privacy is changing. Maybe in the future we'll thank them from pulling us into a brave, new, post-privacy world. My point isn't that Facebook has necessarily been *wrong* in its privacy blow-ups—just that Facebook has been *wrongheaded* in its approach.

In today's social-media world, the crowd rules. When your users and the media cry foul, listen to them. Facebook's history thus far has been to take matters into its own hands, ignoring its users until the din gets deafening. What works better in Web 2.0 is to survey your customers first, before you make a big move, and let your decisions be guided by their feedback.

Smile, You're on Google Street View

Google's Street View project ran afoul of privacy advocates in 2007. Street View involved thousands of street-level photographs of U.S. cities taken by rolling crews of Google photographers and uploaded to the Web. The problem was, when users zoomed into some photos, they started to see disturbing sights, caught on candid camera, as it were: topless sunbathers; a drug bust; cops attending to a traffic fatality; pedestrians picking their noses; a man urinating in public; and an apparent housebreaker scaling a condo fence.

Posting on the Web site Boing Boing, Berkeley, California, resident Mary Kalin-Casey said that when she zoomed into her address on the site, she not only saw the exterior of her apartment, but a highly detailed image of her cat, Monty, sitting in the window. "I'm all for mapping," she wrote, "but this feature literally gives me the shakes. I feel like I need to close all my curtains now."[11]

The feature is still in use, and Google has set up procedures for removal of images flagged as inappropriate, but if the Web site http://www.StreetViewFun.com is any indication, Street View is still responsible for capturing and uploading images that most of us would consider "too much information."

Recently, the same Google Street View program ran afoul of investigators in Germany and the United States when it was disclosed that the same high-tech vans that photograph street scenes had in some cases collected and stored data from unsecured Wi-Fi networks along their routes. "Consumers and businesses rightly expect Google to respect their privacy, not invade it by vacuuming up confidential data," said Connecticut attorney general Richard Blumenthal. "Unauthorized surveillance of wireless network data is the dark side of the new Internet era, and I will fight it."

The lesson here, whether you're a social-media site serving half a billion people, the biggest search site on the planet, or a little mom-and-pop business, is that privacy still matters. The concept may be evolving, but privacy is still a deeply held human value. The line may be blurry, but if you cross it, you'll know it.

So as a business, respect and guard the privacy of your users. If you inadvertently violate their expectations, apologize sincerely and right away. Resolve the issue and ensure it can't happen again to any of your users.

PERSONAL BRAND DISASTERS

In the Web 2.0 world, businesses aren't the only ones with brands to cultivate and defend. Every individual is now a brand whose footprints are revealed with every Google search, with every foray through Facebook, Twitter, LinkedIn, or the blogosphere.

For most of us, that's an unbridled good. No longer must we wait for the right opening to appear in the classifieds, polish our resume and cover letter, send them off to some anonymous HR address, and wait for the best. Yes, plenty of hiring is still done this old-school way (and literally millions of hopeful applicants are slowly languishing on the supply side, often never hearing a single word back from prospective employers). But for many jobs and many applicants, a whole new paradigm of getting connected—either with potential hires, potential employers, business partners, vendors, or B2B customers—is happening online, through the business and social-media networks.

There was always an "old boys' network" that greased the skids for those inside it. But today the network is many times larger, more efficiently connected, instantly updated, and immensely more fluid. With your profile on LinkedIn, the evidence of your professional performance and reputation is signaled with every status update you make, every post from TripIt indicating you're on an apparently important business trip, every friend-of-a-friend you connect with, every blog post you publish. When job openings occur, LinkedIn users often pass them directly to their network, asking for referrals.

That's the positive side of online professional networks. But there's a dark side too. Among the most egregious examples of self-destruction of a personal brand are these three: the Halloween fairy, the Cisco new hire, and the self-infatuated Whole Foods CEO.

The Halloween Fairy

Kevin Colvin, a young intern at Anglo Irish Bank's North American arm, was busted—and fired—when he told manager Paul Davis that he had to miss work due to a family emergency, only to be caught in a lie courtesy of his Facebook account.[12]

While Colvin was supposedly attending to his family emergency, Davis checked out Colvin's Facebook page. There he found a newly uploaded image of Colvin, elaborately dressed as a fairy, beer in one hand, magic wand in the other, obviously enjoying the Halloween party he had skipped work to attend.

Davis downloaded the photo and then attached it to his e-mail reply, saying "Kevin, thanks for letting us know—hope everything is OK in New York (cool wand)."

Colvin was fired from the bank. The e-mail thread and fairy photo quickly circulated around the Internet.

The moral? I suppose it could be: Don't friend your boss or anyone else at work. But let's be realistic. The real lesson is that there's no firewall between your work persona and your social-media one.

How to Torpedo Your Career in 140 Characters or Less

Skye Riley is better known as @theconnor, thanks to her 15 minutes of Twitter fame (or ignominy). A young woman in southern California, she was offered a position at Cisco Systems in 2009. That's when things got weird.

"Cisco just offered me a job!" she tweeted. "Now I have to weigh the utility of a fatty paycheck against the daily commute to San Jose and hating the work."

Such a message may have been fine to kick off a private heart-to-heart with a friend. But theconnor's Twitter account was set (as most are by default) to be public—shared with all of Twitter. Essentially, shared with all the world.

It wasn't long before Cisco employee Tim Levad picked up theconnor's tweet. Like many people today, he receives an alert whenever his company is mentioned in the blogospere, on Twitter, or elsewhere online. He shared this open response to theconnor:

"Who is the hiring manager? I'm sure they would love to know that you will hate the work. We here at Cisco are versed in the Web."

The story circulated virally across Twitter and hit the mainstream media with MSNBC's headline "Twitter Gets You Fired in 140 Characters or Less." The hook of these and other stories was that the new social media presents unprecedented risk to those of us tempted to talk first and think later.

As MSNBC put it, "Never post anything you wouldn't say to your mom, boss, and significant other. Alas, if that message hasn't sunk in by now, it never will. And thanks to Twitter further eroding the wall between your big mouth and a moment required to download some good sense, the Internet is now empowered to get you fired faster than ever."[13]

In an open letter, Riley offered a fairly evenhanded account. "Cisco never did anything to me. I have no complaints about the company and apologize for any damage this situation has done to their image in anyone's mind. What started as one individual calling me out quickly escalated into a major schadenfreude event, which in turn has quickly escalated into a media bandwagon."

Today, Riley is a master's candidate in the UC Berkeley School of Information. She's a smart woman and I have no doubt she has landed on her feet and will be successful in her field. But along the way, she did us all a service of exemplifying just how wrong a 140-character tweet can go.

These two examples depict young, twentysomething Millennials, relatively new to the workforce, raised on the oversharing of social media. Perhaps people just a few years removed from college can be expected to have not fully shucked off the keg-party culture of indiscretion and naïveté.

Keep a Leash on Your CEO

But how do you explain seasoned, adult executives—CEOs no less!—undone by social-media gaffes?

Take Whole Foods CEO John Mackey, a principled vegan and libertarian who pays himself just $1 a year as chairman and chief executive. He's eccentric, perhaps, but surely a respected business leader and visionary.

But that respect took a hit in 2007 with a discovery made by Federal Trade Commission lawyers who were poring through reams of Whole Foods documents, seeking to block the company's acquisition of Wild Oats.

It turns out, Mackey was living a double life. CEO on the one hand, and on the other hand? Mackey was for *seven years* touting his company's stock on the message boards of Yahoo Finance under the pseudonym Rahodeb (a variation on his wife Deborah's name).

In more than 1,100 posts on the Yahoo Finance bulletin board, Mackey slammed the business prospects and management practices of Wild Oats, even as his business was courting it as an acquisition. And he extolled the virtues of Whole Foods as an investment.

Of course, he and his company stood to benefit if Mackey's pseudonymous posts boosted Whole Foods' share price or influenced a decline in Wild Oats.

The story was broken on the *Wall Street Journal*'s Web site.[14]

In a typical post heaping scorn on Wild Oats, Rahodeb wrote: "OATS has lost their way and no longer has a sense of mission or even a well-thought-out theory of the business. They lack a viable business model that they can replicate. They are floundering around hoping to find a viable strategy that may stop their erosion. Problem is that they lack the time and the capital now."

What added color to the whole story was his gratuitous, glowing, and anonymous praise of John Mackey.

"I like Mackey's haircut. I think he looks cute!" Rahodeb posted at one point. The writer later suggested, "Mackey looks like a model for Brooks Brothers!"

After the FTC's disclosure, Yahoo's message boards erupted with chatter about Mackey's secret identity.

As one forum poster commented, "What a hoot! It's so Nixonian!"

Amazon PayPhrase

In October 2009, Amazon introduced an automatic pass-phrase suggestion tool, which it called PayPhrase, to make login faster and easier, both on Amazon and on other Web sites that accept PayPhrase.

Many people got a kick out of the colorful and oddball PayPhrases that Amazon suggested for them: "Feisty Mango," "Feeble Skeleton," and "John's Sudden Availability" to name a few.

The problem was, the random-phrase generator also came up with some creepy and suggestive ideas: "Gil's Splendid Balls," "Amy's Creamy Juices," and "Josh's Special Cucumber" were just a few that were soon bandied about on Twitter, blogs, boards, social networks, and bookmarking sites.

The upside here is that Amazon's new PayPal-killer got a lot of fun, free publicity.

The downside: The awkward and sexual suggestions reflected badly on its brand and made Amazon appear not to have developed the tool with sufficient care. And consider, too, that in this day and age of high-tech hacking, payment account usernames are about the last thing we should be sharing online for a laugh.

Awkwardness aside, Amazon's Pay Phrase feature never rose to the level of a PR boondoggle, and the program is still in use. The lesson here is that any feature you release, any policy you enact, any customer-service message you make through e-mail or instant chat, today has the ability to spread, via blogs and social-media postings and screen captures, far beyond the individual for whom it was written. Don't type or auto-generate anything you wouldn't be comfortable seeing on the Drudge Report or page one of Google results.

Monster Versus Vermonster

The crowd loves an underdog, and as we saw with the Pork Board, you never want to give the impression your organization is a bully. Such was the case when the Nasdaq-traded maker of Monster energy drinks started picking on a small Vermont beermaker over a trade name dispute.

The dispute morphed into another social-media-powered win for David against Goliath.

As with the Pork Board, the case hinged over protection of a trademark and started with a routine cease-and-desist letter—but thanks to the power of social media, no such correspondence should today be viewed as routine. Perhaps we are entering an era where business should take a deep breath, even when they're on the right side of a legal issue, and pick up the phone before firing off a boilerplate threat.

The California-based Hansen Beverage Company, which makes Monster energy drinks, took issue with Rock Art Brewery, a small Vermont brewer that makes a beer called "Vermonster." Hansen's cease-and-desist letter, sent in September 2009 to Rock Art, accused the company of infringing the Monster trademark. Hansen insisted Rock Art stop using the Vermonster name and pay for Hansen's attorneys' fees.

Matt Nadeau, who owns the Rock Art microbrewery with his wife, scoffs that nobody would confuse his craft-brewed American barley wine with the nationally known Monster energy drink. Nadeau consulted five different trademark attorneys and was told he could probably win in court. But that was little consolation because they also assured him fighting the case would likely bankrupt him in the process.

Rock Art's only options seemed either to battle for a pyrrhic victory or roll over and let Monster have its way. But then Nadeau took his battle to the court of public opinion via social media. Nadeau aired the dispute on social-media platforms, blogs, and elsewhere on the Internet, framing it as a classic tale of a large corporation and its big legal team trying to squash a small entrepreneur. Word of the legal fight spread, prompting local and then national media—including the Associated Press—to pick up the story.

A social-media-led boycott campaign sparked stores in Vermont, New York, Maine, and Connecticut to yank Monster energy drink from their shelves in a show of solidarity with the small brewer.

U.S. Senator Bernie Sanders even stepped in, urging Hansen to back off.

"It struck a nerve with everybody when they saw and heard the story," Nadeau said. "They were like, 'You've got to be kidding me. I'm not confused by these products. What do you mean this guy's going to lose his business if he decides to fight for the name that's legally his?'"[15]

Monster's reputation as a hip, positive brand was suddenly under siege. The controversy was enough to get Hansen Beverage to the table with a much different set of demands. Within a couple of weeks, the two sides reached a settlement that let Rock Art to continue to market its Vermonster brew anywhere in the country. Rock Art's only concession was to agree not to sell energy drinks—which it never intended to do—according to Rock Art attorney Douglas Riley.

"It's phenomenal," says Nadeau. "It happened so fast. That's what's just amazing about this new power of traditional media, combined with social media, what tools that we have as Americans to fight against big power."

Tumbling Domino's

Domino's Pizza invests millions in TV commercials and other pricey media buys to tout the quality and value of its pizzas.

All it took to make Domino's come crashing down were a couple of disgruntled employees, a cell phone camera, and a few free uploads to YouTube.

Two now ex-employees videotaped their gross "prank" of stuffing cheese up their noses, then putting the same cheese on sandwiches, violating a host of public health laws. When the videos hit the Internet and went viral, Domino's knew it was facing a public-relations crisis capable of damaging its brand in a matter of days.

The two North Carolina employees were not only fired, but were also charged with criminal food contamination.

Through Twitter, blogs, and YouTube, the videos had been viewed by millions of people, highlighting the power of social media to tarnish a 50-year-old brand virtually overnight.

"Domino's was the latest company to be on the wrong end of a Twitter storm, a spontaneously formed digital mob that rapidly shares information," said ABC News. "The company's swift response to the employees and its wider customer base, using the same Web sites and media that spread the video, has been praised by observers who nevertheless wonder if the company can emerge unscathed."

Domino's put its president, Patrick Doyle, on YouTube with a video apology.

Since the PR disaster, Domino's has been playing damage control, pouring even more millions into image-repairing messages, most notably its "pizza holdout" commercials seeking to prove to skeptics that the quality of its food is high. In a cynical, post-marketing Web 2.0 world where ordinary customers trust each others' opinions and discount the claims of companies, Domino's faces an uphill battle. When they would prefer to be taking the high ground, they're basically starting from an assumption that, "Hey, our product is not bad as you think. Give it a chance and you'll really like it."

In a telling nod to the power of consumer-to-consumer influence, the Domino's pizza holdout ads feature regular folks, visited in their homes, dorms, or workplaces, trying the pizzas and declaring conversationally, "that's pretty good . . . that's very good."

That's not exactly a ringing endorsement, compared to the superlative advertising of yore.

But the message is clear. In a world where we consumers count on the opinions of regular folks just like us—and when amateur videos can torpedo product reputations that have taken decades to build—there's only one route to redemption: Go back to basics, build the best products, then humbly ask the crowd for its honest opinion.

Sumac Ridge Winery

Sumac Ridge Winery is one of the oldest estate wineries of Canada's British Columbia. The company has taken its long heritage and award-winning reputation onto the social-media scene, where it maintains an active Twitter feed @SumacRidgeWine and a Facebook fan page where they share news about winning wine prizes, invite enthusiasts into the winery to taste new vintages, and give advice on food pairings.

Alas, one of Sumac Ridge's ventures into social media was a textbook example of how *not* to do it.

One morning in October 2009, Vancouver passersby began noticing sad little posters, homemade and photocopied, reading: "LOST: My personal diary and my constant companion. It's a little collection of all my gems of wisdom from the past year."

The posters featured a hand-drawn sketch of a journal, and a note at the bottom asking anyone who found it to tweet its owner, David Wicken.

Hannah Stringer's heart sank when she saw the poster taped to a lamp-post on Commercial Drive. "I felt so bad for this guy because he said it's his personal journal," she said, "and I just envisioned people reading it out loud and mocking it. I thought: 'This poor guy!'"

All around downtown Vancouver, people spotted the posters. Then, days later, something amazing happened: Stringer, a nanny, was strolling with the two children she cares for, when she spotted something between a parking meter at 12th Avenue and Main Street. "I thought, 'There's no way this was the journal.' But I picked it up and realized: 'Oh! It is!'"

Her delight at the discovery soon turned to shock, then anger. Opening the journal, she realized it wasn't a person's diary at all—it was a piece of guerrilla marketing from Sumac Ridge. Despite its doodles, handwritten musings about life, and the appearance of taped-in clippings, it was an obviously mass-produced volume.

And 1,999 other copies of the "diary" were scattered about nearby downtown Vancouver streets, waiting to be found and exchanged for a $13.99 bottle of Sumac Ridge Gewürztraminer at a tweetup scheduled a couple days later.

The crowning indignity to those who tweeted David Wicken the good news that his precious journal was found? He isn't even a real person.

In a line vaguely reminiscent of "call me Ishmael," the ersatz David Wicken Twitter profile reads, "I'm a persona—call me David Wicken, assistant winemaker at Sumac Ridge."

But you can't see it today—the Twitter account has been disabled.

To me this story, vividly told by Simon Haupt in the *Vancouver Globe and Mail*,[16] highlights how the biggest asset of social media—its personal authenticity—will backfire every time on the business that is impersonal or downright fake.

Reflecting on the Sumac Ridge campaign, Todd Seiling, a Vancouverite specializing in social media, said he felt "double-punked": first to learn that the diary was a marketing ploy, and second when he learned that David Wicken wasn't even a real person.

"They're breaking one of the first rules of social-media marketing," said Seiling, "which is to be genuine."

"That's so uncool," says Stringer of the whole experience. She added she would go out of her way to avoid drinking Sumac Ridge wines in the future.

Skittles

Positioning the Skittles candy brand as hip, colorful, and quirky has been a big focus of parent company Wrigley's, and in terms of sales and name recognition, the campaigns have been working. Both offline and on, Skittles has done much to appeal to a young, tech-savvy, Web 2.0 audience.

But one creative move aimed squarely at the social Web fell flat on its face. It has become standard operating procedure to integrate one's Web site with one's social-network hubs—thus, we see home pages displaying a snippet of latest postings from a company's Facebook fan page and Twitter stream. We see "Add This" sharing and bookmarking widgets incorporated into the permanent navigation. We see Facebook, Twitter, YouTube, and other social-media logos adorning the footer of every page.

Skittles, however, took it up several notches in March of 2009 by giving over its home page to Flickr images, YouTube videos, and big, prominent, real-time Twitter posts, from any and all regular folks who mentioned the name Skittles in their message. Cool, and definitely engaging and new. The promotion did what it was intended to do: demonstrate how many folks were already talking about Skittles, but more importantly stimulating buzz and conversation by people who wanted to experience firsthand the novelty of typing something about Skittles and—cool!—seeing it appear as front-page news on the Skittles site.

Problem was, the system had no editorial control or governance, as pranksters soon discovered. The message "F**k Skittles!" scrolled across the candy-maker's home page. The creativity of the socialsphere is limitless; soon people came up with devastatingly inappropriate content that flashed boldly across the screen of Skittles.com. Posts talking about bizarre sex acts, pedophilia, drugs, Naziism, racism, homophobia, and more looked like an awful blow to the Skittles brand. Getting the raunchiest, meanest post onto the Skittles home page became a game of one-upsmanship. And while pranksters were having a ball with it, the Skittles brand was being bashed like a piñata.

Plus, in an example of the perpetual archive that has become the Web, these pranks didn't merely disappear the moment new (and hopefully cleaner) posts scrolled onto the screen. Instead, people screen-captured the messages and uploaded them to blogs, Flicker, and other permanent online homes. Google's search results for "Skittles screen grab" yields 30,000 hits.

While all companies that venture online dream of the viral success story, the exponential power of the social Web cuts both ways, and the Skittles dream of social-media coolness became a nightmare: Skittles was the number one trending term on Twitter. The story was picked up by media outlets worldwide, and soon Skittles became the talk of the Web and a significant slice of offline media—but for mostly the wrong reasons.

The company responded quickly, pulling off the social-dynamic content from its Web site and reverting to its previous look.

Ironically, Skittles has never been much of a Twitter user or community member—the @skittles account has a mere 3,000-or-so followers. That may have contributed to its failure to "get" the Twitter ethos or to interact with influential Twitter users as the problem started unfolding.

To its credit, Skittles managed to salvage a happy ending from this debacle. Far from being once burned, twice shy, the company has continued to be active on Facebook and YouTube. In fact, Skittles is the third-largest consumer product on Facebook, after Coca-Cola and Starbucks. Its amazing 10 million-plus Facebook fans were assembled, in part, by distributing free candy vouchers to them.

The Twitter-inspired buzz was good for Skittles in some measure:

• Visits to the Skittles Web site soared 1,332 percent, according to comScore and Alexa.

• Links from blogs and news sources boosted the search-engine credibility of Skittles.com, as well as its national brand awareness.

• Google searches for "Skittles" spiked.

• Facebook fans soared.

Of course, what really matters in the end is whether the efforts increased Skittles brand awareness and sales, and on that score the jury is still out.

The Skittles user-generated tweets fail occurred in part because Skittles was the first company to try it, and therefore the first to attract the massive attention of a trendsetter. Today, prominently displaying your own latest tweets and the hash-tagged tweets of your fans is becoming commonplace. On Indy 500 race day 2010, the Indianapolis Motor Speedway gave home page exposure to its own tweets and those of race fans, exhorting Web site visitors and Twitter followers, "Race Fans lets make #Indy500 the number one trending topic in the world today. You know what to do!"

The appeal of publicly sharing user tweets is still strong: it generates a sense of buzz and enthusiasm about your brand that is contagious, and it encourages tweets on your topic and visits to your Web site (to see it, scroll into view!). Meanwhile, the risk of being defaced with inappropriate content has declined and the negative impact has lessened. Companies are wiser now and can overlay basic filters and controls to weed out inappropriate content. More important, most pranksters have moved on—the novelty of such campaigns has worn off and the thrill of hacking them is gone.

TOP 10 SOCIAL-MEDIA MISTAKES

The previous section on fails and fiascos chronicles in detail some of the most egregious corporate social media screw-ups. But there are just *so many* ways for businesses to shoot their feet off with social media. Here are a few:

1. **The social-media ghost town**. Ninety-five percent of blogs are abandoned. Many never get a single post after their initial creation. While businesses are a bit more dogged than the average Joe, you'd be amazed how many company blogs, Facebook pages, and Twitter feeds are veritable ghost towns, unposted to, virtually memberless, dusty, and forlorn—testimony to nothing but the company's blind social-media "me tooism," its inability to stick to it, and the utter indifference of its audience. Eerie and so sad.

2. **The used-car salesman**. He may seem chummy and full of personality, but he isn't there to get to know you—he's there to sell you a set of wheels. Social media is no place for selling jobs or fake relationships. It's a chance to put a human face on your business, listen to customers, and establish sincere and helpful relationships with them.

3. **Phoning it in**. Okay, maybe you haven't *abandoned* your social-media accounts, but the thrill is gone—you started doing it as an experiment, and you never really found your voice. Social media is too easy to start and too hard for most firms to effectively carry on. It takes time, effort, creativity, and spark. You can't just sleepwalk through it.

4. **Subbing it out**. Everybody's pressed for time, but *don't* hire an outside agency, give them free rein for creative and execution, then take your eye off the ball. That approach guarantees you a program that may look flashy and cool, but is inevitably superficial, soulless, and unresponsive to the customers it hopes to reach. Worst of all is when a

Twitter stream is purportedly from your founder or CEO, but it is revealed to be the work of a hired consultant.

Far be it from me to disparage the use of outside firms to help execute your social-media program. My own company Timberline Interactive provides that service, and done well, it's a boon for a busy business. Specialty firms know the SM landscape, the technology platforms, and the reporting tools, and they've seen a variety of successful campaigns that can be nicely adapted to your special case. But whether you use an outside firm or do SM in house, the imperative is the same: Key strategic and creative people at your firm need to be involved in your program to invest it with authenticity and soul, and in the trenches, in-house CS and social-media staffers need to interact daily to establish the personal connections and resolve any questions or complaints.

5. **The dog ate my homework**. Posting publicly means everyone, *everyone* can see what you're saying, where you are, and what you're doing. Say you're a B2B service business or a real-estate agent. You cancel a client meeting or miss a deadline claiming an unexpected conflict (a key staffer is sick, the flight was cancelled). Meanwhile, your status post on Twitter reveals that you're hobnobbing with cocktails at a networking conference or just finished a great round of golf. Don't laugh—it is happening all over the business and personal worlds, and people of every stripe are getting increasingly good at checking the social networks and catching people in lies.

6. **That was PRIVATE!** With the syndication of status feeds, RSS, the automated connection between platforms, the friend-of-a-friend network effect, and the appearance of tweets and status updates in Google's public search results, don't say anything in blogs, social media (on your own pages or in comments on others), or even in e-mail that you wouldn't be comfortable seeing on the front page of *USA Today*. Whatever the public/private settings are of your various networks, it's just too easy to cut and paste, forward, Digg, retweet, and otherwise make public (and permanent) anything you type.

7. **Every voice from your company is THE voice of your company**. A burned-out CS person fires back a rude e-mail to a dissatisfied customer. A low-level staffer lets something slip and is quoted as a spokesperson. While you need to embrace the freewheeling and decentralized nature of communication on the Web, you also need to train staff on how to interact

with social media, monitor communications, and respond quickly to correct the misstatements of others or undo their harm.

8. **The celebrity crash and burn**. The best corporate social-media programs are those where the voice and image of the company are the voice and image of a real person—the colorful founder, the charismatic leader, or maybe even the pitchman or endorser. That's great as long as the face of your company is conducting himself or herself well. If your spokesperson is a gecko, say, you might be okay, but if the voice of your SM program is a flesh-and-blood person with all of their inherent flaws and foibles, be careful! Real people get in trouble for philandering, stupid public comments, fraud, greed, and stupidity. On a more mundane level, I have seen temperamental CEOs flame grumpy customers via e-mail only to have their dirty laundry aired for all the Web to see. These are worst cases, but even the modest scenario—the person leaves for a new company, as Scoble did—can mean big change to absorb.

9. **The malicious imposter**. I jumped at the scam IKEA offer of a $1,000 gift card. In the end I was mired in page after page of trial sign-up forms for X, Y, and Z. The bad taste it left in my mouth, even though I knew IKEA was a mere victim in this play, was an enduring one; it hurt my enthusiasm for Facebook come-ons across the board and subconsciously probably dimmed my enthusiasm for the IKEA brand.

10. **Expecting the wisdom of the crowd and getting the idiocy of the crowd**. A corollary to the Skittles fail above is that you must (to borrow the phrase from nuclear containment) "Trust in the wisdom of the crowd, but verify." When common citizens discovered the explosive combination of Mentos and Pepsi (or Pop Rocks and a martini), it was good for the popularity and sales of all the brands involved, and no harm was done. Likewise, when Cabana Boy rum gained popularity in the gay community for its hunky mascot, it may have been unexpected, but it was a happy accident. Not so, however, for the Republican Party's "Rebuild the Party" online call for policy suggestions. Among the embarrassments on the largely unmoderated board were such suggestions as "end child labor laws," "build a castle-style wall along the border, there is plenty of stone laying around about there," and "repeal all the amendments to the Constitution." You can bet Comedy Central got plenty of mileage out of that. Any time you maintain a blog, forum, or anywhere else people can post, you have to put structures in place. Hate

speech, fraud, and other unacceptable material will be submitted. Self-policing communities, where members can flag others as being abusive, are the best model for dealing with it.

LEARNING FROM THE FAILURES OF OTHERS

Skittles' response, and the positive perception the brand still enjoys, are a hopeful sign to any company contemplating its own social-media strategy. It would be easy for any businessperson to read this chapter of corporate social-media fails and ask, "If the gains of social media are so tricky to measure and impossible to predict, and if a screw-up like any of these could destroy years of brand equity, why do it?"

Indeed, why not play it safe and sit on the social-media sidelines, watching the bone-crushing hits and the occasional touchdowns from the safety of the bleachers?

Several reasons:

- These examples are the worst of the worst. They're cautionary examples, "perfect storms" of bad vision, bad luck, and usually botched corporate reaction. They're extremely unlikely to replay themselves with your business.

- In some cases, they represent not corporate social media done badly, but *corporate social media not done*. In examples like Domino's and Comcast, negative sentiments sprang up from the grassroots social media, and the companies hadn't established sufficiently strong, well-loved, and well-rooted reputation and voice of their own in the socialsphere. That's why it's so heartening to see how dramatically Comcast turned things around for itself when it started using social media to listen, communicate directly, and solve customers' problems.

- Social media is a proving ground. It's your organization's opportunity to demonstrate the culture and values of your company, to prove your ears are open and you "get it," to humanize your business, and to empower the customer-service people and brand ambassadors at the heart of your social-media program. A social-media blow-up doesn't have to be a public-relations disaster for your company.

You never get a second chance to make a good first impression. But the Skittles story shows us that you can and should act quickly and in a way that showcases the best aspects of your company and its people. While the social Web can be a hostile and bruising place to do business, it's also a fast-moving, fair-minded, and generally forgiving place. If your brand has durable values that people believe in, if you conduct your social-media program with sensitivity and a listener's ear, you will succeed. No doubt you'll hit a pothole or two, but the wheels won't fall off when you do.

Chapter 7

The Future

We've looked at the fast-growing social-media scene and how a business like yours can participate. Now, let's position you at the inside of the next curve. Instead of playing catch-up, let's turn our attention to the future of social media.

SOCIAL MEDIA IS DEAD

Before I wax too enthusiastic about the rosy future of social media, let's consider a possibility:

Social media is dead.

Social media is dead—or at least doomed—for the very same reason that has brought it to the attention of so many users, from Grandma and Grandpa to the businesspeople reading this book.

Like a horde of prospectors trampling and destroying gold-rush California, the many millions of Web users now dabbling in social media are having an impact on it. And some of those impacts could destroy it:

- What was once a purely social stream of posts has started to become polluted with unwanted commercial messages. (Since you've read this book and internalized its lessons, it won't be *your* company mucking up the social stream. But the pollution may happen nonetheless.)
- Spammers, hucksters, frauds, identity thieves, and other bad guys continue to move in, and the controls built in by the social platforms could prove unequal to the challenge.

- As more and more people join the social platforms, the tools (and social standards) for interconnecting become lighter and looser, and each person's network becomes larger and more weakly connected.

The Signal-to-Noise Ratio

Whatever the source—ads, spammers, or random and increasingly peripheral "friends"—the signal-to-noise ratio on social-media platforms has begun to suffer. The signal is the meaningful, emotional, informational, and entertaining input we expect from our online friends and connections. Maybe it's an uploaded album of Caribbean vacation pictures, or a colleague's updating of his job title on LinkedIn, or a timely blog post from a columnist you admire.

The noise, on the other hand, is all of the stuff you either don't care about, or worse—ads, scams, come-ons, and postings that irritate you, bore you, interrupt you, or try to deceive or defraud you.

When the signal-to-noise ratio is high, the user experience is good. Your generally pleasant interactions outweigh the occasional bad ones.

But when the signal-to-noise is low, the roar of static drowns out the music. Your forays onto the social networks become irritating and discouraging. You don't have the time to waste, anyhow. You visit less and less often until you give up altogether.

You Are So Unfollowed

Social-media fatigue can set in, for both ordinary users and uber-users like blogger extraordinaire Robert Scoble, who in 2009 caused a stir by unfollowing everyone—all 106,000 of his Twitter follows—and starting fresh. His motivation was twofold: it was humanly impossible for him to read the tweets of 100,000 people, and he was being deluged by spam posts from what he concluded to be Twitter bots. "When I unfollowed everyone, all my spam just stopped. Dead. No more spam," he wrote later on his blog.

Tech entrepreneur Jason Calacanis, making a crusade against Facebook's privacy stances, publicly deleted his account on TV. "Quit Facebook Day," an international campaign to do just that, mustered just 34,000 account deletions. That's no groundswell, but it's worth noting.

A clever Web site application called Seppukoo allowed Facebook users to elaborately kill off their Facebook identity in the style of Japanese ritual suicide. Seppukoo attracted worldwide coverage in *Figaro, The Globe and*

Mail, L'Express, and the *Los Angeles Times*. But Facebook was not amused: It blocked access to the site from Seppukoo's servers and fired off a cease-and-desist letter accusing Seppukoo of illegal screen-scraping, violating its terms and conditions, and more.

A similar tug-of-war ensued between Facebook and another company, Web 2.0 Suicide Machine.

But dramatic suicides, desertions, and mass unfollows are not the gravest threat to social media. The real enemy of social media is plain fatigue—having hundreds of millions of members shrug their shoulders and move on to the next big thing.

Remember, too, that yesterday's social-media success stories are today's footnotes. When was the last time anybody mentioned Friendster? How much time are you spending in Second Life nowadays?

We have only a limited amount of time in our days; though it seems as if multitasking can expand our diversions indefinitely, there is a real limit to how many online services we can participate in, in-depth and for a significant time. YouTube has stolen hours from television, and Pandora has stolen market share from your local radio station. Social-media sites steal market share from one another and from your real-world social life. "Second Life?" you might ask, "I don't even have enough time for my first life!"

Indeed, in some real-life cases, online role-playing games have absorbed so many hours of their devotees' lives that marriages have ended in divorce, and jobs and homes have been lost. Can we afford to invest more of our busy lives in what might be just a fleeting diversion?

Today we consume three times as much media as we did in 1960. New research shows that the average computer user changes windows, changes applications, and opens messages 37 times an hour.

Some neuroscientists have added to the hand-wringing by suggesting that our compulsive, 24/7 multitasking with computers and cell phones, our ceaseless consumption of e-mails, IMs, and text messages, is rewiring our brains—and not all for the better.

Clifford Nass, a communications professor and an expert in human-computer interaction at Stanford, suggests that obsessive attention to technology, including online social media, can isolate us from real-world family and friends. "The way we become more human is by paying attention to each other," he says. But, he warns, "We are at an inflection point. A significant fraction of people's experiences are now fragmented."[1]

So it seems clear that while social media still enjoys plenty of buzz and rapid-fire growth, some strains are beginning to appear.

Networks Too Big for Their Own Good

Talking about the increasing size but diminishing quality of business networks, Jon Picoult observes in the *New York Times*, "As the definition of people's 'networks' has expanded to include not just colleagues they've known for a decade, but also practically everyone they pass on the street, the quality of those connections has been greatly diluted. What rational conclusions can companies draw from this relationship game?"[2]

Beyond Dunbar's Number, a group really ceases to be an effective interpersonal network. Larger groups require more restrictive rules, laws, and enforced norms to function. Yes, technology may be able to expand our effective networks somewhat. I keep my LinkedIn network tightly focused on businesspeople I know, mostly within my industry, and that network is larger than 150 people. My wife Elizabeth and I send out slightly more than 150 holiday cards each December (or, sometimes, January).

But our networks cannot expand indefinitely without hurting the quality of their connections. As our friend networks grow and bloat, we may find it impossible to compose messages that feel right and relevant to everyone. The status feeds of our countless "friends" scrolling by may become disjointed and unfamiliar.

Have a Little Faith

Now that I've laid out the risks and problems, let me say that I sincerely doubt that social media will crumble under its own weight. It's no passing fad—too many applications are building social aspects into their projects from the ground up. Too many millions of Web users expect social interactions, recommendations, user-generated content, and other social-media innovations to be part of their online life.

New technologies and filters are being invented every day to improve the social-media experience and make it more intuitive and effortless.

Social media helps us make sense of the Web. It makes our online lives richer, more personal, and more satisfying.

Nor will Dunbar's Number write the epitaph of social media's growth. We don't depend on our Twitter followers to help us hunt a mastodon. We don't rely on our LinkedIn network for a barn raising or our Facebook friends for a quilting bee. Web 2.0 social networks are a hybrid: They take some of the best elements of human social life, transplant them to the Internet, extend them, and change them.

Online community may not mean precisely the same thing as community in its pre-Internet sense. But it's clear that online community is a real thing, a powerful thing, and it's here to stay.

THE GAP SCENARIO

John Battelle is one of the Web's intellectual and business leaders. A founder of *Wired* magazine, *The Industry Standard*, and Federated Media, Battelle wrote the best-selling book *The Search: How Google and Its Rivals Rewrote the Rules of Business and Transformed Our Culture*. He is a popular blogger who has invested much thought about what the future convergence of search, mobile, and social will look like.

He describes what he calls the Gap scenario[3] to highlight the intersection of physical and digital spaces in the world of commerce. It's a double entendre: When Battelle uses the clothing store the Gap as his example, he says, "I'm also talking about the 'gap' between where we are as an industry, and where we are headed."

Imagine you walk into a bricks-and-mortar Gap store. You'll have your smartphone, and because you've installed a mobile app that interacts with the environment around you, the moment you cross the Gap's threshold, your phone buzzes.

Battelle pictures the Gap's mobile app of the not-too-distant future messaging you personally, guided by its awareness of your purchase history, preferences, and social network. "The Gap app will welcome you into the store, and perhaps ask if you are enjoying the jeans you purchased at the downtown store last month," writes Battelle. "It also shows that four of your friends have recently been in the store lately, and another three have purchased something online. Would you like to see what they bought?"

You might also be alerted of a special 15 percent off discount "for folks like you, who have 'liked' Gap on Facebook."

You stroll over to a blouse, hold your phone up to it, and focus the camera on the tag. The Gap app immediately scans the tag to display everything you'd want to know about the item: name, price, available inventory in-store and online, customer reviews, related items, and a map function to guide you to those items in the store.

Meanwhile, when you walked through the front door, you were immediately and personally identified as a returning customer: "All the data about your interaction with Gap, as well as any other related data that you have agreed can be publicly known about you, has already been sent to the store, and to the mobile devices of every Gap associate working in the store today."

He pictures a Gap associate who smiles, checks her phone (which lights up with your profile), and says hello. But what does she say next? She knows who you are, what products you've been browsing, what you've bought in the past, and how often you visit. Does she speak to you naturally and with empathy—or is the interaction creepy and corporate?

Battelle is mindful of how wrong it could feel to have this kind of data in the palm of the wrong sort of employee. But he gives his scenario a happy ending: "This day, you've come to your favorite store, where the employees are fluent in the dance between social data, commercial intent, and real-time physical interaction. Your associate simply nods and says 'let me know if I can help you,' smiles, and lets you pass."

You find your favorite jeans, but don't want to dig through the piles to find your size. Instead you point your phone at the stack, and the Gap app tells you the store, alas, is out of size 34. Would you like to purchase them online and have them sent to your home? They'll be there later today, because a store across town has them in stock, and Gap provides same day delivery within a 50-mile radius. You press "Yes," the purchase is confirmed, and, your retail desires fulfilled, you head toward the door.

As you leave, the associate you passed earlier thanks you for your purchase.

What I like about Battelle's Gap scenario is how many pieces need to work in concert: mobile phone app, social-network integration, and the interplay between bricks-and-mortar and the Web store. Yet it is probably not the technology that will be the trickiest piece of the puzzle. It's the new social understanding that will be hardest to pull off gracefully—how comfortable we are with store employees knowing our identity and following, however discreetly, our movements. As consumers, we'll be willing to surrender our privacy as long as it's handled respectfully, and we gain something valuable in return: convenience, efficiency, a "preferred customer" discount, and a more fun and satisfying shopping experience.

SOCIAL SHOPPING

Social shopping puts the reviews, recommendations, and purchase histories of fellow shoppers front-and-center in the online shopping experience. Case studies have amply demonstrated that consumers trust the advice of customers like them, above all else.

Several specialty e-commerce sites have arisen to marry social networking and shopping. These Web sites cater principally to those members of our species who most like to make shopping a social experience—that is to say, fashion-conscious women. Here are some of the best:

- **Etsy**: Specializing in handmade items, Etsy supports its community of artists and craftspeople with chat, forums, blog, Facebook, Twitter, Myspace, Flickr, YouTube, even Meetups.
- **I Like Totally Love It**: Formatted like a Digg bookmarking service for social shoppers, this site covers fashion, green products, pets, food, furniture, and much more. Features include tag clouds and sharing across Twitter and Facebook.
- **Kaboodle**: "Your guide to the Web's best products hand-selected by shoppers like you." Kaboodle is strong on fashion but also covers other product categories, including housewares, furniture, and cosmetics.
- **MyItThings**: A fashion-forward online magazine driven by a social community that shares favorite fashions, as well as books, music, and movies.
- **ProductWiki**: A bit like a wiki-built *Consumer Reports*, this site offers price comparisons, user reviews, and pro and con lists.
- **ShopStyle**: Social shopping focused on designer fashions, it features "looks" assembled by members, stylebooks, and favorites.
- **Woot**: Pioneered the concept of selling just one product a day. These "woot-offs" generate fun and a sense of urgency as the community gives feedback on the item and competes for the limited quantity. Woot was recently acquired by Amazon.
- **Zebo**: Social shopping powered by chats with other social shoppers, product tips, surveys, and more.

If your company sells products online—especially if your target market is mostly women—social-shopping sites should be part of your plan. But no matter what market you serve, male or female, young or old, B2C or B2B, customer-generated reviews and ratings are all-important. Any Web site can now be integrated with review engines like PowerReviews or Bazaarvoice.

More and more, online shoppers will ignore the marketing messages and descriptive copy written by retailers. Instead, they will gravitate to and be guided by the reviews and advice of shoppers like themselves.

Yelp!, the people-powered restaurant-review site, offers social-networking tools for reviewers to establish profiles and build friend networks. The site recently hooked up with the restaurant-reservation system OpenTable so that Yelp visitors can make a reservation without leaving the site. And Yelp's mobile app puts all that power into the palms of its users' hands.

"Social is clearly having a big impact on commerce," said Sameer Samat of Google Product Search in his presentation at the 2010 Social Commerce Summit. "We would like to work with retailers and manufacturers and surface [their product reviews] for users in a number of different ways, in search, in advertising, and mobile."[4]

Increasingly, we'll see this same fusion of social, mobile, and commerce. Netflix and Amazon have continued to build more social interlinking into their "recommendation engines"—the "People who liked X also liked Y." While those features have always been powerful in e-commerce, it's clear that in our increasingly social Web 2.0 world, it's not enough to know the preferences of faceless, monolithic "other people." We want to know the recommendations and preferences of people like us, and of friends and family—real people whose judgment we know and respect.

Netflix, for instance, weights the star rating it displays when you browse movies, based on the ratings of users most like you. If you favor romantic comedies or French art films, you don't want to give too much credence to the opinions of an action-movie nut.

Far from keeping it a "secret sauce," Netflix went public with its quest for an algorithm that would improve the predictive powers of its Cinematch algorithm. "The Netflix Prize," said the company, "sought to substantially improve the accuracy of predictions about how much someone is going to enjoy a movie based on their movie preferences."

On September 21, 2009, Netflix awarded the $1 million grand prize to a team named BellKor's Pragmatic Chaos. It's rather cool that an algorithm that harnesses the tastes of a large network of movie-watchers was developed through crowdsourcing.

"We strongly believe this has been a big winner for Netflix," CEO Reed Hastings told the *New York Times*. "You look at the cumulative hours, and you're getting PhD's for a dollar an hour."

Sadly, we'll not see a sequel of Netflix's innovative approach to bettering its Cinematch algorithm. Although they announced Netflix Prize 2 almost immediately after dishing out the first $1 million, the company had to call it off in the face of an FTC investigation. It seems having outside parties tinkering with the reviews and ratings of a few million people raised the eyebrows of privacy advocates.

Such are the challenges we'll continue to see in social media. While privacy advocates will continue raising objections and influencing the process, social sites will keep pushing the envelope—making their sites more social, more automatically personalized, better able to predict the tastes and wants of each user, and capable of sharing more stuff with more people on more networks and more devices.

AUGMENTED REALITY

The cellular, satellite, and Internet networks have essentially become one massive, global Web. Through mobile phones, PCs, laptops, iPads, PDAs, and other devices, the network is always on and accessible. GPS and IP location constantly broadcasts your whereabouts back to the Web, making possible new levels of locally specific search results, ads, and other information.

More and more, this Web will be personalized—it will know who you are and it will know your social graph: who your friends are, and, thanks to their status feeds shared across open social standards, where they are and what they are doing. Because we grant special attention to the opinions, tastes, and other signals sent by our peers, our experience of the Web, and of the mobile network, will bear all sorts of opinions, ratings, and reviews from our friends, family, and extended network.

Virtually any data can be stored in our smartphones, uploaded to the cloud and effortlessly downloaded, or exchanged with a "bump" to the phone of a friend. In this manner, people who are physically connected, in time and place, can effortlessly join each other's online network, or exchange other digital trappings of their relationship: their contact info, recent photos, and calendars.

Already, the PayPal mobile app lets users transfer money simply by bumping their phones. So in the future, expect to perform your banking by bumping at the ATM, and to buy gas by bumping the pump.

iPhone and Droid apps already mash up social-media data, search data, and GPS location, to let you, for instance, scan your phone 360 degrees and find all of your friends within a range of, for example, a busy convention hall, a New Year's Eve party, or a ski slope.

Though the phone seems to be the killer device for combining all this power and portability, scientists and inventors the world over are coming up with new, more natural, and more intuitive input-output devices. Eventually, the keyboard, mouse, and computer screen will be as outmoded as vacuum tubes. Voice-activated, touch screen, and motion-sensing devices (like the Wii controller) will be our connections to the Web, and the Web will respond to our natural speech and gestures. Experimenters using specially designed helmets have shown that mere *thoughts* can drive a 3-D avatar across a virtual world.

And as our interactions with the Web become more effortless and natural, it will move off the desk and onto our streets, landscapes, cars, and homes. Our "screens" may include augmented glasses, visors, or even helmets, which will show us the world around us as augmented reality—where everything we see will be linked to layers of additional data, much of it social.

Imagine walking down your main street with your augmented reality shades. As you pass stores, their names, products, prices, and perhaps a one-day sale scroll transparently across the lenses. You pass a restaurant and access its menu and daily special; maybe your specs interface with your phone so you can call and get a table. All along, the real stores and sights are augmented by the comments, favorites, ratings, and recommendations made by others—strangers and friends within your circle.

On its Web site http://www.virtualvacay.com, Hotels.com debuted a cool interactive tool it describes as "augmented reality adventures" of several destination cities. The site interfaces either with your smartphone or your Webcam to generate 3-D animated cityscapes you can hold in your hands, move, interact with, and onto which your own image, name, voice, and other customizations can be applied.

The Virtual Vacay site allows you to experience New York, Chicago, Boston, San Francisco, and several other U.S. cities in the palm of your hands. Users interact with the simulated city via cam and microphone, and can follow the guidance of a personal tour guide. Hotels.com feeds local events information and other live data, and you can create your own personalized postcards and e-mail them to your friends.

Layar, an app available for Android phones and iPhones, bills itself as an "augmented reality browser." With AR, you can point your phone at a business, and up pop balloons with Yelp reviews, Wikipedia entries, and Twitter posts concerning whatever you're looking at with the phone's camera. Here are a few of the early adopters of Layar:

- **Berlitz City Guides**: Experience a city's highlights, attractions, restaurants, hotels, coolest places to shop, and best nightlife via augmented reality.
- **"Mouse Reality" for Disney World and Disneyland**: Helps find and navigate all attractions, shows, shops, dining, transportation, and more at Disneyland and Disney World.

- **EyeTour**: Explore Puerto Rico's natural beauty and cultural heritage through exclusive video content when you point your phone at historical sites, museums, restaurants, parks, and more.

- **UK Home Prices**: Interface with "Sold House Price Data 2010" as recorded by the Land Registry—so you can see what that London flat or Lakes District manor house sold for while you're on the move.

Augmented reality is an exciting fusion of your smartphone, the Web, social-media elements, and the physical world around you. It quickly and profoundly answers the question: "What's this place, who else has been here, and what did they think of it?"

BOWLING ALONE? OR WII-BOWLING WITH FRIENDS

In his book *Bowling Alone: The Collapse and Revival of American Community*, the Harvard sociologist Robert Putnam carefully tracked and quantified the declines of American social connectedness on several fronts, including plunges in volunteerism, public-school funding, civic-mindedness, and, of course, bowling leagues.

These trends generally began in the 1960s, and they're so pervasive that Putnam looked almost in vain for a "smoking gun" that could have caused them. His most likely suspect, he concluded, was television. The invention of television, and its soaring use (to eclipse even dinner with family), was said by Putnam to be the factor most clearly correlated to falling community involvement.

At the time he wrote the book, 2000, social media, widespread global connectedness to the Web, and video games were all just beginning to make their mark on our society, so their impact he could only speculate upon. He was not optimistic that the Web would do anything to reverse the trends he had identified, and expressed concern it could worsen them. He issued this call: "Let us find new ways to ensure that by 2010 Americans will spend less leisure time sitting passively alone in front of glowing screens and more time in active connection with our fellow citizens. Let us foster new forms of electronic entertainment and communication that reinforce community engagement rather than forestalling it."[5]

I love Putnam's book. I read it with admiration for his intelligence, and I share his anxiety over the decline in American community involvement. But with more data (albeit anecdotal), it seems we can allay some of

Putnam's worries about the impact of the Web and mobile technology on our social fabric.

It's quite clear now that the world is not necessarily becoming less social—it is becoming social in a far different way than we've ever seen in history. Not since telephones enabled long-distance conversations have as many people, as far-flung across the globe, been suddenly put into reach of one another.

Perhaps the handiest metaphor to answer the notion of *Bowling Alone* is the unexpected appeal that the video game Wii bowling has not just for the stereotypical couch potatoes, but to all sorts of people—including, notably, senior citizens who get healthy stimulation and therapy from the physical exercise of swinging the Wii controller.

Not only have bowling and other Wii games caught on with the blue-haired set, at least on a few occasions high-schoolers have challenged the senior citizens, such as the showdown (and rematch) between St. Petersburg, Florida, high schoolers and the PBT Mighty Bombers Wii bowling team from Philip Benjamin Tower, a retirement community in St. Petersburg, Florida.[6] It's hard to imagine a better example of how technology can unite unlikely partners into the same community.

Casual status-posting and effortless "liking" of causes doesn't do much for our community health. But many community organizers, fundraisers, meetups, and tweetups are using social media to rally the troops, raise money, get out the vote, or just get together for a bike ride, play date, or cup of coffee. Online social media isn't normally an end in itself, and many of its effects are salutary for our neighborhoods, communities, and nations.

On the global stage, Iranian protesters grabbed the world's attention through their Twitter posts. Ethnic violence in Kenya in 2008 sparked the invention of Ushahidi, a Web platform that lets anyone post data via SMS, e-mail, or Web to be visualized on a map or time line. It has been used to collect and pinpoint reports of humanitarian abuses, to aid victims of natural disasters, and to collect news reports that might otherwise be stifled by hostile authorities, communication breakdowns, or both.

For every withdrawn and isolated gamer, there's someone whose connections to other players in a massively multiplayer online game (MMOG) led to a real-life friendship—or even a marriage. And speaking of marriage, how many thousands of people have now met in a chat room or online dating site and gone on to be happily married?

It seems safe to say that far from doing it harm, online media has injected new health and energy into our sense of community.

A WORLD WIDE WEB OF FRIENDS

As ever in popular culture, social-media trends and tastes are set by the young. Over the past several years, social-media platforms were adopted first by high school and college-age kids, and their appeal then spread to their elders and also to ever-younger kids.

Gen-Xers and older generations tend to value the *selectivity* of today's online networking tools, the ability to manage a social network consisting of friends, family, colleagues, and known contacts—and keeping the strangers, spammers, and scammers outside the walls.

But a whole new paradigm for online socializing has arisen, an open social Web where strangers interact freely and sometimes quite intimately. It's not just younger generations who now use the Web to meet strangers, on dating sites, and in multiplayer online games like Second Life, Mafia Wars, World of Warcraft, and others.

The notion of meeting random strangers has been taken to new highs (or lows?) with online text and video chat tools. The leading one, the aptly named ChatRoulette, pairs users with randomly selected chat partners worldwide, face-to-face on Webcams. Andrey Ternovskiy, a 17-year-old high schooler in Moscow, coded ChatRoulette in two days and nights and came up with the name for his creation after watching the roulette scenes in *The Deer Hunter*.

"Nothing can really prepare you for the latest online phenomenon, Chat-Roulette," wrote Nick Biltin in the *New York Times*, which "drops you into an unnerving world where you are connected through Webcams to a random, fathomless succession of strangers from across the globe."[7] And that random succession can include naked guys dancing in Denmark, a guy in a leopard suit, Chinese schoolgirls, skinheads, Spiderman, Darth Vader—and the real Paris Hilton.

ChatRoulette hardly has the market to itself. Similar tools include Omegle, RandomDorm, ShufflePeople, TinyChat Next, 6 Rounds, Anybody Out There, and Camstumble.

Random video chat with strangers may be merely a fad, or it may signal a lasting shift in how open-ended our approach to others online will be. How does this trend apply to businesses participating in social media? My guess is that especially those companies targeting a younger audience, or edgier market, may need to embrace the odd thrill of these new and random social tools. After all, the appeal of socializing online is not necessarily in replicating all the characteristics of your offline social life. Companies wanting to generate real buzz in social media may have to take some risks, push the envelope, and associate themselves with the wilder aspects of the social-media landscape.

GOING MOBILE—AND BRIDGING THE ONLINE-OFFLINE DIVIDE

Mark Mosiniak of Best Buy points out that today, while smartphone visits to their Web sites make up only about 3 percent of all visits, these mobile customers are 25 percent likelier to convert to buyers. "You *have* to engage in mobile. It doesn't really matter where you start—with apps, with a mobile Web site. It's just really important to engage with the mobile channel. Anyone who doesn't start now in mobile is going to find things very difficult in the next three years."[8]

Speaking of the role your own employees can now play in social media on your behalf, Mosiniak urges, "Unleash the power of your people." Best Buy's Home Twelp Force, tweeting and responding to people's electronics-related posts, involves literally hundreds of Best Buy employees with tens of thousands of followers. Because of Twitter's "light weight," Mosiniak says Twelpforce is especially appealing to consumers using smartphones.

Mobile is more than a technology platform—it is, of course, a communications platform. And new developments for data input (2-D bar code scanning, video, and still photography) and interchange (bumping) mobile devices are inherently social. And the social platforms are all jumping into the mobile market. Facebook, Twitter, LinkedIn, YouTube, MySpace, and others all have well-evolved mobile apps and mobile Web sites.

The smartphone is the nexus of our more social, tech-augmented future. A portable device that is connected 24/7 to the Web, its scanning and video capture acting as your digital "eyes" and zapping the physical world—be it bar codes, facial recognition, or video search—and translating that into data. The data then can receive an instant overlay of GPS, Web-based, and social information connected to everything around you, everything your phone sees or bumps or approaches.

Mosiniak of Best Buy sees this as the number one trend of our technology future. Speaking of his company's use of 2-D barcodes and SMS messaging, he says, "On the tag it says 'text this product number' to SPECIFY a number and when they do that on any phone, they'll get customer reviews for that product."

"You have to be transparent. Taking all that online information and making it available in the offline world is a very big trend."

MOBILE PLUS SOCIAL

Earlier we talked about Foursquare, the mobile app you can use to find and review nearby businesses and see what your social network thinks of them. Chad Capellman of Genuine Interactive describes how a local business owner—in this case a doctor's office—can gain advantage by harnessing these new technologies:

"Services like Foursquare are still in their infancy. However, maintaining a presence on these new social platforms can provide a powerful, if subtle, marketing message: You're the type of doctor who 'gets it,' who is open to new approaches and who will be among the first to know about new treatments and new technologies. It's hard to think of a better message to convey about your practice."[9]

Foursquare has generated lots of buzz and has really given us the clearest look at what a future of socially enabled, local business search engines will look like. More and more, our phones—and their socially informed, geographically specific applications—will be the filter through which we view our world.

PROTOTYPING THE REAL WORLD—IN THE VIRTUAL WORLD

In 2009, Linden Lab, creator of the online game Second Life, launched its Linden Prize to recognize an "innovative in-world project that improves the way people work, learn, and communicate in their daily lives outside of the virtual world. This annual award is intended to align with Linden Lab's company mission, which is to connect all people to an online world that advances the human condition."

Chosen from among 130 nominations and 10 finalists worldwide, the winner was San Jose-based "The Tech Virtual" museum. The winner was awarded $10,000—and we are talking good, old-fashioned greenbacks here, not Linden dollars!

Tech Virtual has real-world impacts for modeling and prototyping ambitious projects in the physical world. It went live in late 2007 with a mission to bring faster, more collaborative exhibit development to museums worldwide using an online platform. Typically, says Tech Virtual, museum professionals in the field develop content alone or in small isolated teams. With immersive 3-D modeling environments, museum planners worldwide can collaborate on exhibit design and prototyping.

The technology also makes it possible for individual museumgoers to contribute to museum displays in what Tech Virtual calls "participatory exhibit design."

Kicking off the project on International Museums Day on May 18, 2009, Tech Virtual ran a 45-day program of online screen-share trainings for more than 100 museum and educational professionals. A number of museums across the globe then utilized Second Life to prototype future exhibits. Citilab Cornella in Barcelona designed an exhibit called Expolab, while Science Centre Singapore used the virtual modeling tool to develop an interactive exhibit on the properties and facets of water.

In March 2010, the Smithsonian's Lemelsen Center at the National Museum of American History used Tech Virtual to prototype an upcoming exhibit called Places of Invention.

"We are conducting a grand experiment in open-sourcing the museum content development process, and these virtual exhibits exemplify the collaborative spirit we are striving for," said Peter Friess, president of The Tech. "I look forward to seeing more exhibits come to life in Second Life and make their way into 'First Life,' as curators, artists, and exhibit builders from around the world sign on to this exciting project."

Crowdsourcing is not a new story. Famous Web collaborations include Wikipedia, by far the world's biggest and most speedily updated encyclopedia, and the open-source software phenomenon that gave us Linux, Apache, Drupal, Joomla, etc. Developers have been using wiki Web sites to support invention, testing, refinement, and expansion of complex projects since 1994, when Ward Cunningham created the Web-based collaboration platform he dubbed WikiWikiWeb. *Wiki*, which means "quick" in Hawaiian, is an apt name for the system that supports fast, collective projects by a distributed workforce across the entire World Wide Web.

These companies and projects have a deep and positive footprint in collaboration, education, and social progress for the bricks-and-mortar world in which we (mostly!) live. We can expect to see more projects using social wiki-style organizing principles, crowdsourcing from across the entire planet.

No, the welding of autobody panels is not a likely candidate for a virtual workforce. But an increasingly large portion of the work of producing any product is not in manufacturing, but in conception, design, market research, customer testing, and feedback. Manufacturers no longer must assemble, in one physical location, all of the "knowledge workers" required for these stages of product development. It's hard to imagine any product that wouldn't benefit from online crowdsourcing at these steps in its development. In the relatively near future, products will be conceived, designed, prototyped, and tested using wiki strategies and virtual-worlds tools before the first mold is ever made.

YOUR VERY OWN, PERSONAL WEB

Facebook's Marc Zuckerberg has been a lightning rod of privacy advocates for his company's continually pushing the envelope of privacy concerns and automatic personalization. He has a lot of detractors, a huge surplus of attitude, and all the delicacy of a powder keg. But he may just be right.

Zuckerberg's vision, and that of all major pioneers and visionaries in the social-media space, is of a universal "social graph" that travels with a user as she browses the Web or uses her mobile device.

"I don't know if we always get it right," Zuckerberg says about his site's more controversial features. "But my prediction will be that a few years from now, we'll look back and wonder why there was ever this time when all these Web sites and applications . . . weren't personalized in some way."[10]

When Facebook's Beacon feature reported our purchases on Zappos or Overstock, our rentals on Blockbuster, ticket buys on Fandango, and travel on Travelocity, many of us cried foul, and Facebook abandoned the program. When "instant personalization" on Yelp and Pandora started broadcasting our music tastes or our restaurant reviews to our Facebook network and the wider world, we complained again, and Facebook scrambled to put clear opt-in controls in place so we wouldn't unwittingly share our data with third-party sites.

But make no mistake: The online world is changing, in the direction of more integration and less privacy. In many respects, this represents a much better Internet: Why should I have to remember scads of different passwords, each with their different requirements, as I move from one site to another? Why should I fish for my credit card before buying from my favorite Web sites? Why do I have to rely on a different set of trusted friends in Netflix than I do on Yelp or Pandora?

The future of the Web and mobile is in universal online identities. One username and password, personalization driven by cookies and geo-location, and our social circle accessible everywhere we go—seeing our status, answering our questions, and recommending items when we shop. As we've discovered in the past few years, most everything on the Web is better when it's more social. It sparks more conversation, it draws on more collective wisdom, and it spreads farther and faster. Eventually, every Web site will have the social graph built into its fabric.

This won't happen all at once, and it'll never be completely seamless. After all, Facebook has plenty of incentive to make the Web a more personalized place as long as it's the proprietary Facebook "social graph" that drives the whole machine. But don't expect LinkedIn, Twitter, Facebook, YouTube, or the other big players to throw away their proprietary networks in favor of OpenSocial. Nor should they—all of these individual networks have good reason to be separate because in some real ways they represent different personas of ourselves. The business me that lives in LinkedIn doesn't resemble the Facebook me all that much. Even sharing status posts across Twitter, Facebook, and LinkedIn shows you the limitations of this approach and the need, sometimes, to speak to a particular audience using a particular voice.

But if you have any doubts about a more integrated Web, where everything is connected and everything is social, take a look at how much integrated app development, worldwide and across both the Internet and mobile, is being done for Facebook right now:

- More than one million developers and entrepreneurs from more than 180 countries.
- Every month, more than 70 percent of Facebook users engage with platform applications.
- More than 550,000 active applications currently on Facebook.
- More than 250,000 Web sites have integrated with Facebook.
- More than 100 million Facebook users engage with Facebook on external Web sites every month.
- 67 percent of comScore's U.S. Top 100 Web sites and half of comScore's Global Top 100 Web sites have integrated with Facebook.
- More than 100 million users currently access Facebook through mobile devices.
- People who use Facebook on mobile devices are twice as active as non-mobile users.
- More than 200 mobile operators in 60 countries are working to deploy Facebook mobile products.

THE HOME PAGE, WEB 2.0 STYLE

What's the home page for your Web browser? If you're like most people, it's Google or Bing. Years of Internet use have shown that the quickest and most versatile entry point into the Web is a search engine. People use it not just to search for the unknown, but increasingly they use it to navigate back to familiar sites, rather than typing URLs or selecting bookmarks.

But is the search engine the home page of the future? I don't think so. While search will always be a vital tool on the dashboard of any Web site or Web-enabled gadget, I don't think the Web of the future will be so oriented to finding new stuff. I believe instead it will be about summoning to one place all the people, news, and entertainments we care about. The Web—our own personal Web—will come to us.

This is different than the traditional view of a Web "portal." Portals are an increasingly quaint notion, and the fortunes of AOL, MSN, and Yahoo! (the only two major portals left standing) prove it. The idea all along was that portals could be useful entry points into the Web, aggregating relevant news, entertainment, weather, and other information and links. Portals have made many strides through the years by adding personalized contents, applying a single login to a broad family of sites and services, and adding social networking. The social graph could turn out to be the single, unifying "glue" that makes a browser home page truly your online home— and your bridge between the online and the bricks and-mortar world.

CORPORATE RESPONSIBILITY

Companies have already learned from the black eyes suffered by Toyota, for instance, which was too slow to respond to its auto-safety problems and allowed a significant but not unprecedented customer-service challenge to spiral out of control. It became an international news story, a smudge on a previously stellar brand image. Toyota went from being the most admired and successful brand in automaking to a tailspin in a matter of months.

Companies will know better next time. While the Toyota debacle was not solely a Web phenomenon, its pace of development as a news story and a topic of consumer conversations would never have been as fast and as thorough in the pre-Internet era—or even just a handful of years ago, in the pre-social media era of the Web.

As a result, businesses and organizations now know they need to respond immediately, constantly, consistently, and honestly, and be part of the conversation as it evolves—at the pace of Internet time, and in all the places (the blogosphere and social networks as well as traditional media) where people are talking.

Increasingly, companies will keep a constant ear to the Web, to the feedback of ordinary users and their chatter on Twitter and elsewhere. The social Web will be every company's instant feedback loop, and firms will have to develop the fleetness and agility to respond to it. It's already happening. In June 2010, for instance, Google experimented with letting users personalize Google's famously spare home page with a bright background image from one of several award-winning artists and photographers (a la Bing). But many Google users were shocked by the new look, and also mistakenly thought it was not an optional setting but a permanent design change. Google responded almost instantly, scuttling what had been a longer planned test, and issuing an explanation from Marissa Mayer, vice president of search products and user experience, on the Google blog. "Many people thought we had permanently changed our home page, so we decided to stop today's series early," said Mayer. "We appreciate your feedback and patience as we experiment and iterate."

THE WEB OF THINGS AND THE WEB OF PEOPLE

Mike Laurie is a digital strategist, designer, and user-experience pro at the London agency Made by Many. A frequent contributor to the Web 2.0 blog Mashable, Mike has worked on projects for BlackBerry, Nestle, Sky, and Cancer Research. He sees the future of social media as pervasive, simple, and greatly aided by small and inexpensive devices like RFID tags, GPS transponders, and other technologies.

"In 2019, when you look back at the social media landscape 10 years earlier, you might laugh at how hard you had to work," says Laurie, "You had to type things into forms (ha! remember those?), type URLs in the address bar (how archaic!), and put up with irritating communications about irrelevant products. Social media in the future will be effortless and everywhere."[11]

Arduino

Arduino is an open-source electronics prototyping platform based on flexible, easy-to-use hardware and software. It's intended for artists, designers, hobbyists, and anyone interested in creating interactive objects or environments.

Arduino can sense the environment by receiving input from a variety of sensors and can affect its surroundings by controlling lights, motors, and other actuators. The microcontroller on the board is programmed using the Arduino programming language. Arduino projects can be stand-alone or they can communicate with software running on a computer.

The Arduino team of Massimo Banzi, David Cuartielles, Tom Igoe, Gianluca Martino, and David Mellis were glowingly profiled in *Wired* magazine, and their product won honorary mention in the Digital Communities section of the 2006 Ars Electronica Prix.

As Laurie puts it: "Arduino is a small circuit board commonly used to prototype electronics. Its low cost and ease of implementation has meant that this little device is now leading a hobbyist revolution in connecting real-life objects to social networks, like Twitter. It has allowed one man to create a device attached to a chair that tweets at the presence of noxious natural gasses (ahem), another uses Arduino to monitor when his cats are inside the house or out, and a small bakery and cafe in East London is now able to tweet what's fresh from their oven. This may all seem like pretty pointless stuff, but the pointlessness is the point."

Remember the Weasley family's clock in the Harry Potter series, which uses a clock face and nine hands to report on the location of each family member? Ginny, for instance, might be "traveling," while the hand representing Ron points to "Quidditch." By book six, you might recall, all hands on the clock pointed to "mortal peril" most of the time.

John McKerrell, a Web developer in Liverpool, England, used the Arduino to build a Weasley clock of his own. McKerrell, an inveterate tinkerer, pieced together a broken antique alarm clock, the stepper motor from an old floppy drive, and an Arduino circuit board and software to create a gadget to interact with the Web to automatically report McKerrell's whereabouts. His locations were home, work, traveling, and pub. (No mortal peril? I'll drink to that!)

Thanks to its Arduino and a wireless Internet connection, McKerrell's clock requests his location from the Web, making two http: requests per minute, and then rotates the hands to the proper location based on the answer.

For its location updates, the clock uses Mapme.at, an innovative social-media Web site and application that McKerrell founded in 2007. Mapme.at stores your favorite places and lets you build a network of contacts with whom you can share your location. The site offers a developer API to allow any application to update or make use of your location history, with your permission.

Mapme.at allows you to update your location in several ways:

- Manually by logging into the Web site
- Via posts from e-mail and Twitter
- Integration with ICQ, Gtalk, and other IM statuses
- Integration with mobile devices via Foursquare and other mobile apps
- Integration with Google Latitude, Fire Eagle, GeoRSS, etc.

McKerrell explains: "There are lots of reasons why people want to share their location online with friends and family. Holidaymakers are using the site to keep family and friends at home updated on their travels. People who enjoy running, cycling, and walking are using our Web site to track the routes they take and plan future adventures. Avid photographers use the site to document where and when their photos were taken."

While McKerrell's clock is deliberately whimsical, there's no nonsense in the prototyping of household gadgets that integrate with the Web and social media in real time. Mapme.at already lets users overlay their location and route maps with messages from Twitter. Photo sharing from Flickr and Panoramio and other integrations are planned. It's not hard to imagine Arduino-powered devices broadcasting our own personal entertainment channels based on the feeds, photos, and videos of our friends—and a real-time tracking of their movements.

Critics of geo-status apps have been quick to point out that constant status-posting on the public Web leaves users vulnerable to break-ins. The site http://www.PleaseRobMe.com aimed to raise awareness by "showing you a list of all those empty homes out there." The site, which paired the location of homes with Twitter and Foursquare posts such as "Headed to the airport for a week in Jamaica," recently said it was satisfied it had drawn sufficient attention to "oversharing and location awareness," and so discontinued its service.

"We're acutely aware that security is very important to consumers," says McKerrell. "Our system is built from the ground up to keep your data private while still allowing you to easily select those people and applications that you are willing to share your location with, at the level of accuracy you choose."

iPad

Of course, the Apple iPad and other devices have demonstrated this same appeal: we can have the Web, our e-mail, our social networks, and a host of apps, including games, photo sharing, magazine, newspaper and book reading, and movie viewing, all in one portable device.

There's no up, no down—the only input device is its large, intuitive touchscreen.

As with the iPhone, the gyroscopic sensing has spawned a number of unanticipated applications that rely on your gestural input—like bumping, maze games, and even a silly aerosol air horn and vuvuzelas.

There are five aspects to Apple's technology that will drive the future of our Web devices:

• Multitouch screen
• Wireless Web connection

- Gyroscope
- Accelerometer
- Compass

What we're seeing here is devices that respond to intuitive human gestures and can be programmed to exchange information when bumped together—basically a much more natural way to send and receive information. Between ubiquitous smartphones and smart RFID chips and sensors in all sorts of everyday objects, we'll be navigating a "Web of things" and a Web of people, and it will all be overlaid by our social graph.

OPTICAL-PATTERN RECOGNITION

Smartphones can scan and interpret 2-D bar codes in the physical world, on product labels, posters, etc.—and already in many cases, discounts and promotions are being communicated this way. On the flip side, we can receive e-mails containing bar-coded coupons, airplane boarding passes, etc., and present the screen of our phones to have those codes scanned and redeemed or validated. Soon our phones will be our universal input-output device for bridging the digital and the physical worlds.

Mike Laurie foresees advanced optical scanning—namely, facial recognition—converging with social networking. He pictures that love-at-first-sight moment in a bar: "You're transfixed, your heart starts to race—you're in love. But being the shy type you can't just go over and introduce yourself, so instead you do a quick scan of the room with your cell phone to pick up any latent metadata. Unfortunately, a social-network profile pops up informing you that the object of your affection is in a relationship. Your initial excitement rapidly dissipates and you get on with your reading."

The technology already exists: Biometric face-recognition technology is used by law-enforcement agencies. Google acquired a face-recognition technology company and is reportedly experimenting with it for use on the Picasa photo-sharing site to automatically tag and organize people's photos.

Tochindot's Sekai Camera and Wikitude are collaborating on a project to optically recognize and tag inanimate objects. Can facial recognition, linked into the social graph, be far behind?

OPENID AND YOUR UNIVERSAL ONLINE IDENTITY

As more and more of our life migrates to the Web and to our mobile devices, it becomes impossible to keep straight all the different usernames and passwords—each with their different requirements—that we maintain for everything from our 401-K account to our Twitter feed.

The current "solution"—Web browser settings that can remember your passwords for you and enter them automatically—are no solution at all; they're vulnerable to anyone who uses a public or shared computer. Entering the same names, addresses, and credit card data on each new registration form is tedious in the extreme.

In the future, we can expect to have a near-universal online identity that will move with us, from Web site to Web site, and whether we're using a PC, mobile device, or other gadget.

OpenID is an open source, decentralized authentication system that lets users log into a wide variety of different Web sites using a single set of credentials. It's currently accepted by Blogger, Google, Facebook, Myspace, MSN, Wordpress, Yahoo, and others. It's true, the value of a universal ID is all about adoption: Until your OpenID is accepted everywhere, it won't feel like it's accepted anywhere! That said, OpenID is emerging as a Web standard.

Increasingly, we'll see tools spring up for migrating your profile from one social-networking site to another. These powers should rest in the hands of users, not the services themselves. Currently, in the new-member registration process, social-media sites have gotten eerily aggressive asking you (sometimes in the fine print) to harvest potential "friends" from your Gmail, LinkedIn, Outlook, or other contacts. If you breeze through the sign-up process, you can belatedly find that the system has, in your name, spammed all your personal e-mail accounts to urge them to join the site.

Synchronization of information across disconnected sites will be a great area of opportunity. For example, Trillian, an instant-message aggregator, will connect all your IM services and their contacts into one.

Google established its OpenSocial standard for the social graph—social-networking profiles and friends lists—so that you can port your identity, and your network of friends, from one social-media Web site to many others, including Engage, Friendster, Google Friend-Connect, hi5, Hyves, imeem, LinkedIn, MySpace, Ning, Oracle, Orkut, Plaxo, Salesforce.com, Six Apart, and Yahoo.

OpenID is an open authentication protocol that lets users use a single set of login credentials for every site they visit. It's already in use at hundreds of smaller Web sites, and large sites like Facebook are starting to accept OpenID accounts. Once you've authenticated, a second open protocol called OAuth will help you share data about yourself with other sites you use. OAuth lets you grant authorization to sites to collect data from other places you participate online, which ultimately could eliminate the need to fill in redundant information about your profile and who your friends are at each new site you use. And companies like Cliqset and DandyID are creating platforms that will allow you to share your entire identity graph information from your profile to your contacts to your lifestream.

These technologies could eliminate the need to fill out forms and register for sites altogether.

"Data portability will allow users to theoretically mashup and interact with all of their social media information from a single place," says Josh Catone, writing on ReadWriteWeb."While that won't cut down the number of sites and services tugging at our attention, it does promise to make managing that attention vastly easier."[12]

MIND READING

Anyone seeking the future of search need look no further than http://www.google.com/mentalplex/, wherein Google revealed its MentalPlex, a whirling icon that knows what you want before you even type. The instructions were simple:

- Remove hat and glasses.
- Peer into MentalPlex circle. DO NOT MOVE YOUR HEAD.
- Project mental image of what you want to find.

The MentalPlex was a 2000 April Fools Day joke. (No one knows how many hapless searchers actually bought it!)

But today it may be closer to reality than we guessed.

Predictive searches and personalized search results use stored history to generate suggestions more relevant to each user. In September 2010, Google unveiled "Google Instant," which displays search results instantly, based on the most common search queries for every phrase, word, or even character you type, changing constantly as you type.

Why stop there? Couldn't electrodes or other sensors detect and respond to our thoughts?

"The idea of being able to control an interface without the use of your fine motor skills has massive implications for human-computer interaction," says Laurie. "Consider the ability to tweet what you're thinking without having to pull your phone out of your pocket, type your message, and hit send. Imagine being able to think 'Facebook' and your screen presents you with an overview of your friend's activity stream. This method of interaction is at a very experimental stage but there are proofs-of-concept that exist."

SELLING YOUR ATTENTION

Prior to the Web, virtually all the advertising messages we received were unsolicited. Commercials interrupted our favorite radio and television broadcasts, print ads were interspersed among our magazines and newspapers, and catalogs and junk mail landed in our mail boxes unbidden. Even with do-not-call lists and other consumer protections, all these forms of what Seth Godin called "interruption marketing" are still with us.

What has changed is that with the Web, many of the most successful ads—and therefore the most prolific ones—are now small text ads triggered by relevant search terms. Since they appear only when we have "raised our hands" by searching for something, they are more relevant and are more welcomed by consumers.

The same is true of company e-mail programs. CAN-SPAM legislation governs how companies sign people up for e-mail and how easily people can unsubscribe. Fundamentally, when consumers grant us permission to tell them about our products—and marketers respect and don't abuse that permission—the relationship is lasting and mutually good.

E-mail programs and search ads are examples of what Godin calls "permission marketing," and there's no doubt it is the future of advertising. Every year since their introduction, e-mail and paid searches have increased their share of the advertising pie—at the clear expense of newspaper, TV, catalog, and other traditional ad spending.

What e-mail and paid searching has done is to establish a clear, permission-based relationship between the company and its customers and prospects.

Social media goes further. The relationship between company and customer becomes personal. That's a great opportunity—and a solemn responsibility.

Software architect Alex Iskold describes an attention economy that would provide structure to the current Web landscape, where many advertisers and publishers are vying for the limited attention of consumers, readers, and other Web users: "The basic ideas behind the attention economy are simple. Such an economy facilitates a marketplace where consumers agree to receive services in exchange for their attention."

Iskold pointed to a fledging open-source project launched by Steve Gilmour and Seth Goldstein, called AttentionTrust, which distributed free software designed to act as an interface between Web users and those jockeying for their attention. Though the project went nowhere, the concept is provocative: "Something as big as an attention economy needs a solid foundation," says Iskold. "This marketplace needs participants who play by the rules, as defined by an independent entity." He went on to define the pillars that would undergird this new relationship between consumers and marketers:

- **Property**: You own your attention and can store it wherever you wish. You have CONTROL.
- **Mobility**: You can securely move your attention wherever you want, whenever you want to. You have the ability to TRANSFER your attention.
- **Economy**: You can pay attention to whomever you wish and receive value in return. Your attention has WORTH.
- **Transparency**: You can see exactly how your attention is being used.[13]

In the new attention economy, ordinary users are in full control of what they watch and hear. With social media at the heart of all we do online, we'll maintain only those connections that feel personal and mutually rewarding to us. Companies that can relate to us personally and keep us engaged by their message will retain us as connections. The rest will fall outside our network, and their ad messages will increasingly fall on deaf ears.

In the new attention economy, we may express willingness to learn more from a company—but the company may have to pay us for the privilege, in gift cards, discounts, or even in cash. Unlike those intolerable vacation timeshare sales pitches, we won't be captive audiences. To earn and keep our valuable attention, businesses must produce remarkable products and communicate to us in inherently interesting and entertaining ways.

It won't happen overnight, but the evolution is underway. We're moving, as a society, from interruption marketing, to permission marketing, to a truly consumer-centric attention economy.

NATURAL-LANGUAGE PROCESSING

Natural-language processing (NLP) aims to get computers to understand verbal requests from their human users. Firefox's Ubiquity, Google Voice, and Google Mobile are a few projects changing how we interact with the Web by allowing people to use natural-language commands. We're still a long way to the kind of vocal commands issued to computers and robots in vintage science fiction, but that day will come, in some form. "Further, in the future," suggests Mike Laurie, "applications might exist that could analyze your tweets or comments with NLP, and suggest people or brands for you to follow."

THE END OF E-MAIL

While older Millennials still spend an average of 9.5 hours a week writing or receiving work-related e-mails, mid-Millennials already in the workforce say they spend just 7.7 hours a week on e-mail. High school and young college students spend far less time with traditional e-mail—less than two hours a week—instead preferring newer (and more immediate) alternatives such as text messaging, instant messaging, and communicating on social-networking sites.

Futurists have begun predicting the end of e-mail as we know it. IDC Research predicted that by the second half of 2010, instant messaging will overtake e-mail as the world's leading form of business communication. Kevin Marks, then a Google engineer and a veteran of Technorati, in a 2008 talk about Google's OpenSocial project and Social Graph APIs, called e-mail a "strange legacy idea."

"E-mail has died away for a group of users," said Marks. "For the younger generation, they don't use e-mail. They see it as this noisy spam-filled thing that annoys them every day . . . they see it as how you talk to the university, how you talk to the bank."[14] Marks pointed to Facebook messaging and mobile texting as the future of communication.

These forms offer both immediacy and an element of social control—of interacting only with those contacts you have personally invited into your circle.

Meanwhile, Web-based e-mail is getting a social makeover. Google Buzz makes Gmail more of a social networking/chat/status-reporting tool. WindowsLive and Yahoo Mail have added the same suite of social features. And the social networks are getting into the e-mail game, with MySpace Mail and Facebook's Titan Webmail. Make no mistake: The social feed and the e-mail inbox are converging.

PRIVACY IS SO 2005

Last chapter we mentioned Facebook CEO Mark Zuckerberg's apparent inability to understand—and foresee—his users' privacy needs and sensitivities. And yet there's plenty of evidence that our expectations for privacy have become a fluid, fast-moving target. Not only are all of us individually modifying our own privacy needs and the discretion of our online behavior. Generationally, the perspective of Millennials is much more blasé than that of the aging Baby Boomers and older generations.

Some of the best and most popular sites on the Web, Facebook among them, are by necessity blazing fresh trails and pushing past conventional notions of privacy.

"A few years from now we'll look back and wonder why there was this time when all these Web sites weren't personalized," says Zuckerberg. "The world is moving in this direction where everything is designed around people."[15]

Zuckerberg sounded similar notes onstage at a 2010 awards ceremony with TechCrunch founder Michael Arrington:[16]

> When I got started in my dorm room at Harvard, the question a lot of people asked was "Why would I want to put any information on the Internet at all?". . .
>
> And then in the last five or six years, blogging has taken off in a huge way and all these different services that have people sharing all this information. People have really gotten comfortable not only sharing more information and different kinds, but more openly and with more people. That social norm is just something that has evolved over time.
>
> We view it as our role in the system to constantly be innovating and be updating what our system is to reflect what the current social norms are.
>
> A lot of companies would be trapped by the conventions and their legacies of what they've built, doing a privacy change—doing a privacy change for 350 million users is not the kind of thing that a lot of companies would do. But we viewed that as a really important thing, to always keep a beginner's mind and what would we do if we were starting the company now, and we decided that these would be the social norms now and we just went for it.

Though Zuckerberg has been alone under the glare of the hottest privacy spotlights, he is not alone in wrestling with these issues. Speaking at the 2010 Google Zeitgeist event in London, Google founder Larry Page too suggested that privacy was an evolving notion with no roadmap: "It is clear life has changed—the Internet has affected people's lives in many new ways and we don't know where this is headed," said Page. "Social networking has created a ton of data that has been made public and semi-public that didn't used to be . . . This is a very important, very complex issue for society that is going to be debated for the next 50 years."[17]

Chapter 8

Conclusion

We've explored the various social networks, how they work, and how businesses large and small have been participating in them. Here are a few key points I think are critical for the success of your business's social-media program:

- Start by listening on Twitter and the blogosphere to ongoing conversations about your industry, brand, and products.
- Establish your beachhead on the major social-media platforms by reserving your company's name.
- Apply your company's mission statement to your social-media program-to-be.
- Create rules of engagement, including a minimum posting schedule.
- Assign social media responsibility to a full-time, in-house staffer.
- Develop your program on the major networks, Twitter, Facebook, and YouTube, and establish your own professional profile on LinkedIn. Do these things with an eye toward customer service and networking first, with sales a distant second.
- Once your community is well established, extend your presence to newer or second-tier networks.
- Try advertising on social networks.
- Make ever stronger and more memorable connections to the members of your online community; host real-world events, contests, meetups, and tweetups. "Friending" someone is only the beginning!

Because the whole idea of social media is to connect *socially*, and personally, to the real individuals out there in your customer base, I'd like to close by reexamining the idea of evangelists and influencers. We know that from a customer-service perspective, it makes sense to connect with your customer, any customer.

But do we also believe that in a corporate social-media program it pays to identify and connect with the super-users, the most influential people in your market niche?

SOCIAL-MEDIA POWER USERS, EVANGELISTS, AND INFLUENCERS

Malcolm Gladwell, in his best-selling book *The Tipping Point*, championed the notion that super-connected, super-influential people serve as the hubs of taste-making networks. Though tiny in number, their impact is enormous, thanks to the network effect. Thus, fewer than 100 urban hipsters brought the Hushpuppy shoe back from the brink of death and made it cool again, simply by wearing it.

Gladwell describes three classes of well-connected and persuasive people:

Connectors: The hubs in any network, connectors know everybody. They are sociable, energetic, and eager to introduce people to each other.

Mavens: They may not know everybody, but they seem to know every-*thing*. Mavens love to share information and are always trying to help others. They're the people who kick off word-of-mouth epidemics.

Salesmen: Charming persuaders, salesmen have a lot of charisma and are trendsetters.

"The success of any kind of social epidemic is heavily dependent on the involvement of people with a particular and rare set of social gifts," Gladwell wrote in *The Tipping Point*.

According to MarketingVOX, more than $1 billion is spent each year on word-of-mouth campaigns targeting influentials. That amount has been growing at 36 percent a year, faster than any other segment of marketing and advertising.

Yet some researchers have recently suggested that the theory of online influentials is pure bunk. Duncan Watts, principal research scientist at Yahoo and previously a network-theory scientist at Columbia University, analyzed e-mail patterns and concluded that highly connected people do not perform any critical function as social hubs. He has written computer models of rumor-spreading that found that well-connected people are no more likely than an average user to start a big new online trend.

"It just doesn't work," says Watts. "A rare bunch of cool people just doesn't have that power. And when you test the way marketers say the world works, it falls apart. There's no there there."[1]

But what if your goal is not to start a huge new trend? What if all you want to do is strengthen your connections with your core audience, your best customers?

The social-media company Syncapse performed a research study, reported by *Forbes*,[2] which found that customers who friend a brand on a social network like Facebook spend more money buying the company's products than customers who don't "friend." On average, fans spent $71.84 more than customers who hadn't friended the brand. Clearly, your customers who are active social-media users and who are willing to "friend" your brand represent an elite, core, and highly motivated group. Like a loyalty or "preferred customer" program, your fan page brings together your most valuable customers.

CUSTOMER OUTREACH

When I interviewed her for the Skechers case study in chapter 5, I found that Sandie Mainwal-Price really personifies the new Web 2.0 mode of active consumers interacting with the companies from which they buy. She readily gives feedback, good and bad, on a wide range of products. Sometimes she may post on a company's social-media pages, other times she'll respond to customer surveys. She also enrolls in volunteer product-testing programs.[3]

"I do a lot of product testing from foods to shoes," she says. "I am a member of about 10 different survey companies, though not for Skechers. I am also a New Balance product tester. It's a lot of fun. Most pay you in points that can be redeemed for gift certificates and sometimes cash. I just get a kick out of trying different products, especially the food-related ones."

But Mainwal-Price is not in it just for the freebies. As any expert will tell you about the new Web 2.0 consumer—especially women—there is a powerful sense of engagement and a desire to create positive change. "I enjoy giving feedback to companies. I only hope to help them improve their products for us the consumer."

Such programs go by many names: Product Testing Panel, Consumer Advisory Panel, Market Opinion Board, and so on. They are being run for many brands, including Johnson and Johnson, Good Housekeeping, New Balance, Intuit, and M&M/Mars. Today their application forms can be found online, and getting started is a snap.

With the Web's powerful new social-media tools, it's easier than ever to engage in a consumer-research program, reach a well-defined segment of customers, and foster robust connections between testers and the company—and among individual testers if you so desire. And businesses needn't engineer and launch their own stand-alone product-testing sites: They can partner up with a testing and sampling-and-promotion company that will conduct the campaign for them on their software, with their network of registered product testers. Many of these networks are designed with social-media virality built right in: Buzzheads, BzzAgent, and Scatterbee are just a few of the new word-of-mouth oriented networks.

Many of these networks make aggressive claims about the word-of-mouth (WOM) benefit their services will bring. Take such claims with a grain or two of salt. If you're making or doing something truly remarkable, sure, you have potential to go viral. But don't expect a product-testing or WOM campaign to turn an ugly duckling into a swan.

As we've seen with the "mommy blogger" networks, product giveaways, contests, surveys, and sampling can motivate consumers. They can be some of the most effective promotional moves a company can make online today.

Another point to make about consumer opinion panels: The people who join such panels tend by nature to be evangelists—the most social and enthusiastic citizens, outspoken and full of energy. They're well connected and they care pretty deeply about the stuff they buy and use. Make something shoddy or overpriced and they'll let a thousand people know in an instant, to your lasting detriment. They are the hubs. The 80–20 rule is alive and well here: This small minority of active evangelist consumers have the loudest voice and the most potent impact on the new social Web.

Did I say "80–20?" Most experts say the rule is even more starkly disproportionate when it's applied to the social-media world. In a phenomenon dubbed "participation inequality," it has been observed that some 90 percent of people on any social network are mere "lurkers"—they visit, they check things out, but remain mute on the sidelines.

A Harvard Business School study found that 10 percent of Twitter users account for 90 percent of tweets.[4]

Web site usability guru Jakob Nielsen calls it more of a 90–9–1 rule, saying: "In most online communities, 90 percent of users are lurkers who never contribute, 9 percent of users contribute a little, and 1 percent of users account for almost all the action."[5]

- 90 percent of users are lurkers (i.e., they read or observe, but don't contribute).

- 9 percent of users contribute from time to time, but other priorities dominate their time.
- 1 percent of users participate a lot and account for most contributions.

Of the super-contributing 1 percent, Nielsen says, "It can seem as if they don't have lives because they often post just minutes after whatever event they're commenting on occurs."

If a mere 1 percent of a network conducts almost 90 percent of the conversations, it's hard to imagine they could be anything but enormously influential on the other 99 percent of people in the room who either chip in only occasionally or lurk without saying a word.

Social-media trends show us consumers engaging in a more direct and reciprocal relationship with brands and businesses. To be successful in this day and age, consumer-product companies cannot make product decisions in a vacuum or send down marketing messages from on high. The successful business today has both ears open to what its customers think. These companies are plying channels—social media among them—where listening to consumers is easy, fast, and of primary importance.

Feedback cycles that include customer surveys, focus groups, product testers, and mystery shoppers do two very healthy things:

1. They provide companies with valuable insights into their marketplace and the appeal of their products and services, and
2. They provide consumers with a sense of connectedness to the brands they buy, a feeling of being important and helpful to the company—and a resulting sense of loyalty to the brand.

Add to this the prevalence of user-submitted product reviews and ratings, which you'll now find on about many e-commerce sites and growing daily.

Getting people to be walking commercials for your products—and for them to feel good about it—is simply the ultimate. If anything crystallizes the spirit of marketing 2.0, this is it. Remember, the two most trusted sources of product recommendations are people we know personally, and other consumers whose opinions we read online. When it comes to deciding what to buy, 90 percent say they trust people they know, according to a Nielsen survey (unrelated to Jakob Nielsen) of 25,000 Internet purchasers from 50 countries. Some 70 percent of us trust consumer opinions posted online.

Table 8.1   Most trusted forms of advertising and promotion

Recommendations from people known:	90%
Consumer opinions posted online:	70%
Brand Web sites:	70%
Newspaper and other articles:	69%
Brand sponsorships:	64%
TV commercials:	62%
Newspaper ads:	61%
Magazine ads:	59%
Billboards:	55%
Radio ads:	55%
E-mail (promotional):	54%
Search-engine ads:	41%
Online video ads:	37%
Online banner ads:	33%
Text ads on mobile phones:	24%

Interestingly, customers still place high degrees of trust in company Web sites (70 percent trusted) and editorial content, like newspaper or blog articles (69 percent trusted); see Table 8.1. Nielsen theorized that the revolution in consumer-generated content, and the jaundiced eye that consumers now cast on old-school marketing hype, had compelled brand Web sites and the media to adopt a more balanced and low-key approach to consumers. In other words, Web 2.0 may have ushered in the era of the soft sell.[6]

What are your business goals in using social media? According to a recent Chief Marketer social-media survey,[7] here's how companies responded (they were allowed to name multiple objectives); see Table 8.2.

Michael Lazerow, chairman and CEO of the social-media marketing agency Buddy Media, sees social media not primarily as a PR or prospecting channel, but as a loyalty and retention channel. "The companies that harness social best look at it as part of a loyalty program," says Lazerow. "They use social to manage and build better relationships with their most profitable customers."[8]

As marketers and businesspeople, we need to have all of these objectives at the heart of our social-media programs. We must be active in social media because that's where the customers are, and where they are increasingly placing their attention and trust—instead of in traditional advertising channels.

Table 8.2   Business goals in using social media: Companies' responses as per Chief Marketer social media survey

69%	Drive traffic to your company Web site
59%	Identify and speak directly to the company's fans
46%	Generate leads
40%	Generate sales
28%	Generate e-mail signups
20%	Keep up with competitors
16%	Collect customer suggestions or improve customer service

We must reach out to the influentials, the well-connected folks who can serve as our brand ambassadors to a larger community. But in chasing the brass ring of an influential customer, we must remember that good listening, humility, sincerity, and good, old-fashioned customer service are what really make our social-media programs tick. Treating the customer right, and connecting with her personally and directly, is simply the right thing to do. If she turns out to be an influential customer, an evangelist who can multiply our efforts—then so much the better!

Appendix A: Glossary of Social Terms and Technologies

Aggregator: A Web site that systematically combines information from multiple online sources. Popular aggregator sites are dedicated to news, blog posts, videos, reviews, products, poll results, etc.

Astroturfing: A fake grassroots campaign (Astroturf is artificial grass, get it?). An Astroturf campaign tries to create the impression of being truly people-powered buzz, but it's really just a marketing campaign fueled by an ad agency. This is not the way to stimulate trust with your online community.

Avatar: An animated or other visual representation of the user. Created for online virtual worlds games, avatars have begun to be used in other social-media environments.

Backchannel: During a seminar, speech, classroom lecture, or other presentation, the "backchannel" is the audience's networked communication and comments about the presentation. Backchannel conversations may be had on Twitter and by using text messaging or IM. In a project called ClassCommons, academic researchers are experimenting with using backchannel conversations to encourage student participation.

Behavioral targeting, or BT: BT uses cookies to track a Web user's past behaviors and predict which advertising he will best respond to.

Blog: An online journal, updated on a regular basis with entries in reverse chronological order. Blogs typically enable comments by other readers and are richly interlinked with other sites.

Blogosphere: The collective ecosystem of all the Web's blogs. Bloggers and their audiences form a community—or, actually, more than 100 million overlapping communities. Bloggers link to each another and inspire each other's work. The result is a network that both reflects and influences our culture.

Bot: As in "robot," this is a program that runs repeatedly and automatically—to crawl the Web, for instance. (The word "bot" can also describe a computer that has been taken over by a Web virus.)

Bulletin board: An older term describing online public posting systems. *See* forum.

CAN-SPAM: An acronym for the 2003 Congressional Act, whose full name is the "Controlling the Assault of Non-Solicited Pornography and Marketing Act." In the words of the FTC, it "establishes requirements for those who send commercial e-mail, spells out penalties for spammers and companies whose products are advertised in spam if they violate the law, and gives consumers the right to ask e-mailers to stop spamming them."

Chat: Real-time communication between people online. Today this can be text chat, audio/video, or some combination.

Collaboration: Working together, with the aid of online networking tools, on a common project or toward a common goal. *See also* crowdsourcing and wiki.

Collective intelligence: *See* wisdom of the crowds.

Comments: Posts allowed on most blogs, social-media-sharing sites, and social networks (on Facebook, it's a "wall post"). *See* user-generated content.

Comment spam: Posts containing links back to the poster's Web site, for no purpose other than to sell something or gain search-engine benefit.

Community building: Personal, direct outreach to community members for the sake of strengthening the relationships and growing the network.

Conferencing: Online meetings facilitated by technologies like GoToMeeting, WebEx, or Acrobat Connect, combining online screen sharing, remote access, and VOIP or traditional telephone conferencing, and in some cases streaming real-time video.

Crowdsourcing: Enlisting the aid of a large online community to develop a project.

Flash mob: A group that comes together, aided in its planning and logistics by using online tools, to suddenly stage an act of performance art or other public event.

FOAF file: Friend of a friend is a specification for the Semantic Web that is particularly relevant to programming for social networks. FOAF describes people and the relationships between them.

Folksonomy: When users—ordinary folks—can tag and classify your content, the resulting hierarchy, tag cloud, and other structures are called a folksonomy.

Forum: An online chat room or message board system.

Friends, fans, followers, connections: The terminology varies from Web site to Web site, and whether you're a business or a person. But whatever the term, these are the direct relationships developed between you and your customers and prospects—your online community.

Hash tag: A tag that when used in a Twitter post allows Twitter users to search for all posts (by any users) that contain that tag. A hash tag is a word or concatenated phrase, preceded by the # sign, for example #tourdefrance, #hugochavez, #oscars, etc.

Link juice: The search-engine ranking benefit you get when someone else's site links to you (*see* page rank).

Lurkers: Members of a social network, especially a forum or chat room, who read but do not post. An estimated 90 percent of members of today's social sites are lurkers—while the 10 percent most active members produce the lion's share of posts.

Mashups: Programs that combine two or more sources of online data to produce something new.

M-commerce: Online transactions conducted over a PDA, Web-enabled cell phone, or other mobile device.

Meetups: Real-world meetings, events, or other gatherings, promoted and organized online, typically at the Web site Meetup.org. *See also* tweetups.

Microblogging: A form of blogging characterized by very short, usually more frequent posts than traditional blogging, and with a social component in which users follow or subscribe to one another's posts. Twitter is the biggest and most notable microblogging platform, but others include Plurk, Jaiku, Seesmic, Posterous, Tumblr, and Yammer.

Microsite: A small, purpose-built Web site with its own look and feel and domain name, distinct from its corporate parent site and aimed at supporting an individual marketing campaign, contest, promotion, brand, product, movie, etc. Microsites are gaining favor as landing pages for online advertising campaigns and more because they're often more effective at sharpening a message and cutting through online clutter.

.mobi: The top-level domain for mobile Web sites, i.e., Web sites designed and formatted for the small screens and keypads of cell phones, PDAs, and other Web-enabled mobile devices. There's no consensus whether the .mobi domain-name extension will take off as a convention for hosting mobile Web sites, or whether site owners will simply employ user-agent sniffing to identify mobile devices and serve up appropriate mobile content at their main Web site domain.

MMOGs ("massively multiplayer online games") or MMORPGs ("massively multiplayer online role-playing games"): Online video games like World of Warcraft, Second Life, etc., where players worldwide can interact with each other in a virtual world.

Multivariate test: These tests display alternative versions of your home page, say, or important navigation elements or "landing pages," and they track which version—or which combination of several variations—delivers the best conversion rate. Such tests are performed in real time, with variations served up randomly to segments of your audience.

Online community: A social network of individuals who interact through online media to pursue mutual interests or goals.

OpenID: An open sign-in system that allows users to log into many different sites using a single username and password. While OpenID is accepted by many sites—some of them major ones—its adoption is currently far from universal.

Open source: The opposite of "proprietary software" or "licensed software," open-source software is available for free. Its underlying source code is also open to modification and improvement, wiki-style, by a community of independent developers. The business model of open-source software companies is to give away the software and make money on premium services like installation, configuration, tech support, training, consulting, etc.

Open video: Video files employing the HTML5 format and not requiring proprietary viewers like Flash or Silverlight.

OWL: In the semantic Web, OWL is the Web ontology language used to describe the classes and relations between Web documents and applications.

Page Rank: The term coined by (and sort of named after) Google founder Larry Page as a means of ranking the importance of any Web page based on the number and quality of other sites linking to that page.

Participatory Web: Describes the characteristic of Web 2.0 in which ordinary users can easily interact with other people online and easily alter and create online content. They can chat online; participate in forums; post comments; share, rate, and review photos and videos; and launch their own blogs, social-network profiles, etc.

Persona: A personification of a typical customer or of a brand image. Businesses carrying out social-media campaigns are also said to have a social-media persona; ideally, these are the real people behind your company's program! The social-media persona exemplifies the voice, style, values, and ethics of your business.

Photo sharing: On Flickr, Facebook, and elsewhere, the uploading of your photos and albums for public view, tagging, and commentary.

Podcast: Syndicated online video or audio, usually employing feed technology like RSS or Atom, for playback in a computer or portable media player (like an iPod; hence the name).

Predictive search: When search engines use personal stored history to generate suggestions more relevant to each user.

Profile: A page detailing an individual user of a social-media Web site or social network. It usually features a photo or avatar of the person, their name and/or username, interests, links, etc., as well as thumbnails of the user's friends or followers.

RDF (resource description framework): This is a markup language for the Semantic Web. Loosely based on XML, it is for describing information and resources on the Web and their relationships to each other.

Retweet: To indicate your approval of someone else's Twitter post, or tweet, by reposting it to your own followers. When retweeting, you prefix the post with "RT." It's the main mechanism on Twitter that causes items and topics to trend, or become virally popular.

RSS: Really simple syndication technology that delivers blog posts and any other content in a highly portable form, including tagged "metadata" such as publishing date and authorship, so they may be read in a user's personalized home page or "feed reader" software.

RT: *See* retweet.

SaaS: Software as a service. Software applications that are hosted on the Internet and delivered on demand through a Web browser. SaaS is the Web 2.0 answer to the traditional software model of shrink-wrapped products installed on a user's PC or local network.

Screencasting: Sharing your computer screen across the Internet, either in real-time through conferencing tools like GoToMeeting or WebEx, or via sharing a video recording. Screencasting is a popular way of performing software demos or sharing presentations.

Semantic Web: Coined by Tim Berners-Lee, the Semantic Web is envisioned as a network that is able to describe things in a way that computers can understand by structuring data into fields and defining the properties of things (like dimensions, prices, age, and/or location) and the relationships between things (one entity is a member of another). The Semantic Web introduced a logical language that human programmers could use to inform computers of the relationships between data with the goal of replacing the old Web of links with a new Web of meaning.

Smart mob: A group that uses Internet and mobile networking to organize itself as a social network. Howard Rheingold coined the term in his book *Smart Mobs: The Next Social Revolution. See also* flash mob, a special smart mob that carries out performance art or other public events.

SOAP (simple object access protocol): A means for transferring XML-based data across the Internet. SOAP is a basic messaging framework used in Web services.

Social advertising: Placing ads on social-networking Web sites. Social marketing covers advertising as well as the online participation, personal outreach, guerilla marketing, and other tactics companies are employing (to mixed effect!) to spread their brands, products, and services in the social-media space.

Social bookmarking: The practice of tagging news items, blog posts, videos, and other offbeat or interesting content for the enjoyment of others within an online community. While traditional bookmarking simply remembers your favorite pages within your Web browser, social bookmarking on sites like del.icio.us, Digg, Reddit, Furl, and others allows you to share your opinions publicly with other users and also vote on their suggestions.

Social graph: The social graph or social network diagram is, in the words of Brad Fitzpatrick (founder of LiveJournal, chief architect of SixApart, and now working at Google), "the global mapping of everybody and how they're related." Social graphs underpin today's social-networking sites—and whose output is expressed in, for instance, your "friend news feed," social graphs, and Google's OpenSocial API.

Social media: Broadly, any Web site or online technology that enables people to create and share content and interact with other users. Narrowly, social media refers to the online content typically shared—such as video (YouTube), photos (Flickr), writing (blogs and microblogs), and music (Napster, once upon a time).

Social network: Aka social media, any Web site like Facebook, MySpace, LinkedIn, Friendster, Classmates.com, etc., whose central purpose is to facilitate the connection of individual members. Members establish profiles, create links to a network of friends, and use the site for entertainment, communication, and networking.

Social-network analysis: Mapping and measuring relationships and message flows between people, groups, and organizations. Social-network analysis is a method for visualizing connections between people or the emergence of topical trends. SNA tools like Friendwheel, MentionMap, Twitter Venn, and TouchGraph can produce some beautiful and informative maps.

Social search: Applying human wiki and social-networking power to improve search-engine results. The new search engines Wikia and Mahalo are chief examples of this concept.

Social shopping: Enlivening online shopping by adding social-networking elements such as the sharing of wish lists or recent purchases and rating or commenting on others' shopping exploits.

Spider: Also known as a "Web crawler," this is a program that visits Web pages by following the links from one page to another for the purpose of indexing and (in the case of search-engine spiders) ranking them.

Streaming media: Video and audio files that are transmitted from a Web server to the end user. Streaming media basically starts playing a large file immediately without requiring the user to download the entire file before viewing.

Tag cloud: A visual representation of user-created tags, each linking to appropriately tagged items. In a tag cloud, the most frequently used terms are rendered in a bigger, bolder font.

Tags: Descriptive keywords added by users to videos, blog posts, photos, product reviews, etc., to help others find or sort for items relevant to them.

Trackback: A special URL presented by a blog author to his or her readers. Whenever readers use that URL on their own Web sites, the author knows immediately who has linked back to them.

Troll: An unsavory denizen of a chat room, message board, or other online social forum whose posts are mean-spirited, profane, abusive, off-topic, or otherwise unwelcome.

Tweemes: Twitter memes, or popular cultural memes trending on Twitter.

Tweet: A Twitter post.

Tweetup: A real-world get-together of people that is promoted and organized on Twitter.

Universal search: Breaking down the walls between content types that previously had lived in their respective silos on specialized search sites: images, videos, news, blogs, maps, and local business listings.

URL shortener: A service like Tinurl.com or Bit.ly that creates short, sweet URLs which then redirect to your long, cumbersome Web addresses—a must for posting links on Twitter, in blog comments, and elsewhere that impose a tight character limit on your posts.

User-agent sniffing: For Web sites, identifying what sort of device a visitor is using—a particular PDA or cell phone, say, versus a desktop or laptop computer—and displaying content designed specifically for that device.

User-generated content (UGC): Any posting, comment, review, profile, or uploaded files submitted not by the owner of a Web site but by its visitors or users. Web sites enabling user-generated content tend to grow exponentially.

Video sharing: As on YouTube, Hulu, and other leading Web sites, the uploading of user-created videos for public sharing, rating, and commenting.

Viral: Growing exponentially, as with hot online news, fads, trends, videos, sites, or marketing campaigns where each person touched spreads the word to more than one other person. In pre-Internet days, most marketing investments produced linear growth. But with the frictionless ease of e-mail and hyperlinking, consumers on the Web spread word-of-mouth at an exponential rate. Needless to say, successful computer viruses also chart a viral growth pattern.

Virtual worlds: 3-D online game worlds where the "game" consists of unscripted role-play interactions among their thousands of players.

VLOG: Video log, an online video diary. Powered by the author's cam, it's the Web 2.0 answer to a plain old blog.

WAP: Wireless application protocol, an open standard for wireless applications used by cell phones and other mobile devices to access the Web.

Web 2.0: The technologies and cultural trends characterized by a "new," more interactive, and dynamic World Wide Web—post-Internet bubble. The term Web 2.0 was popularized by John Battelle and Tim O'Reilly and encompasses the social-media trends and technologies described in this book.

Webinar: An online presentation or seminar conducted using online screencasting, audio, or videoconferencing tools.

Web service: Any software system designed to support interoperable machine-to-machine interaction across the Web.

Widgets: Small, freestanding programs—pieces of html and programming code—that can be pasted to any Web page. They use JavaScript, DHTML, Flash, or another language to carry out some dynamic action. Web visitor counters, mini games, clocks, calendars, horoscopes, weather forecasts, and stock tickers are all examples of common widget applications. They may also be called "snippets" or "plug-ins," and Google likes to call them "gadgets."

Wiki: Meaning "quick" in Hawaiian, it is an approach to online collaboration made most famous by Wikipedia, the user-created and edited Web encyclopedia. Aka "crowdsourcing" or "distributed workforce."

Wisdom of the crowds: The notion that the consensus opinions and judgments of millions of networked Internet and mobile users can bring efficiency and intelligence to many tasks and topics—including shopping for products, buying stocks, or creating an online encyclopedia. The wisdom of the crowds is typically seen either in (1) evolutionary, wiki-style development projects; (2) predictive markets, like stock markets and oddsmakers; and (3) ratings and recommendations systems, like those used by Netflix, Amazon, Pandora radio, and others.

WML: Wireless markup language, the format of Web sites meant to be viewed by WAP mobile devices.

WOM: Word of mouth—in contrast to paid advertising, WOM is the natural, unpaid, person-to-person spreading of information. In the Web era, it's also known as "word of mouse."

X3D: An open standard for developing 3-D objects, virtual reality, and virtual worlds online.

XML: Extensible markup language—a formatting language that breaks data into fields and puts it into a form that can be used, manipulated, and re-presented anywhere on the Web.

Appendix B: Social Media Reading and Resource List

CONFERENCES AND EVENTS

New social media and Web 2.0-oriented conferences are proliferating, and many of the traditional marketing and media conferences now offer social-media tracks. Here is a sampling of some of the higher-profile marketing and strategy-related shows:

DMA—Direct Marketing Association Conference and Exhibition
http://www.the-dma.org/conferences
A general-interest direct-marketing conference with strong Web 2.0 tracks.

Future of Mobile
http://future-of-mobile.com
London event for thinkers and practitioners in the mobile industry.

GEL Conference: Good Experience Live
http://www.gelconference.com/
Not strictly a social-media conference, GEL is dedicated to "exploring good experience in all its forms—in business, technology, art, society, and life." Founder Mark Hurst has captured a zeitgeist and attracted a community that is very Web 2.0; attendees are a diverse bunch, and include many from leading Web companies.

Internet Retailer Conference and Exposition
http://www.internetretailer.com
A leading Internet retailing conference, the IRCE brings together a huge swath of online merchants and industry experts and dedicates a lot of programming to Web 2.0 topics.

Mobile Content Strategies
http://www.mobilecontentstrategies.com/
Addresses the business of supplying content for mobile devices.

Mobile Internet World
http://www.mobilenetx.com
This European conference series recently crossed the Atlantic for an event in Boston. It covers business strategy, emerging technologies, and best practices for targeting the mobile Internet.

NewTeeVee
http://live.newteevee.com
A new conference targeting the online video and entertainment industry.

OMMA Social
http://www.mediapost.com/events/
Online Media, Marketing, and Advertising's focus on Social takes place in New York and San Francisco.

SaaScon
http://www.saascon.com/
ComputerWorld-sponsored conferences on software-as-a-service, Web services, and cloud computing.

Search Engine Strategies
http://www.searchenginestrategies.com/
A U.S. and international conference series dedicated to paid search advertising and search-engine optimization—including Web 2.0 and mobile topics.

Shop.org
http://www.shop.org
Trade group and conference and seminar sponsor for online retailers.

SMX: Search Marketing Expo
http://searchmarketingexpo.com/
The new search-engine marketing and SEO conference series led by a leading voice in the field, Danny Sullivan.

SocialTech 2010
http://www.socialtech2010.com
Organized by the Marketing Profs research firm, SocialTech puts a lot of social-media visionaries on the podium.

SXSW: South by Southwest Interactive Festival
http://www.sxsw.com
Part of a larger music and arts event, the interactive festival "Celebrates the creativity and passion behind the coolest new media technologies."

SYS-CON Events
http://events.sys-con.com/
For Web 2.0 developers and CIOs, SYS-CON hosts several events, including Ajax World, SOA World, Virtualization Expo, iPhone Developer Summit, and more.

Virtual Worlds Conference and Expo
http://www.virtualworlds2008.com/
Conference series devoted to MMOGs and online virtual worlds.

VoiceCon
http://www.voicecon.com/
Conference series devoted to voice communications across the Internet: IP telephony, Unified Communications platforms, and "converged networks."

Web 2.0 Expo
http://www.web2expo.com/
The newer and less expensive "companion event" to the Web 2.0 Summit, this U.S. and international conference series is intended for a broader audience, not just the A-players offered an invitation to the summit.

Web 2.0 Summit
http://www.web2summit.com/
The exclusive, cutting-edge, invitation-only event launched and moderated by John Battelle and Tim O'Reilly, the guys who coined the term "Web 2.0."

Word of Mouth Supergenius
http://gaspedal.com/supergenius/nyc/
The How to Be Great at Word of Mouth Marketing conference.

BLOGS AND WEB SITES

John Battelle's Searchblog
http://www.battellemedia.com
Thoughts on the intersection of search, media, technology, and more.

Mashable
http://www.mashable.com
A leading source of social-media news and information. According to Mashable, it has 25 million page views a month, and its audience includes early adopters, social-media enthusiasts, entrepreneurs, influencers, brands and corporations, marketing, PR and advertising agencies, Web 2.0 aficionados, and technology journalists.

O'Reilly Media
http://www.oreilly.com/
Books, online training, blog posts, and more dedicated mostly to the technologies, trends, and programming languages that power the Web.

Programmable Web
http://www.programmableweb.com/
Keeping you up-to-date with mashups, APIs, and the Web as a platform.

ReadWriteWeb
http://www.readwriteweb.com/
Web apps, Web technology trends, social networking, and social media.

Seth Godin
http://www.sethgodin.typepad.com
Daily and dependably brilliant marketing insights.

SocialBrite
http://www.socialbrite.org
This learning hub and sharing community brings together experts in social media, causes, and online philanthropy.

TechCrunch
http://www.techcrunch.com/
This blog captained by Michael Arrington and Erick Schonfeld covers the latest Internet technology, gossip, buyouts, and Web 2.0 business stories.

Technorati
http://www.technorati.com
The authority on blogs, online news, and social bookmarks. When last we looked, Technorati was tracking 112.8 million blogs and over 250 million pieces of tagged social media.

Valleywag
http://valleywag.com/
Tabloid-style news and gossip about Silicon Valley.

MAGAZINES

Business 2.0, http://money.cnn.com/magazines/business2/

DMNews, http://www.dmnews.com/

Internet Retailer, http://www.Internetretailer.com/

Multichannel Merchant, http://multichannelmerchant.com/

Wired, http://www.wired.com/

BOOKS

Brennan, Bridget. *Why She Buys: The New Strategy for Reaching the World's Most Powerful Consumers*. New York: Crown, 2009.

Brogan, Chris. *Social Media 101: Tactics and Tips to Develop Your Business Online.* Hoboken, NJ: John Wiley & Sons, 2010.

Brogan, Chris, and Smith, Julien. *Trust Agents: Using the Web to Build Influence, Improve Reputation, and Earn Trust.* Hoboken, NJ: John Wiley & Sons, 2009.

Cairncroft, Frances. *The Death of Distance: How the Communications Revolution Will Change Our Lives.* Boston: Harvard Business Press, 1997.

Gillin, Paul. *The New Influencers: A Marketer's Guide to the New Social Media.* Sanger, CA: Quill Driver Books, 2007.

Gladwell, Malcolm. *The Tipping Point: How Little Things Can Make a Big Difference.* New York: Little, Brown, 2002.

Gladwell, Malcolm, and Godin, Seth. *Unleashing the Ideavirus.* New York: Hyperion, 2001.

Godin, Seth. *Meatball Sundae: Is Your Marketing Out of Sync?* New York: Penguin, 2007.

Godin, Seth. *Permission Marketing: Turning Strangers into Friends and Friends into Customers.* New York: Simon & Schuster, 1999.

Godin, Seth. *Tribes: We Need You to Lead Us.* New York, Portfolio, 2008.

Israel, Shel. *Twitterville: How Businesses Can Thrive in the New Global Neighborhoods.* New York: Portfolio, 2009.

Keller, Ed, and Berry, John. *The Influentials.* Florence, MA: Free Press, 2003.

Kirkpatrick, David. *The Facebook Effect: The Inside Story of the Company That is Connecting the World.* New York, Simon & Schuster, 2010.

McConnell, Ben, and Huba, Jackie. *Citizen Marketers: When People Are the Message.* New York: Kaplan Publishing, 2006.

Safko, Lon, and Brake, David K. *The Social Media Bible: Tactics, Tools, & Strategies for Social Media Success.* Hoboken, NJ: John Wiley & Sons, 2009.

Scobel, Robert, and Israel, Shel. *Naked Conversations: How Blogs Are Changing the Way Businesses Talk with Customers.* Hoboken, NJ: John Wiley & Sons.

Sernovitz, Andy. *Word of Mouth Marketing: How Smart Companies Get People Talking.* New York: Kaplan Business, 2006.

Tapscott, Don, and Williams, Anthony. *Wikinomics: How Mass Collaboration Changes Everything.* New York: Penguin, 2006.

Tobin, Jim, and Braziel, Lisa. *Social Media Is a Cocktail Party: Why You Already Know the Rules of Social Media Marketing.* Cary, NC: Ignite Social Media, 2008.

Tuten, Tracy L. *Advertising 2.0: Social Media Marketing in a Web 2.0 World.* Westport, CT: Praeger, 2008.

Weber, Larry. *Marketing to the Social Web: How Digital Customer Communities Build Your Business.* San Francisco: John Wiley & Sons, 2007.

SOCIAL MEDIA TOOLS AND PLATFORMS

What do all those tools, widgets, services, and platforms do? Here is a brief and selective guide to major players—and some emerging ones—on the social-media scene:

AddThis: Widget for adding pages to social bookmarking sites.

Angie's List: Ratings and reviews.

Badoo: Social network.

Bizrate: Ratings and reviews.

Blogger: Blog software.

Classmates: Social network focused on connecting school/college classmates.

Crowdstorm: Ratings and reviews.

Del.icio.us: Social bookmarking.

Delicious Tagometer: Shows how many users have tagged a post and with what categories.

Digg: Social bookmarking.

Digg Alerter: Desktop app that displays Digg trends, including buries.

Digg Alerts: Sign up to be alerted when anyone Diggs a given subject; based on keywords.

Digg Notify: Desktop app that displays a notification box whenever someone Diggs one of your items.

Digg Toolbar: Browser toolbar that provides most of the common Digg functions.

Digg Web site Widget: Lists your latest Digg submissions on the sidebar of your Web site.

Epinions: Ratings and reviews.

EventBox: Integrates the top social networks into a single program.

Facebook: Social network.

Flickr: Photo share.

Flixster: Movie network.

Flock browser: A specialized Web browser designed around social media. It integrates with dozens of services and makes it easier for you to stay connected.

Foursquare: Mobile phone app combining elements of local search and social media.

FriendFeed: Combines your different social networks into a single feed. Makes you easier to follow, and makes it easier to follow others.

Gathera: Browser plug-in that aggregates social media, e-mail, messaging, etc.

GoodReads: Book and reading network.

Google Buzz: Instant messaging/social network.

Habbo: Kids' social network.

hi5: Social network.

HootSuite: Manage multiple social-media platforms from one dashboard.

Howcast: Video share.

iLike: Music share.

Infegy Social Radar: Social-media monitoring tool that helps track the Web.

iTunes: Podcasting network.

Jott: Voice-to-text, task organization, and much more. Post to Twitter and many other services by calling in from your phone.

LibraryThing: Book and reading network.

LinkedIn: Social network for businesspeople.

MocoSpace: Mobile social network.

Movable Type: Blog software.

MSN Messenger: Instant-messaging platform.

MyLife: Social network.

MySpace: Social network.

Nielsen BuzzMetrics: Social-media analytics tool that lets you search the blogo-sphere and track/find trends.

Ning: Blog 2.0 software platform that enables niche social networks.

OpenID: A single sign-on solution supported by many Web apps and networking sites.

OpenSocial: A common API for social applications across multiple Web sites. With standard JavaScript and HTML, developers can create apps that access a social network's friends and update feeds.

Orkut: Social network.

Picasa: Photo share.

Ping.Fm: Update your social networks by connecting the most popular networks into one service.

Plaxo: A service designed to make it easier to stay in touch with people you care about.

Plurk: Microblogging.

Posterous: Microblogging platform.

Redditt: Social bookmarking.

Scribd: Social publishing and reading network.

Second Brain: Organize all of your content in one place, including bookmarks, files, etc.

Seesmic: Microblogging platform.

SlideShare: Presentation sharing.

Spoke: Social network for businesspeople.

Spokeo Search: Social-media search that makes it easy to find information from 41 different networks.

StumbleUpon: Social bookmarking.

StumbleUpon Buttons: Buttons that make it easy for visitors to stumble your articles.

TripAdvisor: Ratings and reviews.

Tumblr: Microblogging platform.

TweetBeep: Sign up to be alerted when anyone tweets on a given subject, based on keywords.

TweetDeck: Adobe Air application that helps organize and make sense of your tweets. You can group tweets based on search terms, time frame, and many other ways.

Twhirl: Desktop Twitter client. It adds the ability to cross-post tweets to other sites, post images to TwitPic, and search tweets (among other things).

Twidget: Microsoft dashboard widget that lets you keep up with your Twitter account.

TwitBin: Firefox extension that allows you to receive and send tweets anywhere in your browser.

Twittelator Pro: iPhone app for Twitter.

Twitter: Microblogging platform and social network.

TwitterBerry: A mobile twitter client for Blackberry users. It works over the data network with no need for SMS.

TwitterFeed: Takes your latest post titles and posts them to your Twitter account.

TwitThis: A social button to put on your Web site that helps promote your articles on Twitter.

TypePad: Blog software.

Vimeo: Video share.

Vox: Blog software.

Wikipedia: Wiki encyclopedia project.

WordPress: Blog software.

WordPress Twitter Tools: WordPress plug-in that let's you pull your tweets into your blog.

Xanga: Blog software.

XING: Social network for businesspeople.

Yahoo! Messenger: Instant-messaging platform.

Yammer: Microblogging platform.

Yelp: Ratings and reviews.

YouTube: Video share.

Yumeo: A social network that allows users to control many other social sites in one place.

Notes

CHAPTER 1: INTRODUCTION

1. Heather Dougherty, "Hitwise Intelligence, North America," Experian Hitwise, http://weblogs.hitwise.com/heather-dougherty/2010/03/facebook_reaches_top_ranking_i.html.

2. "The BlogHer—iVillage 2010 Social Media Matters Study," Ketchum and Nielsen.

3. *The Global Social Media Check-Up*, Burson-Marsteller, 2010.

4. Forrester Research, Inc., "U.S. Interactive Marketing Forecast, 2009 to 2014," July 2009.

5. "The Value of Social Media Report," Econsultancy, 2010.

6. Dianna Dilworth, "Travel Campaigns On, Despite Cuts," *DMNews*, May 17, 2010.

7. "The Value of Social Media Report," Econsultancy, 2010.

8. Remarks at the Search Engine Strategies Conference, New York, March 24, 2010.

9. Marianne Kolbasuk McGee, "YouTube Videos Stir Up New Sales for 'Will It Blend' Maker," *InformationWeek*, September 27, 2007.

10. David Wilson, "The ROI of Social Media," July 23, 2009, http://social-media-optimization.com/2009/07/the-roi-of-social-media/.

11. iModerate.com, "Engaging Consumers via Facebook, Twitter Makes Them More Likely to Buy, Recommend," press release, March 10, 2010.

12. Ibid.

13. "Does Social Media Sway Online Shopping?" *BusinessWeek*, August 31, 2009.

14. Danny Brown, "The Real Social Media ROI—Risk of Ignoring," December 2, 2008, http://dannybrown.me/2008/12/02/the-real-social-media-roi-risk-of-ignoring/.

15. Reid Hoffman, "Reid Hoffman: My Rule of Three for Investing," TechCrunch, April 19, 2009, http://techcrunch.com/2009/04/19/reid-hoffman-my-rule-of-three-for-investing/.

16. John Jantsch, http://www.ducttapemarketing.com/blog/2010/05/25/why-social-media-doesnt-matter-anymore.

17. Shel Israel interview of Jim Deitzel on his blog Global Neighbourhoods, http://redcouch.typepad.com/weblog/2008/12/twitterville–5.html.

CHAPTER 2: GETTING STARTED—THE STRATEGY

1. Marissa Tarleton, remarks made at Retail Marketing Conference, Orlando, Florida, March 2010.

2. Max Kalehoff, interview with the author.

3. Jim Tobin, *Social Media Is a Cocktail Party: Why You Already Know the Rules of Social Media Marketing*, CreateSpace, 2008.

4. Max Kalehoff, interview with the author.

5. Lynn Ricci, interview with the author.

6. "Millennials at the Gates," Accenture, February 21, 2009.

7. Ibid.

8. Ed Moran, "Tribalization of Business" survey, Deloitte.

9. "The Global Social Media Check-Up, 2010," Burson-Marsteller.

10. Mark Mosiniak, remarks made at the Retail Marketing Conference, Orlando, Florida, March 26, 2010.

11. Eric Fulwiler "10 Things Your Grandmother Can Teach You About Social Media," OpinionatLarge.com, April 22, 2010, http://www.opinionatlarge.com/social-media/10-things-your-grandmother-can-teach-you-about-social-media/.

12. Megan Casey, "Tie a String Around Your Finger," SquidBlog, September 30, 2008, http://blogs.squidoo.com/squidblog/2008/09/30/tie-a-string-around-your-finger/.

13. Derek Sivers, "A Real Person, A Lot Like You," http://sivers.org/real.

14. Max Harris, remarks made at the Vermont New Hampshire Marketing Conference, May 2010.

15. Robert Scoble and Shel Israel, *Naked Conversations: How Blogs Are Changing the Way Businesses Talk with Customers.*

16. Burnes, Rick, "Study Shows Small Businesses That Blog Get 55% More Web Site Visitors," http://blog.hubspot.com/blog/tabid/6307/bid/5014/Study-Shows-Small-Businesses-That-Blog-Get-55-More-Website-Visitors.aspx.

17. "Social Media Metrics Neglected by Most," eMarketer, September 22, 2009, http://www.emarketer.com/Article.aspx?R=1007286.

18. Seth Godin, e-mail interview with the author.

19. Sophos social-media security study.

20. Mark Mosiniak, "Realizing Innovation," remarks made at the Retail Marketing Conference, Orlando, Florida, March 26, 2010.

21. Aaron Uhrmacher, "10 Social Media Tasks for Summer Interns," http://disruptology.com/10-social-media-tasks-for-summer-interns/.

22. Phil Terry, interview with the author.

23. Guy Kawasaki, "The Art of Evangelism," revised and collected in *What Matters Now*, an e-book and print book by Seth Godin, originally blogged January 12, 2006, on http://blog.guykawasaki.com/2006/01/the_art_of_evan.html.

24. "What Men and Women Are Doing on Facebook," Jenna Goudreau, April 26, 2010.

25. Elisa Camahort Page, e-mail interview with the author.

26. Seth Godin, e-mail interview with the author. Godin tells the Blendtec story in detail in *Meatball Sundae: Is Your Marketing Out of Sync?*, New York: Penguin, 2007.

CHAPTER 3: GETTING STARTED—THE PLATFORMS

1. "The Global Social Media Check-Up, 2010," Burson-Marsteller.

2. Mike Mosiniak, "Realizing Innovation," remarks at Retail Marketing Conference, Orlando, Florida, May 26, 2010.

3. Nielsen/BlogHer, "Social Media Matters 2010."

4. Shel Israel, *Twitterville*.

5. "As the Economy Sours, LinkedIn's Popularity Grows," February 14, 2009, http://techcrunch.com/2009/02/14/as-the-economy-sours-linkedins-popularity-grows/.

6. Jessica Guynn, "Business Card? He Has Your Profile," *Los Angeles Times*, July 8, 2008.

7. Reid Hoffman, interview on Charlie Rose.

8. YouTube, Quantcast.

9. Tam Vo, comScore Video Metrix, "YouTube Still Rules Online Video, U.S. Viewing Time Leaps 40 Percent," January 5, 2009.

10. *Internet Retailer*, December 2009.

11. Forrester, January 2010.

12. eMarketer, January 2009.

13. Bill Siwicki, "Blending Video and E-commerce," *Internet Retailer*, January 2007.

14. Ben Cohen, remarks made at Vermont Businesses for Social Responsibility Spring Conference awards dinner, Burlington, Vermont, May 16, 2010.

15. Glenn Allsopp, http://www.viperchill.com/important-blogging-analysis/.

16. The E-tailing Group and PowerReviews survey of 1,000 customers, March 2010.

17. Max Harris, remarks made at the Vermont New Hampshire Marketing Conference, May 2010.

18. Matt Cutts, "Google Searchology 2009: Search Options, Google Squared, Rich Snippets," May 12, 2009, http://www.mattcutts.com/blog/google-searchology-2009-search-options-google-squared-rich-snippets/.

CHAPTER 4: TAKING IT TO THE NEXT LEVEL

1. Dale Nitschke, "Realizing Innovation," remarks at Retail Marketing Conference, Orlando, Florida, May 26, 2010.

2. Mike Mosiniak, ibid.

3. Adam Ostrow, "Inside Gatorade's Social Media Command Center," Mashable, http://mashable.com/2010/06/15/gatorade-social-media-mission-control/

4. Chad Capellman, "Check-Ins for Check-Ups: How to Corner the Local Market with Foursquare," *MediaPost,* June 4, 2010.

5. Christopher Heine, "How Gap's 'Groupon' Went Crazy Viral," ClickZ, August 24, 2010, http://www.clickz.com/clickz/news/1729509/how-gaps-groupon-went-crazy-viral

6. Jon Swartz, "Once-Fading MySpace Focuses on Youthful Reincarnation," *USA Today*, March 10, 2010.

7. Mitch Wagner, "Linden Lab Holds to Grand Plans for Second Life," *Computerworld*, April 20, 2010.

8. Max Kalehoff, interview with the author.

9. Kim Boatman, "Let Your Fans Shop Without Leaving Facebook," Inc., April 12, 2010, http://www.inc.com/internet/articles/201004/facebook.html.

10. Diana Dilworth, "Direct Sales Through Social Clicks," *DMNews*, June 7, 2010.

11. Kim Boatman, ibid.

12. ibid.

13. ibid.

14. Brad Stone, "A Friend's Tweet Could Be an Ad,"*New York Times*, November 22, 2009.

15. Dick Costolo, "The Twitter Platform," May 24, 2010, http://blog.twitter.com/2010/05/twitter-platform.html.

16. Paul Boutin, "Idealab Founder Bill Gross: Why I'm Running a Twitter Startup," *Venture Beat*, April 12, 2010, http://venturebeat.com/2010/04/12/idealab-founder-bill-gross-why-im-running-a-twitter-startup/.

17. Jessica Guynn, "Promoting for Dollars Is New Twitter App," *Los Angeles' Times* April 15, 2010, http://articles.latimes.com/2010/apr/15/business/la-fi-twitter-hire15-2010apr15.

18. Ibid.

19. LinkedIn media kit, 2010.

20. Karl Greenberg, "NBA Reaches Out to Hispanics with Enebea," *MediaPost*, October 19, 2009.

21. Max Harris, remarks made at the Vermont New Hampshire Marketing Group Annual Conference, Whitefield, New Hampshire, May 21, 2010.

22. *Internet Retailer*, May 2010.

23. Brian Hashemi, e-mail interview with the author.

24. Andrew Ran Wong, "My Interview with Scott Herfernan," http://webstudio13.com/2010/03/09/interview-with-meetup-founder-scott-heiferman/.

25. Ibid.

26. Megan Casey, "Worldwide Squidoo Meetup Day!" http://www.squidoo.com/squidoo-meetup-day.

27. Some of these suggestions come from Joshua Tabb, "Learn the Lingo: F is for Flash Mobs, Mobilizing Your Mob," http://www.casefoundation.org/blog/learn-lingo-f-flash-mobs-mobilizing-your-mob.

CHAPTER 5: SUCCESS STORIES

1. "Realizing Innovation," Marissa Tarleton, remarks at Retail Marketing Conference, Orlando, Florida, May 26, 2010.

2. Kevin McKeefery,"HP to Launch 'Let's Do Amazing' Campaign," *DMNews,* March 11, 2010.

3. Michael Lyman, interview with the author, March 29, 2010.

4. Samuel Axon, "How Social Media and the Web Helped Avatar Make $1 Billion," http://mashable.com/2010/01/08/avatar-social-media-web/.

5. David Siegel, "Realizing Innovation," remarks at Retail Marketing Conference, Orlando, Florida, May 26, 2010.

6. Jeffrey Pape, remarks at Internet Retailer Conference and Expo, Chicago, June 8, 2010.

7. Jill Walker Rettberg, "Case Study: Fisk-a-teers—A Community for Fiskars Scissor Users (aka Scrapbookers)," http://jilltxt.net/?p=2406. The case study was presented at the BlogHer annual conference, September 26, 2009.

8. Andy Sernovitz, "How Fiskars Created Their Amazing Fan Community," June 3, 2010.

9. Spike Jones, "How to Create a Fan Community," remarks made at Word of Mouth Supergenius Conference, April 20, 2010, http://gaspedal.com/blog/newsletter/3-minute-wom-lesson-lessons-from-the-amazing-fiskars-fan-community-live-from-word-of-mouth-supergenius/.

10. "Lego Click: A Well Decorated Case Study for Social (and Viral) Media," http://www.psfk.com/2010/06/lego-click-a-well-decorated-case-study-for-social-and-viral-media.html.

11. Joan Voight, "Block by Block: How LEGO Stacks Up," *OMMA Magazine,* May 2010.

12. Augie Ray, Forrester Research.

13. Karlene Lukovitz, "Mountain Dew Lets Fans Plan Tour Events," *Media-Post Marketing Daily*, June 28, 2010.

14. Max Harris, remarks at Vermont New Hampshire Marketing Group annual conference, Whitefield, New Hampshire, May 21, 2010.

15. Kevin McKeefery, "In Search of the Adventurous," *DMNews*, June 7, 2010.

16. Rebecca Jennings, e-mail interview with the author.

17. Sandie Mainwal-Price, e-mail interview with the author, May 16, 2010.

18. Paul Kalemkiarian, remarks made at Retail Marketing Conference, Orlando, Florida, May 27, 2010, reported by Tim Parry, "How to Be a Social Media Superstar," *MultiChannel Merchant*, May 27, 2010.

19. Steve Elkins, remarks at Internet Retailer Conference and Expo, Chicago, June 8, 2010.

20. Thad Rueter, "Social Media's Google Juice," June 8, 2020, http://www.internetretailer.com/2010/06/08/social-medias-google-juice.

CHAPTER 6: FAILS AND FIASCOS

1. Molly DiBianca, "Another Reason Employers Need a Social-Media Policy: New FTC Regulations," Delaware Law Blog, January, 29, 2010, http://www.delawareemploymentlawblog.com/2010/01/another_reason_employers_need.html.

2. Dan Frosch, "Venting Online, Consumers Can Find Themselves in Court," *New York Times*, May 31, 2010, http://www.nytimes.com/2010/06/01/us/01slapp.html.

3. Ibid.

4. Ibid.

5. Meghan Casserly, "Dell's Revamped 'Della' Site for Women," May 22, 2009.

6. Dell, "The Lifestyle Connection," http://en.community.dell.com/dell-blogs/b/direct2dell/archive/2009/05/15/the-della-connection.aspx.

7. Laura Petrecca, "Offended Moms Get Tweet Revenge over Motrin Ads," *USA Today*, http://www.usatoday.com/tech/products/2008-11-18-motrin-ads-twitter_N.htm.

8. Nicholas Carlson, "Well, These New Zuckerberg IMs Won't Help Facebook's Privacy Problems," *Silicon Alley Insider*, May 13, 2010, http://www.businessinsider.com/well-these-new-zuckerberg-ims-wont-help-facebooks-privacy-problems-2010-5.

9. Katherine Kaplan, "Facemash Creator Survives Ad Board," *Harvard Crimson*, November 19, 2003, http://www.thecrimson.com/article.aspx?ref=350143.

10. David Kirkpatrick, *The Facebook Effect: The Inside Story of the Company That Is Connecting the World*, New York: Simon & Schuster, 2010.

11. Sam Knight, "All-Seeing Google Street View Prompts Privacy Fears," *Times* Online, June 1, 2007, http://technology.timesonline.co.uk/tol/news/tech_and_web/article1870995.ece.

12. "Bank Intern Busted by Facebook," http://valleywag.gawker.com/321802/bank-intern-busted-by-facebook.

13. Helen Popkin, "Twitter Gets You Fired in 140 Characters or Less," MSNBC, March 23, 2009, http://www.msnbc.msn.com/id/29796962/.

14. Kara Scanell, "SEC Opens Informal Inquiry of Whole Foods CEO Postings," *Wall Street Journal,* July 14, 2007.

15. Lisa Rathke, "Vermont Brewery Settles Dispute with Energy Drink-Maker Monster, Can Keep 'Vermonster' Name," Associated Press, October 22, 2009.

16. Simon Houpt, "Lost Boys, Lost Diaries and Other Marketing Mistakes," *Vancouver Globe and Mail*, October 23, 2009.

CHAPTER 7: THE FUTURE

1. Matt Richtel, "Hooked on Gadgets, and Paying a Mental Price," *New York Times*, June 6, 2010, http://www.nytimes.com/2010/06/07/technology/07brain.html.

2. Jon Picoult, "Networks Too Big for Their Own Good," *New York Times*, October 17, 2009.

3. John Battelle, "The Gap Scenario," April 30, 2010, http://battellemedia.com/archives/2010/04/the_gap_scenario.

4. Remarks at the Social Commerce Summit, Austin, Texas, April 20, 2010.

5. Robert Putnam, *Bowling Alone: The Collapse and Revival of American Community*, New York: Touchstone, 2000.

6. Mina Asayesh-Brown and Kelley Benham, "Wii Bowling Match: High School Seniors Vs. Retirement Home Seniors," *St. Petersburg Times*, April 28, 2010, http://www.tampabay.com/news/aging/lifetimes/wii-bowling-match-high-school-seniors-vs-retirement-home-seniors/1090647.

7. Biltin, Nick, "The Surreal World of Chatroulette," *New York Times*, February 19, 2010.

8. Mike Mosiniak, "Realizing Innovation," remarks at Retail Marketing Conference, Orlando, Florida, May 26, 2010.

9. Chad Capellman, "Check-Ins for Check-ups: How to Corner the Local Market with Foursquare," MediaPost, June 4, 2010.

10. Remarks made at the All Things Digital Conference, Palos Verdes, California, June 2, 2010, reported by Alexei Oreskovic, "Facebook CEO Says No Date in Mind for IPO," Reuters.

11. Mike Laurie, "7 Technologies Shaping the Future of Social Media," http://mashable.com/2009/06/01/social-media-future-tech/.

12. Josh Catone, "Visualizing Social-Media Fatigue," ReadWriteWeb, February 8, 2008, http://www.readwriteweb.com/archives/visualizing_social_media_fatigue.php.

13. Alex Iksold, "The Attention Economy, An Overview," ReadWriteWeb, March 1, 2007, http://www.readwriteweb.com/archives/attention_economy_overview.php.

14. Remarks made at the Future of Web Apps Conference, Miami, February 28, 2008, reported by Caroline McCarthy, CNET News, "The Future of Web Apps Will See the Death of E-Mail," http://news.cnet.com/8301-13577_3-9883380-36.html.

15. Marc Zuckerberg, remarks made at D8, All Things Digital Conference, June 2, 2010.

16. Marc Zuckerberg, remarks made at the Tech Crunch Crunchies Awards, San Francisco, January 8, 2010.

17. Larry Page, remarks made at Google Zeitgeist London, May 18, 2010, reported by Jemima Kiss, *The Guardian*, "Google's Eric Schmidt: Privacy Is Paramount," May 19, 2010.

CHAPTER 8: CONCLUSION

1. Clive Thompson, "Is the Tipping Point Toast?" *Fast Company*, February 1, 2008, http://www.fastcompany.com/magazine/122/is-the-tipping-point-toast.html.

2. Victoria Taylor, "A Brand's Facebook Fans Are Valuable Consumers," June 11, 2010, http://blogs.forbes.com/marketshare/2010/06/11/a-brand%E2%80%99s-facebook-fans-are-valuable-consumers/.

3. Sandie Mainwal-Price, e-mail interview with the author, May 16, 2010.

4. Bill Heil and Mikolaj Piskorski, "Men Follow Men, and Nobody Tweets," *Harvard Business Review*, June 1, 2009.

5. Jakob Nielsen: "Participation Inequality: Encouraging More Users to Contribute." *Alert Box*, October 9, 2006, http://www.useit.com/alertbox/participation_inequality.html.

6. Nielsen Global Online Consumer Survey, April 2009.

7. Chief Marketer Social Media Survey, 2009.

8. Michael Lazerow, "Social's Prime Function: Retention," *DMNews*, April 5, 2010.

Index

About the Author

TOM FUNK is the author of *Web 2.0 & Beyond* (2008, ABC-CLIO) and a speaker at marketing conferences in the U.S. and abroad. He has been involved in e-commerce and Web publishing since 1995. In his six years managing the Web sites of the Vermont Teddy Bear Company, Funk saw online revenues triple, and the company's sites were named to Internet Retailer's "Best of the Web" Top 50. Funk is currently VP of Marketing for Timberline Interactive, a Web development and online marketing consultancy.